DATE DUE

GAYLORD			PRINTED IN U.S.A.

THE SYMBOLIST MOVEMENT

THE SYMBOLIST MOVEMENT

BY KENNETH CORNELL

ARCHON BOOKS, 1970

ISBN: 0-208-00947-7
Library of Congress Catalog Card Number: 70-121755
Printed in the United States of America

FOREWORD

THE LITERARY MOVEMENT which during the last years of the nineteenth century transformed French poetry not only in its themes but in its expression has now become a vast subject, often international in scope, closely bound with many of the great names of our times and enriched by a constantly increasing body of critical literature. At times the word symbolism assumes connotative values which extend from Ballanche to T. S. Eliot. Again the word may be reduced to concentration on a single meaningful sentence of Mallarmé, Rimbaud, or Valéry. But whether we consider symbolism in its broad implications, in its world-wide manifestations, or in its revelation of individual artistic vision, one of our primary tasks should be to investigate the tumultuous years when traditional French poetic ideas underwent important and lasting change.

Those who participated in the French symbolist movement have left us many accounts. From Kahn, Ghil, Retté, Fontainas, Merrill, Fort, and Henri de Régnier we learn of the enthusiasms, the rivalries, the friendships, and more especially of the confusing and conflicting currents which characterized the epoch. Unfortunately, sometimes because of bias, always because of the reminiscent nature of their books, these writers offer only incomplete reports and an abundance of anecdotes. They fail to give us an exact story of how poetry, beginning as a little-favored literary form, became for some years a matter of prime concern. By the number of short-lived periodicals they mention, by the number of personalities they cite as having played a part in poetic evolution, we become immediately aware of complicated patterns, conflicting theories, examples of transitory literary renown, and rapid transformation of the poetic idea. Other immediate and definite problems soon become apparent. Among them we may mention the absence of a single directive force, the almost simultaneous action of Baudelaire, Mallarmé, Verlaine, and Rimbaud on poetry, as well as the ambitious attempts of several lesser writers to attain leadership. Moreover, the bonds as well as the dissidences between French and Belgian poets and periodicals require analysis.

In the history of a confused literary movement, it will often be necessary to describe and enumerate. Many of the new periodicals were ephemeral but not unimportant. Numerous reviews where poets presented their work and in which their accomplishment was discussed came into being, underwent alteration, and disappeared. Change of ownership, of editors, or even of critics gave to some magazines a series of disparate existences. The writers themselves suddenly shifted from one theory to another, formed new groupings, or isolated themselves from their fellows. Out of this confused activity, however, emerges a lofty aim, the constant search for the proper realm of poetry and its appropriate expression. Whatever their failures or their excesses, the symbolists courageously invaded an unexplored world of human emotion and feeling, deeper than mere sensation, more difficult to seize than logical reasoning. Accessory circumstance, narrative development, and descriptive detail yielded to the more difficult problem of expressing delicate shadings of mood. These innovations led to experiments in musical effects, in imagery, and vocabulary which have proved of lasting importance, and also to less felicitous efforts which were soon discarded.

In discussing this search for the new, without minimizing the importance of the really great poets, we must not neglect a number of lesser talents. The symbolist movement is not merely the story of how four or five writers emerged from obscurity to permanent fame. Gustave Kahn is not only an editor who played an important part in publishing the work of Laforgue and Rimbaud. He is also the poet who penned his impressions of the subconscious world in *Les Palais nomades* and created a new kind of love poem in *Domaine de fée*. While Moréas was helpful in giving Verlaine a place of honor, his own activity as theorist and poet has also its importance, perhaps not because of his ostentatious showmanship but by reason of such attempts as the suppression of time and space in *Les Cantilènes*. In Mallarmé's rise to fame must be counted the names of Dujardin and Mauclair, but they too have their small creative roles, the first in the liberation of versification, the second in the suggestive mystery of words.

Nor must we forget those whose activity was marginal. Personalities like Félix Fénéon, Téodor de Wyzewa, and Albert Aurier, whose criticism of painting and of music throws light on the parallel development of poetic ideas, magazine editors who made publication of verse possible and in whose periodicals were printed the critical commentary on new volumes, must necessarily be included. Mockel of *La Wallonie,* Deschamps of *La Plume,* Vallette of the *Mercure de France,* Natanson of *La Revue blanche,* and Mazel of *L'Ermitage* loom as most important; but a score of others, even to Rodolphe Salis of *Le Chat noir,* cannot be neglected. Like most magazines, those of the symbolist period are a combination of faults and virtues. They revealed talents but often overestimated the worth of their contributors. They agitated poetic ideas but many of these were of no permanent value. Their book reviews, in large part written by poets, were often inspired by friendship or personal antipathy. But these very prejudices help to complete the picture of the period.

Several monographs on symbolist poets have, through their chronological exactitude, cast new light on the period. Studies on larger aspects of the movement usually have adopted a different approach. Questions of esthetic aims or of prosody, valuable and stimulating as they are, often neglect points of reference as to time. The evolution of poetry after 1885 is so much a product of relationships and oppositions that slight distortions of the truth are likely unless the poet and his work are viewed in regard to the specific moment, the place, and the literary group. Needed information is largely contained in rare volumes and magazines completely available only in the Bibliothèque Nationale or the splendid collection gathered by Jacques Doucet.

The present volume is an endeavor to trace the movement from its source rather than from the viewpoint of our outlook today. In order to keep the work in reasonable limits, it has seemed preferable to take the modest role of chronicler, excluding critical amplification and concentrating on the factual. Information on the past has by implication many ramifications with the present. Rimbaud, for instance, as he was judged by the poets of the 1890's, stands in sharp contrast with his literary significance after surrealism. Gide's insistence on the merits of Emmanuel Signoret's poetry invites examination of the latter's reputation in his lifetime. Mallarmé's work, in enlarged critical editions, fortified by the study and commentary of such scholars as Mondor, Thibaudet, and Noulet, assumes today an importance and meaning which his contemporaries failed to grasp. Laforgue's prestige in our time leads us back to the years, after his death, when loyal friends first revealed his work.

A history of the symbolist period should also assign to their proper place many obscure names, both of persons and periodicals, which receive passing mention in almost all literature on the subject. It is only by fitting these tiny matters of detail into the pattern of the times that we may obtain a reasonably accurate representation of the epoch. Long ago Baudelaire inserted in his "Le Peintre de la vie moderne" a few paragraphs of admonition which may be pertinent to us today. After telling of those who think they possess literature in reading Bossuet and Racine, or art in contemplation of Titian or Raphael, he concludes:

Par bonheur se présentent de temps en temps des redresseurs de torts, des critiques, des amateurs, des curieux qui affirment que tout n'est pas dans Raphaël, que tout n'est pas dans Racine, que les *poetæ minores* ont du bon, du solide et du délicieux; et enfin, que pour tant aimer la beauté générale, qui est exprimée par les poëtes et les artistes classiques, on n'en a pas moins tort de négliger la beauté particulière, la beauté de circonstance et le trait de mœurs.

I wish to express my gratitude to the staffs of French and American libraries and to Professors Henri Peyre and Theodore Andersson for their invaluable assistance. I am deeply indebted to the John Simon Guggenheim Memorial Foundation for financial aid which enabled me to complete my documentation abroad. A substantial portion of the publishing expenses has been borne by the same Foundation and by Yale University.

K. C.

CONTENTS

Chapter I: THE CRADLE OF THE MOVEMENT, 1866–70

To SPEAK of the symbolist movement is almost invariably to conjure up the names of Baudelaire, Mallarmé, Verlaine, and Rimbaud and in so doing to group as precursors men who were born thirty-three years apart, yet who, by reason of their greatness, as well as by certain original attitudes of spirit, determined the destinies of poetry during the last fifteen years of the nineteenth century and the beginning of the twentieth. From another point of view it might be said that what is designated as the symbolist movement was the period when these same names were recognized at their real worth by an understanding group of literary artists. But whether envisaged as guides or as recipients of praise, whether as dynamic forces or objects of veneration, these four innovators tend to enlarge the chronological scope of symbolism and to bring the period known as Parnassian into its history. Perhaps for this reason Ernest Raynaud begins his *Mêlée symboliste* by the study of certain aspects of the 1870's, while Pierre Martino combines, in a volume admirable for its concision, the story of both the Parnassian and symbolist movements.[1]

There are furthermore in every literary trend the dual elements of continuance and inherited traits together with those of innovation, often of revolt. That three of the forerunners of the symbolist movement were once enrolled with the Parnassians assumes significance when one contrasts their somewhat cautious changes in form with their courageous originality in theme and expression. Even the youngest of these four precursors, when he was not yet sixteen years old, sent Théodore de Banville three poems written in impeccable alexandrines with the request that he be included in the second *Parnasse contemporain*.[2]

In March, 1867, when Verlaine's first volume of verse appeared, Rimbaud was a twelve-year-old schoolboy in Charleville studying Latin versification,[3] and Baudelaire, who had been brought to Paris from Brussels in 1866, was lying mortally ill. Mallarmé, as we now know from his letters, had already undergone at Tournon a spiritual experience in which the search for beauty and perfection had brought him close to the abyss of nothingness. He had

1. *Parnasse et symbolisme.*
2. Rimbaud's letter from Charleville, dated May 24, 1870.
3. In 1868 Rimbaud sent an epistle of sixty Latin verses to the imperial prince.

suffered anguish of which the intensity, although on a different intellectual plane, recalls best that of Baudelaire. He had made the vow to renounce publicity, to consecrate his life to the elaboration of the study of self, the expression of the noble illusion of existence. In May, 1867, he wrote a credo which was the glory and the despair of his career:

Il n'y a que la Beauté; —et elle n'a qu'une expression parfaite—la Poésie. Tout le reste est mensonge—excepté pour ceux qui vivent du corps, l'amour, et cet amour de l'esprit, l'amitié— Pour moi, la Poésie me tient lieu´de l'amour, parce qu'elle est éprise d'elle-même, et que sa volupté d'elle retombe délicieusement en mon âme.[4]

Verlaine, about two years younger than Mallarmé, had felt in 1867 but little of that spiritual questing and had much more readily received diverse influences, such as those of Leconte de Lisle and Glatigny. Like Mallarmé he had felt the enchantment of Baudelaire, but, to judge by his essay of 1865,[5] few of the philosophical implications in the work of this author impressed him. In 1867 Verlaine was in correspondence with Poulet-Malassis concerning the publication of Les Amies, his own version of the "Pièces condamnées." Two extremely diverse personalities were already maturing and each, after his own manner, was later to gain the admiration of a whole generation of poets.

Thus it becomes useful to cast a retrospective glance on the years immediately preceding the Franco-Prussian War, and especially on the Parnasse contemporain of 1866, which by its list of collaborators seems the cradle of both symbolism and Parnassianism. The volume is chiefly remembered for the number of sonnets it contains and for the grouping of authors who, following the example of Gautier, made art and plasticity their chief concerns, or, taking their inspiration from Leconte de Lisle, strove to temper the expression of their emotions. Thus the general tone of the anthology is descriptive; the poets, often by the use of the third person, sublimate the romantic ego and interpose a veil of impersonality between the feelings and their expression; the tendency to moralize is constantly apparent.

There is present in the collection, however, another element, one which gives the volume a certain variety and charm and makes it much better than the two subsequent books which bear the same name. The phenomenon occurs in those lyrics which offer the direct statement of an emotion, often one of remembrance it is true, but one which is vibrant with feeling. Leconte de Lisle himself presents such a poem in "Les Spectres," François Coppée in "Vers le passé," and Léon Valade in "Rêve d'été." Valade's great friend,

4. Mallarmé's letter to Cazalis, dated May 14, 1867.

5. "Charles Baudelaire," L'Art, November–December, 1865. See Paul Verlaine, Œuvres posthumes, II, 7–30.

Albert Mérat, who was later to be called a good poet by Verlaine [6] but at the same time be accused of British coldness, wrote in "L'Image" some lines which in their intimate, personal tone and even by reason of the pauses in the verse are the antithesis of the didactic:

> Seul, dans l'apaisement des soirs silencieux,
> Suivant l'éclosion lente et mélancolique
> Des étoiles, j'ai pu reconnaître ses yeux.[7]

In addition to these examples of the personal lyric, the volume of 1866 contains poems by those Parnassians who are generally accepted as direct ancestors of the symbolist movement. With them, indeed, examples of inner emotion are numerous. Baudelaire's "Madrigal triste," together with "A une Malabaraise" and the passionately gentle "Recueillement," Verlaine's "Il Bacio" and his nostalgic, simple "Mon Rêve familier," Mallarmé's intimate creations of mood in "Les Fenêtres," "A celle qui est tranquille," "Soupir," and "Brise marine," and finally Villiers de l'Isle-Adam's "A un enfant taciturne" relieve the volume of pomposity and moralizing. Numerous enough to be important, these poems do not triumph over a general impression of Leconte de Lisle's influence, the tendency to a noble style. An example of this, exemplified in a poet of lesser talent, occurs in Emmanuel des Essarts' "A celle qui est trop loin." Here the tone and diction seem so closely modeled upon those of the author of "Midi" that the author's own personality seems to have small part:

> Viens! des cieux rajeunis s'épanche une vertu
> Fluide, et qu'on dirait par un Dieu distillé.
> Octobre est glorieux et de soleil vêtu.[8]

This preoccupation with artistic form and exterior description has as its source not only Leconte de Lisle but also the ancestor of all the Parnassians, Théophile Gautier. It happens that this very poet, two years after the publication of the *Parnasse contemporain,* undertook the task of evaluating the "progress" that French poetry had made between 1830 and 1868.[9] His essay comes at an interesting moment, the very year he wrote a long preface for an edition of *Les Fleurs du mal,* whose author had died in August, 1867. Gautier's history of French poetry after the crisis of romanticism, by its nature retrospective and by virtue of its author's sympathies somewhat biased, is nevertheless an interesting document. Keenly aware that the public of 1868 was satisfied with recognizing only three or four "étoiles de première grandeur,"

6. Paul Verlaine, *Œuvres complètes,* V, 423–430.
7. *Le Parnasse contemporain* (1866), p. 203.
8. *Ibid.,* p. 188.
9. Published in Gautier's *Histoire du romantisme* (1874).

he suggests that some vague gleams in the poetic sky may in the future be revealed as important worlds. He sees the period of 1868 as one when poetry is very little read, when magazines and newspapers disdain verse, and when poets vainly seek a publisher. In the midst of materialism, of scientific investigations, and of triumph of the novel the publication of the *Parnasse contemporain* appears to him an oasis, and an important one, since he regards its tone as modern and its contents representative of current poetic art. According to Gautier, who as author of the essay omits reference to his own influence, the sun about whom the lesser stars revolve is Leconte de Lisle; the principal theme in current poetry is Hellenism. Those contributors to the *Parnasse,* who were later to be recognized among the symbolists—Verlaine, Villiers de l'Isle-Adam, Stéphane Mallarmé—are only mentioned, save for a brief sentence about the latter, "dont l'extravagance un peu voulue est traversée de brillants éclairs." When one considers that this remark was made concerning Mallarmé's first and most orthodox poetic manner, he can surmise that Gautier might not have remained sympathetic to the later evolution of the poet.

Although Gautier is apparently not deeply impressed by Verlaine and Mallarmé, he finds challenging matter for examination in Baudelaire's contributions to the *Parnasse.* Of these he speaks with some perspicacity, indicating the author's mysterious and fascinating grace. He even discusses in more general terms the volume which had been dedicated to him, and perhaps succeeds better than most of his contemporaries in presenting the meaning of Baudelaire's tone and manner. But Gautier is convinced that the *Fleurs du mal* are like dangerous exotic drugs. Using such terms as "monomanie," "outrance," and "paroxysme," he reveals to what degree he is troubled by this form of art. In his discussion he prefers to ask questions of the reader rather than to make judgments. Baudelaire's world is a sunset realm bathed in hallucinatory gleams. But does this represent decadence? Does it merit contempt and scorn? Even if this sunset is followed by inevitable night, will not flashing of stars, moon, and comets create their own poetic values? Gautier seems to be pleading for the weird beauty of Baudelaire's volume, yet in his heart finding it overly morbid and eccentric. United with Baudelaire in horror of death, Gautier's mind probably grasped but a part of the younger poet's spiritual and intellectual qualities. Wholehearted enthusiasm for *Les Fleurs du mal* was to be found among members of later generations; among them Verlaine and Rimbaud.

Verlaine had already published, in November and December, 1865,[10] three articles on Baudelaire. Here, reproving the public for its lack of comprehension, he praised the author of the *Fleurs du mal* for revealing the anguish

10. In Xavier de Ricard's *L'Art.*

of man in nineteenth-century civilization. With critical acumen which he rarely showed in later articles, Verlaine intimated the relationship of Poe's poetical creed with that of Baudelaire, emphasized the importance of imagination in the composition of verse, and lastly, like a good Parnassian, praised Baudelaire's absolute mastery of lyric art.

In the mind of a youthful genius, a few years later, admiration for Baudelaire was to take the form of lyric adoration, which remains celebrated in the sentence fragment: "Baudelaire est le premier voyant, roi des poètes, *un vrai Dieu*." [11] Rimbaud's regrets that Baudelaire did not invent new poetic forms to express the hitherto unknown may well be the key to a development which, passing through a liberating period, was to culminate in the revolutionary era of free verse.

Gautier did not feel Baudelaire's originality so profoundly as did Rimbaud, but his printed words in 1868 and the measure of comprehension he showed were important. He was the well-known author whose *Poésies* had been a landmark in the now distant Romantic revolution of 1830 and whose *Emaux et camées* in ever larger editions after 1852 had determined the form and tone of so much poetry of the nineteenth century. A leader of the "Jeune France," he had long ago defended the artist's right to the world of his own imagination, and in company with his friends Gérard de Nerval, Pétrus Borel, and Arsène Houssaye he had proclaimed the anguish of the poet in the modern world. When he compares Baudelaire's work with that of the poets of the Latin decadence, his memories probably go back to 1834, when Désiré Nisard's volume attacked romanticism through these very comparisons. This is reaching far back into the past, yet the poetic urge for originality, the war against the commonplace and utilitarian is as important a manifestation in 1885 as in 1830. A pink waistcoat, a daring poetic image, an unusual sequence of rhythms, all these are refinements which seem to win the epithet of decadence in the nineteenth century. The sequence of Nisard's *Poètes latins de la décadence,* Gautier's introduction to the *Fleurs du mal,* a celebrated line from Verlaine's sonnet "Langueur," the literary taste of des Esseintes, the title of Anatole Baju's little magazine, and Remy de Gourmont's *Le Latin mystique* suggest a unity of conception much more definite than a vague term such as "mal du siècle." Poetry, finding itself in hostile surroundings, expressed its reactions in several ways. Sometimes it declaimed its displeasure, sometimes retired into haughty detachment. Because poetic sensitivity tried to ally itself with the landscape or the dream and because it sought delicate shadings of ideas or arresting images, it was labeled decadent. New forms were more readily evaluated as twilight in artistry than as valid change in artistic concept. Eccentricity, insanity, artificiality were the common accusa-

11. Letter from Rimbaud to Paul Demeny, May 15, 1871.

tions made throughout the nineteenth century against all important poetic trends, whether romantic, Parnassian, or symbolist. Gautier was enough a hater of banality to appreciate Baudelaire's originality, but he did not embrace the elements which the symbolists were to make their own, the complicated music, the suggestion, the interrelationships of the senses.

Gautier in 1868 is much concerned with the indifference of the public toward poetry. What he says will be true for the following decade of the seventies and is certainly accurate for that of the sixties, when the few critical articles on the subject proclaim the fact. In 1861 A. de Pontmartin speaks of the "déclin de la poésie" and of "les poètes qui gémissent de l'indifférence du public." [12] In 1866 C. Martha writes: "La poésie a disparu des lettres françaises, ou du moins tout le monde croit qu'elle a disparu." [13] D. Ordinaire says that although people may be unjust in calling poetry a dead literary form, little promise of revival is indicated by the volumes one reads.[14] These articles appeared in a magazine whose overconservative tendencies from 1833 to the end of the century seem highlighted by a single departure, the publication of eighteen of Baudelaire's poems in 1855.[15] Periodicals seemed to be content to sound the death knell of verse without offering very much to whet the readers' appetites. Thus a magazine such as the *Correspondant* chose for its favorites Victor de Laprade, J. Autran, X. Marmier, and of course the ubiquitous André Theuriet.

The decade of the sixties, it is true, had not been overly rich in poetic events. Hugo's *Chanson des rues et des bois* made a much less powerful impression than his novels, *Les Misérables* and *Les Travailleurs de la mer.* Publication of the second and third editions of the *Fleurs du mal* (1861, 1868), Leconte de Lisle's *Poèmes barbares* (1862), Vigny's *Destinées* (1864), Sully-Prudhomme's *Stances et poèmes* (1865) and *Solitudes* (1869), Coppée's and Verlaine's first volumes in 1866 and the latter's *Fêtes galantes* in 1869, however dear they may be to the literary historian, cannot conceal the general apathy concerning poetic expression. The short story and the novel were the

12. *Revue des deux mondes,* 2ᵉ époque, XXXIV, 697.

13. *Ibid.,* LXII, 1013.

14. *Ibid.,* LXXI, 523.

15. Even this event is made ludicrous by the apologetic editorial note with its advice that Baudelaire should broaden his horizons, and by the utter silence the magazine preserved while Baudelaire's fame was becoming established. The *Revue des deux mondes,* like other established periodicals, did not exclude poetry but seemed to favor mediocrity and restricted its pages to a few favorites. During the decade 1860–70 poems of Edouard Pailleron were published in ten issues, those of André Theuriet and of Blaze de Bury in seven. The other poets who made more than one appearance during the period were Auguste Barbier and H. Cantal. Eight other poets were represented by selections in single issues. Finally, in 1870, Sully-Prudhomme's poems appeared on four occasions.

forms of creative literature which attracted authors and readers, and discussion of fiction and the theater occupied to such an extent the critical portions of periodicals that poems seldom seem more than a second-rate filler. Thus if Pailleron, Theuriet, and Laprade, whose verse is as unobjectionable as it is unoriginal, assume places of importance, the causes must have been in part indifference and conservative taste.

Catulle Mendès and Xavier de Ricard, the animators of the Parnassian movement, had sought through the establishment of periodicals such as the *Revue fantaisiste* (1859) and *L'Art* (which was transformed into the first *Parnasse contemporain*) to react against the endless imitations of Lamartine and of Musset, the "pleurards" and the "débraillés" of whom Mendès speaks in his *Légende du Parnasse contemporain*. The Parnassians admired poets for whom the writing of verse was often a kind of technical triumph; they showed preference for those who sought in Hellenism, in exterior description, and in faultless form surcease from the iterated expression of the "moi." While exalting the names of Gautier, Banville, and Leconte de Lisle, they often forgot to consider one in their midst who held a higher truth: that poetry is the portraiture of the inner self and that its expression need not be a direct statement but rather the creation of a mood through a superb blending of imagery and music. Gautier however does include Baudelaire among the four poets who, to his way of thinking, are exerting the greatest influence among the young generation of 1868. His epithets for the work of each of these masters is interesting: he speaks of the "grandeur farouche" of Hugo, the "ampleur harmonique" of Banville, the "sérénité impassible" of Leconte de Lisle, and the "âpre concentration" of Baudelaire.[16]

For Gautier the *Parnasse contemporain* was like a springtime bouquet which gave much promise for the future. But scarcely had the volume appeared when a small book of parodies, the *Parnassiculet contemporain* (1867), gaily attacked the collection. The Parnassians are accused in a preface, signed "L'Editeur," of merely wishing to be eccentric and of using exotic names in order to revive a form of outmoded romanticism. The author of the preface adopts a bantering tone and concludes with the hope that some of the group will reform:

Cependant, comme quelques-uns d'entre eux lui paraissent plus sainement doués que les autres, il y a des chances pour qu'ils rejettent au vestiaire de Babin les costumes bizarres dont ils se sont affublés pour ne pas ressembler à tout le monde

16. This epithet, applied to Baudelaire, is revelatory. It suggests the kind of inspiration which Aloysius Bertrand found in Rembrandt. Bertrand, in the preface of *Gaspard de la nuit*, calls Rembrandt the philosopher "qui se consume à pénétrer les mystérieux symboles de la nature." The debt acknowledged by the author of "Correspondances" to Bertrand for the form of the "petits poèmes en prose" may extend to the exhausting search of the mystery of existence.

et qu'ils comprennent enfin qu'il vaut mieux être original en français que ridicule en sanscrit.

That Alphonse Daudet and his friends were the authors was immediately suspected, and indeed the colony of Clamart [17] (Daudet, du Boys, Arène) had with the help of Alfred Delvau composed the satire. They understood quite well certain peculiarities of Parnassian technique: the descriptive detail, the role of mythology and folklore, the affection for rich rhymes and sonorous syllables. As a result, their parodies are quite good. The curious thing is that the preface contains much the same accusations as those later leveled at the symbolists. The "Sanscrit" will perhaps signify neologisms and distortions of meaning, but the poets will be accused in the same way of wishing to be isolated from the crowd.

The *Parnassiculet,* so frankly farcical in tone, probably did not harm the group at which it was poking fun and indeed may have been good advertising. More serious and less well-intentioned were the "Médaillonets" which Barbey d'Aurevilly published in the *Nain jaune* in the early part of 1867 and in which, through a series of caricatural portrait-sketches, he poked fun at Gautier, Leconte de Lisle, and especially Verlaine.[18] Sainte-Beuve preserved silence on the group in the last articles he wrote for the *Constitutionnel,* but in these last years of his life he was so much more occupied with political questions than literature that such reticence may not indicate utter hostility.

Verlaine's first volume, published the same year as the *Parnasse contemporain,* found a contemptuous critic in Barbey d'Aurevilly but no great admirers. With its proclamation of impersonality and its poems in which the influence of Leconte de Lisle is all too evident, it is still the collection which contains the "Chanson d'automne," the little poem whose suggestion and music quite well synthesize symbolist art, and it offers lines where melody and mood are fused in a new and original form. These are the verses which provoke John Charpentier to say:

Verlaine, en tout cas quand il croit faire œuvre parnassienne, en publiant en 1866 les *Poèmes saturniens,* rompt, le premier, avec le matérialisme ou le positivisme des disciples de Leconte de Lisle.[19]

If one were to judge by lines such as the following, this statement would seem perfectly accurate:

17. See A. de Bersaucourt, "La Dédicace manuscrit," *Les Marges,* July 15, 1921.

18. An article published by Verlaine in *L'Art* (see Paul Verlaine, *Œuvres posthumes,* II, 306–323) is supposed to have been the origin of this enmity. Later in his biography of Barbey in "Les Hommes d'aujourd'hui," Verlaine is malicious but seems not to have kept rancor against the author of the *Diaboliques.*

19. John Charpentier, *Le Symbolisme,* p. 12.

Souvenir, souvenir, que me veux-tu? L'automne
Faisait voler la grive à travers l'air atone
Et le soleil dardait un rayon monotone
Sur le bois jaunissant où la bise détone.[20]

Other verses offer a gentle, hesitant music and a simple, nostalgic form of expression that was later to receive its full measure of praise and the consecration of imitation:

Et les soucis que vous pouvez avoir sont comme
Des hirondelles sur un ciel d'après-midi,
Chère,—par un beau ciel de septembre attiédi.[21]

If the inspiration of Leconte de Lisle is evident in such a poem as "Çavitri," that of Baudelaire is not to be discounted, ranging as it does from a bold transcription in a few lines of "Sub urbe" to the images in the sections "Mélancholia" and "Paysages tristes." The inception of a new art, the continuation of Baudelaire are thus present but hidden among a dominant sequence of lines where the emotion becomes exteriorized and restrained.

Verlaine's volume and poetic collections by Coppée and Xavier de Ricard began the series of volumes of verse that were to make illustrious the name of Lemerre as editor of the Parnassians. The immediate influence and rapid rise to fame of Coppée, in contrast with the retarded recognition of Verlaine, remains one of the curious facts of literary history. Within the younger group of the *Parnasse contemporain* of 1866 were most of those who would shape the destinies of poetry until the twentieth century. In the 1870's the reigning themes would be those of antiquity, represented by José-Maria de Heredia, of every-day existence chosen by Coppée, of the philosophical and meditative disquisition elected by Sully-Prudhomme,[22] and the intimate, descriptive landscapes of poets such as Albert Mérat.

The music, the delicate shadings of the inner self, the courageous departure from traditional form and expression were to abide their time. Verlaine, before embarking on the adventure which was to separate him from French letters for many years, had sufficiently voiced not only in *Les Poèmes saturniens* but in *Fêtes galantes* and *La Bonne Chanson,* much of the fragile and suggestive melody that would make him one day celebrated,

20. Paul Verlaine, *Œuvres complètes,* I, 11.
21. *Ibid.,* p. 16.
22. Both Coppée and Sully-Prudhomme were extremely fecund in publications during the 1870's. The former is the author of: *Les Humbles* and *Promenades et intérieurs* (1872); *Le Cahier rouge* (1874); *Olivier* (1875); *Elégies* (1876). Sully-Prudhomme published *Croquis italiens, Impressions de guerre, Les Destins,* all in 1872; *La Révolte des fleurs* and *La France* (1874); *Les Vaines Tendresses* (1875); *La Justice* (1878).

but perhaps that very fragility caused the volumes to go unnoticed in a world more accustomed to the sonorities of Victor Hugo or Leconte de Lisle. Mallarmé's slow and careful elaboration of the search for absolute beauty, scattered here and there at rare intervals, was not available to the general public; even Rimbaud, who read with attention the second *Parnasse contemporain,* was apparently unmoved by the "Hérodiade," [23] and Gustave Kahn's narration of visits to the Rue de Rome in 1879 and 1880 [24] indicates only a faint hint of coming popularity. Even in 1883 Ernest Raynaud was led to desire further acquaintance with the work of Mallarmé by the Verlaine article in *Lutèce.*[25]

Just on the eve of the Franco-Prussian War a poet who called himself the Count of Lautréamont died in complete obscurity. By his imagery, sarcasm, rhythmic prose, and exploration of the subconscious he is often counted among the precursors of symbolism. His work does indeed present valid affinities with that movement but until the surrealist period he seems to have been almost totally unknown. Edouard Dujardin, certainly not uninformed concerning the literary conversations of the last fifteen years of the nineteenth century, is able to state that he did not hear the name of Lautréamont pronounced a single time during the symbolist period. Except for Léon Bloy [26] and Remy de Gourmont,[27] the former of whom considers Lautréamont insane, the author of the *Chants de Maldoror* seems to have aroused little interest. Yet he seems one of those so marked by destiny to figure among Verlaine's "poètes maudits," to have played a part in Rimbaud's "dérèglement des sens," and to have a part in the irony of Jules Laforgue that the publication of the first canto of the *Chants de Maldoror* in 1868 and the unfinished, enigmatic essay called *Poésies* (1870) deserve mention. The revolts of Villiers de l'Isle-Adam, Rimbaud, and Isidore Ducasse are so nearly contemporaneous that, regardless of the question of possible influences, they constitute what Léon Bloy saw as the exasperation of idealism in materialistic society, a portion of the somber message contained in the work of Baudelaire.

Thus between 1866 and 1870 evidence of dissent from the traditional is not lacking in the realm of poetry. The desire for innovation even appears vigorous when one examines the early work of Mallarmé and Verlaine. But it would be false to assume much appreciation of their originality on the part of the gen-

23. Rimbaud's letter to Paul Demeny, May 15, 1871.

24. Gustave Kahn, *Symbolistes et décadents,* pp. 23–25.

25. Ernest Raynaud, *En Marge de la mêlée symboliste,* p. 39.

26. Bloy's interest in Lautréamont antedates the publication of the Genonceaux edition of 1890, for he laments the complete obscurity of the *Chants de Maldoror* in *Le Désespéré* (1887). His article in *La Plume,* II, 151–154, entitled "La Cabanon de Prométhée," comes just before the publication of Lautréamont's work in the small and expensive edition of Genonceaux.

27. La Littérature Maldoror," *Mercure de France,* II (February, 1891), 97–102.

eral public or from men of letters. Even Baudelaire's reputation, in the years immediately following his death, remained far from secure. It is because of its divergence from current opinion that Gautier's attempt to make a critical evaluation of the *Fleurs du mal* is remarkable. While some of the most meaningful texts for poetry of suggestion and music had appeared before 1870, they gained almost no notice and found no immediate following.

Chapter II: POETIC LETHARGY
IN THE 1870's

GAUTIER'S HOPES for a revival of interest in poetry through the publication of the first *Parnasse contemporain* were not destined to be fulfilled. Very soon political events occupied the foreground, beginning with the outbreak of the Franco-Prussian War in July, 1870, and extending through the Commune until 1873, when the German invaders finally left the country. The period was one of anguish and uncertainty, of civil unrest in the face of disaster and discouragement. This state of affairs gave to poetry a temporary orientation toward past events and the immediate problem of the French nation. Personal lyricism yielded to patriotic themes, expressed by the very titles of volumes of verse published during the period: Bergerat's *Poèmes de la guerre*, Manuel's *Pendant la guerre*, Banville's *Idylles prussiennes*, all published in 1871, were followed the next year by Hugo's *Année terrible*, Déroulède's *Les Chants du soldat*, and Sully-Prudhomme's *Impressions de la guerre*.

Meanwhile the second *Parnasse contemporain*, ready since 1869 but retarded by the war, appeared in 1871. It boasted fifty-seven contributors, twenty more than the first *Parnasse*, but it is of inferior quality. Its monotony of tone is perhaps ascribable to the inclusion of many unoriginal and imitative poets. There are few departures from descriptive verse. Women writers in the collection, such as Madame Blanchecotte and Louisa Siefert, give free rein to their emotions but offer only a belated form of romanticism. Albert Glatigny's "A Cosette," Armand Silvestre's "La Gloire du souvenir," and André Lemoyne's "Rosaire d'amour," though of intuitive inspiration, seem singularly unoriginal. A weight of reticence burdens the lyric utterance, and even Charles Cros, so enthusiastic by nature, seems to be asking pardon for not accepting the lesson of "Les Montreurs":

> Car ce mal est trop grand pour que seul je le garde;
> Aussi j'ouvre mon âme à la foule criarde.[1]

Verlaine, who was shortly to be cut off from contact with the Parnassians when he left Paris in the company of Rimbaud, is still represented in this anthology. His five poems, some of which had been written as far back as 1862, are unimpressive either in form or content. In the volume one poem,

1. *Le Parnasse contemporain* (1871), p. 309.

Mallarmé's "Hérodiade," stands apart, a spiritual foreigner, published at a time when understanding and appreciation would seem negated by current fashions, and awaiting the moment when Huysmans and Verlaine could unveil its significance to a more receptive world.

The author of the "Hérodiade" had written, in 1864 and 1865, when he had begun composing the first version of the poem, a series of letters to Cazalis, in which he had given his ideas of poetic innovation.[2] Had these meditations, based to some degree on Poe's theories, been disseminated, printed, and read, they might have given new strength to those who admired Baudelaire. But Mallarmé's confidences to personal friends were concerned with the possibilities of accomplishment rather than with elucidations of doctrine. He hoped to be able to produce a mysterious effect on the reader by a combination of sounds and connotative values. He felt at times that he had found a strange and intimate manner of noting fugitive sensations, but he passed through alternate periods of doubt and hope concerning his actual realization of the absolute beauty he dreamed.

Thus, to a marked degree, to cite the date of publication of an important poem by Mallarmé is to give an unsatisfactory truth. Often, and this is the case of the "Hérodiade," one may propose a valid date only by spanning two decades and more, from the time of the inner struggle of creation, through modifications and the appearance in print, to the years when the poet's lines really began to have existence in the interest and admiration of a public. The music and intention of the "Hérodiade" certainly fell on deaf ears in the 1870's; aided somewhat by Verlaine and Huysmans, the poem was to take on new life after 1884.

The *Parnasse* of 1871 was mercilessly condemned in Rimbaud's letter of May 15, 1871, to Paul Demeny. It is strange that he does not mention Mallarmé's name, but interesting that he accords talent to Léon Dierx, François Coppée, and Sully-Prudhomme. Among the young generation of the Parnassians, Rimbaud finds that only two, Verlaine and Mérat, are worthy of the designation of "voyants," the poets who, by a "long, immense et raisonné dérèglement de tous les sens," have arrived at the unknown. Equally incisive is Rimbaud's judgment on the older generation of the Parnassians, the poets who were hailed as masters and blindly copied:

Les seconds romantiques sont très *voyants:* Théophile Gautier, Leconte de Lisle, Théodore de Banville. Mais inspecter l'invisible et entendre l'inouï étant autre chose que reprendre l'esprit des choses mortes, Baudelaire est le premier voyant, roi des poètes, *un vrai Dieu.*[3]

2. Mallarmé's intentions, revealed through his letters, are carefully studied in Henri Mondor's *Vie de Mallarmé.* See especially the numerous quotations from letters, pp. 100–150.

3. Arthur Rimbaud, *Œuvres complètes* (Pléiade ed.), p. 257.

These two sentences, which follow a diatribe against Musset and a summons to seek new poetic forms and ideas, constitute a vigorous and significant manifesto. In them one may discover the repudiation of Parnassian Hellenism, the invitation for the poet to explore the depths of his own personality, and the selection of a proper guide from the older generation. Although this invitation for poetry to embark on new paths, written in an obscure letter by a sixteen-year-old boy, was not printed until 1912, the concept, imparted to Verlaine and later revealed in poetry itself, was to have rich and abundant harvest. Rimbaud, penetrating the meaning of *Les Fleurs du mal* as had no one before him, unprovided as was Laforgue with Hartmann's study of the unconscious as a breviary, foresees an art in which the sensations will be but the crude tools with which to unearth the mystery of beauty. But the hour had not yet come for the revelation.[4]

The 1870's belong essentially to realism and to Parnassianism. The landmarks of *Madame Bovary* (1857), *Germinie Lacerteux* (1865), *Thérèse Raquin* (1866), preluding the series of the Rougon-Macquart through the seventies, and the publication of the *Roman expérimental* and the *Soirées de Médan* in 1880 give an impression of solidarity and continuity.

Elements of realism meanwhile found their way into poetry. The method was not that of Maxime Du Camp, who had the none too happy idea of celebrating railway locomotives and electric telegraphy in *Les Chants modernes* (1855). The incursion took the form of description of commonplace and humble existence. Victor Hugo had pointed the way in "Les Pauvres Gens"; [5] Verlaine had composed "La Soupe du soir," which was printed in the second *Parnasse contemporain;* Eugène Manuel's *Poèmes populaires* appeared in 1871. The best-known example was that of François Coppée, whose volume *Les Humbles* was the model for some of the most prosaic verse written in the French language. Coppée had at least the traits of tenderness, irony, and a certain delicacy to relieve banality. What such themes became in less gifted poets may be illustrated by the opening lines of two poems published in *La Renaissance artistique et littéraire* on August 31, 1872:

> Elle était pauvre et seule, et voulut rester fille.
> De bonne heure, elle avait adopté pour famille
> Les enfants sans parents, délaissés ici-bas.[6]

4. Rimbaud's conception of the hidden world into which poetry alone can penetrate offers certain similarities with ideas of Novalis. The German romantic poet speaks of the invisible realm beyond mere sensation, which allies poetry with mysticism (*Fragments*, p. 125). The whole romantic movement presents, however, these points of contact with Symbolism: the penetration of the inner self, the poet as seer, the importance of dreams. See A. Béguin, *L'Ame romantique et le rêve.*

5. In *La Légende des siècles* (1859).

6. The author is Auguste Baluffe.

This form of expression, which has very little to do with poetry, is under-standable, if not pardonable, when the author is relating a story. Unfortunately the same pedestrian muse seems to have officiated at the birth of lines which involve an idea rather than a narration:

> A rester tout le jour incliné sur un livre
> On se fatigue, il faut de l'air à qui veut vivre,
> De l'air au cerveau lourd, à l'œil appesanti.[7]

The point of departure is probably not very different from that of Mallarmé's "Brise marine" and causes one to reflect on the importance of expression as opposed to thought in verse. But it is quite true that the tendency to stop at the exterior aspect of things, to describe without penetrating the soul, is a constant phenomenon in the 1870's. Many of Francis Jammes's poems will have subjects as simple and commonplace as those of Coppée, but will seem infinitely more lyric by the intervention of the writer's dream.

Another aspect of realism, more vulgar than Coppée's and at the same time satirical of the middle classes, is that of the three "vivants," Jean Richepin, Maurice Bouchor, and Raoul Ponchon. Bouchor's *Chansons joyeuses* (1874) and Richepin's *Chanson des gueux* (1876) both were considered somewhat too frank in expression, and the latter volume resulted in a short imprisonment and fine for its author. Ponchon wrote abundantly, his rhymed "gazettes" were famous but not published in book form until 1920 when a selection of his verse appeared. The title, *La Muse au cabaret,* recalls the numerous groups which formed during the symbolist period for the recitation of verse. In them the most serious of poetic efforts were heard with ironical or ribald songs. About 1878 Emile Goudeau formed the literary club called the "Hydropathes," to which Bourget, Maupassant, Hennique, Paul Arène, Rollinat, and Sarah Bernhardt belonged. This group, which its founder calls the negation of a literary school, set the pattern for other gatherings of writers, artists, and musicians. Though sometimes frivolous and eccentric, they are not without importance in literary evolution. The "Hirsutes," the "Zutistes," and later the meetings of the "Chat noir" and the "Soirées de *La Plume,*" with their tendency to make fun of what was established and traditional, were useful for the gestation of new ideas and forms.

One of the curious mementos of such activity in the early 1870's is the *Album zutique,* in which are to be found autograph poems of Rimbaud, Verlaine, Charles Cros, Camille Pelletan, Léon Valade, Germain Nouveau, E. Cabaner, E. Carjat, Raoul Ponchon, Richepin, and others. Signed derisively with the names of many of the Parnassians, with the actual author's initials usually below, these facetious poems seem to have been added at various times

7. The author is Julien Lugol.

between 1871 and 1875. The album may have had some relation with the "Vilains Bonshommes," [8] if, as Félix Régamey writes, the meeting place of the group frequently changed.[9]

The *Album zutique* is one of the few souvenirs left of Rimbaud's brief visit to the world of letters of Paris in 1871–72. His name and that of Verlaine in the same collection symbolize a meeting which was to have far-reaching effects, first of all by the influence of a child prodigy on the author of *La Bonne Chanson,* and secondly by the revelation, a decade later, of Rimbaud's work through the writings of Paul Verlaine. In so far as French literature is concerned, Rimbaud's immediate influence seems to have been limited to the one poet, although certain of the ironic lines in Charles Cros's *Le Coffret de santal* (1873) and the brutal clarity of some of his prose at the end of the same volume invite speculation on the nature of literary conversations while Rimbaud was being sheltered beneath Cros's roof.[10] The commentary of Verlaine on Rimbaud's appearance among the Vilains Bonshommes indicates this limited sphere of influence:

Sauf un petit groupe de Parnassiens indépendants, les grands Parnassiens (Coppée, Mendès, Hérédia) n'admirèrent que mal ou pas du tout le phénomène nouveau. Valade, Mérat, Charles Cros, moi donc, excepté, il ne trouva guère d'accueil dans la capitale revisitée.[11]

There is, to be sure, the testimony of a letter from Léon Valade to Emile Blémont, written soon after Rimbaud's arrival in Paris, in which the writer states his belief that the newcomer is a budding genius,[12] but the scandal of the Verlaine-Rimbaud relationship soon silenced comments on their work and virtually exiled them from French literature for a decade.

One of the few friends who remained loyal to Verlaine through all his vicissitudes was Emile Petitdidier, known in literature as Emile Blémont.[13] Most of our knowledge of Verlaine's life and literary activity during the 1870's is derived from letters written to him or to Edmond Lepelletier, but

8. See Paul Verlaine, *Œuvres posthumes,* II, 258–259.

9. The notes of the *Œuvres complètes* of Arthur Rimbaud (Pléiade ed.), by Rolland de Renéville and Jules Mouquet, discuss fully the various questions which arise concerning the *Album zutique.* See pp. 667–673.

10. The poems in the *Coffret de santal* are extremely diversified in tone and inspiration, ranging from the ironic to the sentimental, and employing both severe and popular diction. The portion called "Grains de sel," as its name would indicate, contains the most sharp commentaries on society, and the "Fantaisies en prose" have passages of strange, evocative power, which may have some affinity with the *Illuminations.* For example (p. 273): "Mais quand la fièvre pesante m'a égaré et fait redescendre, puis-je vivre seul et sans soleil entre des murs de haine?"

11. Paul Verlaine, *Œuvres posthumes,* II, 271.

12. See Marcel Coulon; *La Vie de Rimbaud,* p. 160.

13. Ernest Raynaud has written an interesting sketch of Blémont in his *En Marge de la mêlée symboliste,* pp. 169–177.

in 1872 he is more important as one of the cofounders (with Jean Aicard) of the *Renaissance artistique et littéraire*. This weekly periodical, which appeared, with interruptions, between April 27, 1872 and May 3, 1874, is the most interesting of the decade in so far as poetry is concerned. Ernest Raynaud, in the opening pages of his *La Mêlée symboliste* utilizes it to illustrate the essence of the poetic spirit after the Franco-Prussian War, and with some justice, for in its ninety-nine numbers almost an equal number of poets are represented. Their names give a representative list of the older generation and of the young poets who were just beginning to be known.

That the tone is largely Parnassian, that the endless number of sonnets and eight-syllable quatrains repeat the descriptive and carefully wrought themes of Leconte de Lisle and of Gautier, is undeniable. Admiration for Gautier, whose death occurred during the life span of the magazine, is equaled only by the veneration accorded Victor Hugo, whose letter of greeting was printed not only in the second number of the year 1872 but also in the first number of the following year. The lists of the most frequent contributors reveal no great names; in addition to the founders, the poets most frequently represented are Albert Mérat (1840–1909), Léon Valade (1841–84) and Léon Dierx (1838–1912). Thus, beyond the fact that the group represents that portion of the Parnasse which preferred modern, intimate themes to Hellenism or philosophy, this poetic fellowship seems without significance.[14]

However great the number of conservative poets who figured among the collaborators of the *Renaissance* during its first year of existence, there are indications of affinities and interests which are forecasts of the future rather than restatements of the past. In the first number is an article by Théodore de Banville on Baudelaire.[15] Largely a description of Baudelaire's apartment, it is yet full of admiration and understanding and is perhaps an indication of that continuous and hidden influence which was to become evident in the next decade. Later in the same year, in a bibliographical note [16] concerning *Charles Baudelaire, souvenirs, correspondances, bibliographie* by Cousin and Spoelberch, the author of the *Fleurs du mal* is designated "le poète exquis et

14. Fantin-Latour's painting of 1872, entitled "Coin de table," shows some of the collaborators of the *Renaissance* when Verlaine was still among their number. Blémont and Aicard are standing behind the table with Elzéar Bonnier. The presence of Rimbaud in the picture, seated beside Verlaine, caused Albert Mérat to demand that his likeness be scraped away. Valade, d'Hervilly, and Pelletan, however, remain.

15. When one considers that this article, so descriptive in character, is the only important one which mentions Baudelaire, one understands with difficulty the words of Ernest Raynaud: "En attendant, les poètes de la *Renaissance* exaltent Baudelaire" (*La Mêlée symboliste*, I, 17), and even less those of Guy Michaud: ". . . début du culte rendu à Baudelaire, dans la *Renaissance*" (*Message poétique du symbolisme*, I, 224).

16. *La Renaissance artistique et littéraire*, April 27, 1872.

profond." But these are the only contributions [17] to Baudelairian criticism in the entire history of the magazine and it is rather by isolated poems that one realizes the profound effect of certain aspects of Baudelaire's art. Thus when Maurice Rollinat begins a poem with the line:

> Chopin! frère du Gouffre, amant des nuits tragiques,[18]

or when Charles Grandmougin speaks of:

> Beethoven, mer aux flots sinistres et grondeurs,[19]

the memory of "Les Phares" is inescapable. But other poets to some degree seem to have felt the "frisson nouveau." Even such a staunch admirer of Leconte de Lisle as was Léon Dierx becomes at times mysterious and subjective. The atmosphere, the vocabulary, the music of such a stanza as the following, published in the *Renaissance* on June 22, 1873, seem the antithesis of the objective and might indeed be defended as a model of symbolist poetry:

> Tout se fait suave et se vaporise,
> Et tout s'abandonne aux vagues langueurs,
> O mots embaumés flottant sur la brise!
> Quel fécond silence embrase nos cœurs?

Verlaine's verse appeared in the *Renaissance* in two early numbers,[20] shortly before his departure from Paris with Rimbaud. The two poems are among the most beautiful from his pen, they being "C'est l'extase langoureuse" and "Le piano que baise une main frêle," [21] which were to become a portion of the "Ariettes oubliées." They are a valedictory to Verlaine's publication in French periodicals until 1882. Although Blémont was one of Verlaine's good friends, and Verlaine continued to be interested in the *Renaissance,* the magazine does not mention his name until 1874 when a brief bibliographical notice gave this reticent praise:

Nous recevons un volume de Paul Verlaine, *Romances sans paroles,* d'un art très subtil et d'une bien étrange morbidesse. C'est l'œuvre d'un vrai poète, mais maladif et tourmenté.[22]

Thus the poems which Verlaine wrote in Brussels, London, and Jéhonville during 1872 and 1873, and which under the influence of Rimbaud were to

17. *Ibid.*, October 5, 1872.

18. *Ibid.*, November 30, 1873.

19. *Ibid.*, December 28, 1873.

20. A third poem, Verlaine's "Pantoum négligé," a parody of Alphonse Daudet's *Les Amoureuses,* was published in the *Renaissance* (August 24, 1872). The poem is signed with the name of Daudet, the magazine suggesting that the verses had been simply left in its mailbox and that Daudet may perhaps be the author. Is connivance between Verlaine and Blémont indicated?

21. *La Renaissance,* May 18 and June 29, 1872.

22. *Ibid.*, April 19, 1874.

reveal a poetic manner in which suggestion and music dominated thought, were denied much publicity. Verlaine sent Blémont three poems on September 22, 1872, and two others on April 22, 1873, but these were not published in the *Renaissance*. There was apparently much hostility among the collaborators of the magazine toward Verlaine. When, thanks to Edmond Lepelletier, the Sens edition of *Romances sans paroles* appeared in March, 1874, Verlaine had been in prison for some eight months and the publication met with most complete indifference.[23] It was not until 1884 that the unsold copies were placed in the hands of Verlaine's new editor, Léon Vanier, who reprinted the poems in 1887 with success.

Meanwhile, in the summer of 1875, Verlaine sent some offerings for the third *Parnasse contemporain,* employing Emile Blémont as intermediary. The committee's refusal, Anatole France's harsh words concerning Verlaine's character and the worth of the poetry [24] were followed by trips to Lemerre's office, where Blémont evidently spoke in favor of Verlaine and encountered difficulty in securing return of the manuscript.[25]

Almost complete silence meanwhile surrounded the name of Verlaine's companion, Rimbaud. It is not strange that the pistol shot at Brussels and the imprisonment at Mons should have been ignored. Nor could one expect comment on *Une Saison en enfer,* published in Brussels in 1873, and long thought to have been almost completely destroyed by its author. Léon Losseau's discovery of the entire edition, moldering in a warehouse, in 1901, became known only in 1914. Only one short poem, "Les Corbeaux," appeared in print at this period, in the *Renaissance* on September 14, 1872, and this publication, according to Verlaine,[26] was without the sanction of Rimbaud. Written in the regular meters which Rimbaud had renounced by 1872, it probably excited little attention and remains one of the bibliographical curiosities of the few poems by Rimbaud published before 1883.[27]

In the *Renaissance* Mallarmé published many of his translations of Poe's poems, wrote an appreciation of the poetic work of Léon Dierx,[28] and published a politely scathing attack on the jury which rejected two out of three paintings by Manet in the 1874 national exhibition. Villiers de l'Isle-Adam,

---

23. Lepelletier's son, Saint-Georges de Bouhélier, tells of having found a considerable packet of the Sens edition in his father's house. Very few of the three hundred copies must have been sold. See Saint-Georges de Bouhélier: *Le Printemps d'une génération*, p. 106.

24. It is true that Anatole France redeemed himself somewhat by laudatory articles concerning Verlaine in *Le Temps*, April 19 and November 15, 1891.

25. *Correspondance de Paul Verlaine*, II, 3–11.

26. Paul Verlaine, *Œuvres complètes*, IV, 29.

27. A chronological listing of published works of Rimbaud may be found in the Pléiade edition of the *Œuvres complètes*.

28. *La Renaissance artistique et littéraire:* June 29, July 20, August 17, October 5, October 11, November 16, 1872.

who like Mallarmé was to become one of Verlaine's *poètes maudits,* is also represented in the magazine by the first part of the drama *Axel,* published in three installments, by a short poem "Sara," and by two stories, "La Découverte de M. Grave" and "La Machine à gloire," both of which are indictments of commercial and materialistic civilization.[29]

Ernest Raynaud lists three volumes published in 1873 which were to have enormous influence on the symbolist movement and to which he says that no one paid any attention. They are: *Une Saison en enfer, Les Amours jaunes,* and *Le Coffret de santal.* It is interesting to note that while the *Renaissance* does not speak of Rimbaud's work, and while it gives more honor and importance to Hugo's *La Libération du territoire,* Mérat's *L'Adieu* and *Villes de marbre* than to the volumes of Tristan Corbière or Charles Cros, it does not entirely neglect these two poets.

Charles Cros, the author of *Le Coffret de santal,* who was to found the ephemeral little periodical, *La Revue de monde nouveau,* in 1874, and was to be the moving spirit of the Zutistes in the early 1880's, made occasional verse or prose contributions to the *Renaissance.* His is one of the obscure names which have their importance in the evolution away from objectivity. In the magazine's review of his poetry [30] this character is more or less recognized, for he is described as "plus intime que descriptif, plus poète que peintre" and his favorite theme is designated as a subtle and faithful analysis of love, in the varied shading of feeling, almost in the most fugitive of sensations. His poems, the article continues, are songs, not simply words written for tunes, but such harmonies as would tempt a musician's talent. Notation of qualities of delicate shading, of the fugitive and of the musical (which might have been so well applied to Verlaine's *Romances sans paroles,* published the year after the *Coffret de santal*) indicate at least an appreciation of suggestive rather than declamatory art.

In truth, while the *Renaissance* is an isolated example of a publication which welcomed certain innovations in literature, it rarely broke entirely away from tradition. This is seen in the review of Tristan Corbière's *Les Amours jaunes,* where the opening paragraph reveals the degree of acceptance and rejection in the reviewer's (most probably Blémont's) mind:

Des idées baroques, *étrangement* sceptiques rendues dans une forme saccadée, nerveuse, blême et surtout irrégulière; çà et là quelques beaux vers et quelques conceptions très-larges, comme *Décourageux, Le Renégat;* souvent de l'humour et une façon propre de voir les choses: telle est l'œuvre de M. Tristan Corbière.[31]

29. Villiers de l'Isle-Adam's contributions are in the following numbers of the *Renaissance:* October 12, December 7, December 14, 1872; July 13, November 30, 1873; March 22, 1874.
30. *Ibid.,* June 22, 1873.
31. *Ibid.,* October 26, 1873.

It is in 1874, in the last numbers of the expiring *Renaissance,* that an open note of revolt is sounded. An unsigned series of articles on the literatures of several countries during the year 1873 terminates with these conclusions on contemporary poetry:

En poésie, l'école plastique semble incliner partout vers la décadence. . . . La poésie n'est vraiment supérieure que quand elle pénètre jusqu'à l'âme des choses et des êtres; quand d'un trait, d'un mot, elle fait voir et sentir la vie et la beauté, quand loin de décrire minutieusement l'homme et la nature, elle note et condense en une phrase, en une parole, l'impression que les sites et les scènes produisent sur le cœur et l'esprit.

L'école plastique doit se compléter, se transformer, pour triompher. Et en effet l'art s'imprègne d'une vie nouvelle; il y a commencement de transformation.[32]

The author of this article—and because of the emphasis on foreign literatures Blémont would seem the most likely candidate—speaks of the influence of Hugo, Whitman, and Swinburne as precursors of the coming change which will sweep aside impassibility and description "devant un immense et irrésistible mouvement d'aspirations naturistes et humaines." In the following number of the magazine Jean Richepin is even more revolutionary, saying that all the formulas of literature seem worn out, that the past must be abandoned, that a new literature, a rejuvenated theater, and a modern poetry are necessary. He is particularly harsh on the Parnassians, whom he calls the offspring of romanticism, even as worms are offspring of a corpse, and who fail to see the horizon since they are eternally contemplating the ends of their noses.

These articles suggest no French poet as a model to follow, save for the mention of Victor Hugo, and doubtless the form envisaged was not that finally assumed by symbolism; yet the protest against the objective and the descriptive is there, and the summons for originality is as imperative as in Rimbaud's letter to Demeny. But if the *Renaissance* proposed to breathe new life into literature, it hardly had the chance, since it ceased existence at the beginning of May, 1874. Charles Cros, reassembling many of the collaborators, tried unsuccessfully to launch the *Revue du monde nouveau* in 1874, and later in the decade Villiers de l'Isle-Adam, with the *Spectateur* and the *Croix et l'Epée,* attempted to establish a periodical of religious idealism but elicited no response. The *Revue des deux mondes* had accepted Coppée, Sully-Prudhomme, and José-Maria de Heredia, who appeared in its pages with Eugène Manuel, Theuriet, and Albert Delpit. Verlaine's erstwhile companions, Valade and Mérat, enjoyed a passing renown; André Lemoyne and Charles Grandmougin were well regarded. The dominion of dream and introspective fan-

32. *Ibid.,* March 1, 1874.

tasy seemed relegated to the privately printed *L' Après-midi d'un faune* (1876) and the first volume of a mystical dreamer from Flanders, Georges Rodenbach.[33]

The general stagnation of poetic art is reflected by the third and last *Parnasse contemporain*. True, it contains two important sections: twenty-four "Rondels" by Théodore de Banville and as many sonnets from the pen of José-Maria de Heredia. The former are scarcely more than proofs of skill, composed after the manner of Charles d'Orléans, and the brilliant descriptions of the past contained in the poems of *Les Trophées,* however great their art, do not allow for more than imitation. The sixty-two other contributors, who by reason of their number might militate for variety and originality, unfortunately have little merit. They are able versifiers, but neither their thought nor their expression sets them apart from their fellow poets. Indeed a few minor authors falsely take on an air of originality, simply because from their verse emanates an atmosphere of emotion or of mystery. "Forêt, la nuit" by Henry Cazalis, "Les Cheveux" by Rollinat, Armand Silvestre's "Fantaisies célestes," and even the rustic poems, "A travers champs" or "La Source" by Anthony Valabrègue, none of which is great verse, are refreshing oases amid so much descriptive and expository poetry.

Toward the end of the decade, in 1878, appeared a magazine which, by its title at least, promised a rebirth of letters. This was *La Jeune France*. Founded by Albert Allenet, it had as literary advisers Jules Claretie, Alphonse Daudet, and Mario Proth. Two of these were born in 1840, and indeed it is that generation, no longer so young, which is chiefly present in its pages. The phenomena which it represents are not those of a new development in poetry; François Coppée and Léon Valade are its chief contributors of verse. The publication during 1878 and 1879 of Allenet's translations of the poems of Poe [34] and the marked hostility toward Zola are the sole indications in the magazine of future literary trends.

The interest in Poe is a consistent element in the 1870's. Mallarmé's translations, begun in *La Renaissance,* were continued in Catulle Mendès' *La République des lettres* (1875-77), a periodical which is still known in literary history for such diverse publications as prose poems by Mallarmé,[35] Zola's *L'Assommoir,* Richard Wagner's "Un Musicien étranger à Paris," and certain short stories by Villiers de l'Isle-Adam. In poetry the magazine represents the whole Parnassian school: Théodore de Banville, Leconte de Lisle, Sully-Prudhomme, Heredia, Mérat, Valade, and Silvestre. Rollinat and Emile Goudeau, it is true, appeared among the contributors, but their poems were not of the

---

33. *Le Foyer et les champs* (1877).
34. *La Jeune France,* I, 145, 300, 386, 464; II, 66, 142, 185, 264, 318, 463.
35. "Frisson d'hiver," "Plainte d'automne," "Le Spectacle interrompu," "Le Phénomène futur," published in the first number of the *République des lettres,* December 20, 1875.

sensational type for which they later became known. In general the lesser poets are docile and imitative; Adelphe Froger, who appears quite often in the *République*, took subjects for his sonnets from the Bible and created "Kaïn," "Le Spectre de Sodome," and "La Mort de Moïse."

The docility of the Parnassians in following established formulas for poetic expression is at once their chief characteristic and their principal fault. The accusation of impassiveness was somewhat inaccurate, for many of the lesser poets consciously tried to write modern, intimate verse. But the form, the imagery, the diction are seldom more than carefully wrought. The poems suggest models rather than spontaneity. Laudable as was the desire to escape sentimentality, its effect in hobbling the lyric impulsion was disastrous. Poizat's conclusions on the group, while overly harsh, contain a grain of truth:

Les Parnassiens crurent avoir fixé la poésie. C'était avouer qu'ils comptaient s'arrêter au soin du détail et que leur horizon ne dépassait guère leur table de travail. En réalité leur préoccupation secrète était de désespérer par leur perfection ceux qui viendraient après eux et de s'imposer à leurs successeurs comme des maîtres.[36]

A manifestation of anxiety and unrest, a deep melancholy which at times verges on despair and nihilism, appears in the work of a poet who is difficult to ally with any movement and whose poetic life is confined to the years 1875–83. This is Paul Bourget, whose three volumes of verse, *La Vie inquiète, Adel,* and *Les Aveux,* are in their diction more akin to the romantic movement and yet whose themes, particularly in his last book of verse, are sometimes similar to those of Baudelaire. Debauchery, boredom, and death are the subjects of a delicate and refined analysis which conquered the admiration of Laforgue, an admiration which may have been in part the expression of gratitude for Bourget's kindness but even more the appreciation of a sincere inner struggle.

Bourget, first a frequenter of Goudeau's Hydropathes and later briefly enrolled with Verlaine and Moréas in the group centered around *La Nouvelle Rive gauche,*[37] was to have a short-lived influence on the decadent phase of symbolism. His evolution, terminating in conversion to Catholicism and in the abandonment of poetry for the novel and essay, has left a reputation which bears little relationship with his youthful writings. Yet his verse remains as testimony of another state of mind, one which causes Henri Chantavoine to speak of his poetry as the last, graceful charm of a rather tired generation which is dying away.[38] Unoriginal in imagery, in *Adel* the author of lines which are much like those of Coppée, he is yet one of the poets who abandoned the universal for the individual and who sought in the depths of his own sensation and meditation the subject for lyric expression. As such, he typifies the poetry of the years to come.

36. Alfred Poizat, *Le Symbolisme,* p. 40.
37. See *La Nouvelle Rive gauche* for February 23 and March 30, 1883.
38. Petit de Julleville, *Histoire de la langue et de la littérature française,* VIII, 63.

Chapter III: THE CONCEPT
OF DECADENCE

SHORTLY BEFORE 1880 the hidden but persistent influence of Baudelaire began to show itself openly. After 1878, among the group of the Hydropathes, Rollinat, accompanying himself on the piano, delighted and terrified his audiences (among them the actress Sarah Bernhardt) by recitations of poems of death and decay.[1] In a preface dated August, 1879, for the first edition of Théodore Hannon's *Rimes de joie*, J.-K. Huysmans violently attacked the Parnassian school but reserved a place of honor for the author of the *Fleurs du mal*.

Among the Hydropathes was the young poet whose first volume, *La Vie inquiète* (1875), had revealed a sense of anguish in search of faith and idealism in the conditions of existence. In an article published in 1881,[2] possibly identifying his own problems with those of Baudelaire, he strove to analyze the reasons for the pessimism, the ideas on love, and the nature of decadence as observed in Baudelaire. By this essay, which antedates Verlaine's "Langueur," the *Poètes maudits,* and *A rebours,* Paul Bourget stimulated interest in the idea of decadence. He saw as cause of Baudelaire's pessimism the lack of harmony between realities and the needs of civilized man. What had been a form of skepticism in Musset and a proud rebellion in Vigny have become in Baudelaire a horror of existence and a desire for annihilation. In considering these judgments of Bourget, one must not forget that the budding critic was still the pessimistic, almost nihilistic poet whose anguish was expressed in lines such as the following:

> La matière se meut en sa stupidité,
> L'affreuse solitude est à jamais la même
> Et l'homme seul répond à l'homme épouvanté.[3]

In these verses and in many others where the futility of effort and the spectacle of death, as well as the desire for faith, furnish the theme, we have the immediate spectacle of Bourget's conflict and understand to what degree he expresses his own preoccupations in speaking of Baudelaire. In a section of his essay entitled "Théorie de la décadence" Bourget defines decadence as

1. His popularity is attested by several writers, the best account being that of G. Guiches in *Au Banquet de la vie.*
2. *La Nouvelle Revue,* XIII (November 15, 1881), 398–416.
3. Paul Bourget, *Poésies 1876–1882,* p. 294.

the state of society which produces too great a number of individuals incapable of taking their proper place in the work of the world. As for a decadent style in literature, he finds that its chief element is the yielding of a book's unity to the individual sentence, indeed to the individual word. The portrait of Baudelaire, with his qualities of "mystique, libertin, et analyseur," is summed up in the sentence:

Voilà l'homme de la décadence, ayant conservé une incurable nostalgie des beaux rêves de ses aïeux, ayant par la précocité des abus tari en lui les sources de la vie, et jugeant d'un regard demeuré lucide l'inguérissable misère de sa destinée, c'est à dire,—car voyons-nous le monde autrement qu'à travers le prisme de nos intimes besoins?—de toute destinée.[4]

A few years later Bourget had passed the crisis of his own soul and, convinced of the possibilities of scientific analysis of the mind according to the principles of Stendhal and Taine, used these very characteristics of Baudelaire to warn the young generation; but first he was to express the ideas he later abhorred:

> Ah! que ta froideur me pénètre,
> Lune pâle des nuits du Nord,
> Et verse-moi l'horreur de l'être
> Dans l'amour profond de la mort! [5]

The circle of the Hydropathes was the scene of a meeting in 1880 of two men about twenty years of age who were to have an important role in poetic innovation. The one, Gustave Kahn, had come from Metz to study in the Ecole des Chartes and that of Oriental languages, but had as early as 1880, according to his own statement,[6] ideas of reforming prosody. The other, Jules Laforgue, after schooling in Tarbes and at the Lycée Fontanes in Paris, began to write verse. Encouraged by Paul Bourget, who enjoyed some prestige in 1880 as the author of *Adel,* a long, personal narrative poem, Laforgue had developed artistic and philosophical interests. His favorite book was the *Philosophie de l'inconscient* by Hartmann,[7] which had been translated into French in 1877.

Both Kahn and Laforgue attended meetings of the Hydropathes in 1880. At the end of that year Kahn departed for military service and in 1881 Laforgue too, accepting a position as reader for the Empress Augusta, left Paris. The letters [8] written by Laforgue to Kahn, after their brief acquaintanceship in the

4. *La Nouvelle Revue,* XIII, 411–412.

5. Paul Bourget, *Poésies 1876–1882,* p. 272.

6. Gustave Kahn, *Symbolistes et décadents,* p. 19.

7. In the first of the *Lettres à un ami,* dated December, 1880, Laforgue mentions Hartmann twice. Thereafter in his correspondence are many references to the German philosopher.

8. Jules Laforgue, *Lettres à un ami;* introduction and notes by G. Jean-Aubry.

French capital,[9] reveal much concerning the literary ideas of the period. Before his departure Laforgue heard Bourget read translations of Tennyson and Shelley; together they examined an old copy of Catulle Mendès' *République des lettres,* in which were four of Mallarmé's prose poems. In 1881 Laforgue speaks of the ever new admiration he feels for Baudelaire, and in his exile he managed to procure the authors (Verlaine, Huysmans, Villiers de l'Isle-Adam) who interested him most. He makes acute critical judgments, stating his conviction that Richepin was following literary fads, confessing his difficulty in reading Ghil for pleasure, despite his realization of a certain talent. Two authors, whom he knows only by fragments, he admires most; they are Mallarmé and Rimbaud.

While he was in Germany Laforgue procured Verlaine's *Sagesse* and the first poetic volume by Jean Moréas, *Les Syrtes.* While Kahn and Laforgue were away from Paris, a little magazine had been founded, which in truth laid the groundwork for a new poetic school, rehabilitated Verlaine's literary reputation to some degree, and published the verse of Moréas, a young Greek who had come to Paris and whose strong personality had been first revealed among the Hydropathes. First known as *La Nouvelle Rive gauche,* this periodical soon took the name of *Lutèce.*

Verlaine, after a decade of wandering, tragedy, and scandal, won his way back slowly into the literary life of Paris. In 1880 he had great difficulty in finding a publisher for *Sagesse.* His first reappearance in periodical literature was in 1882, in *Paris moderne,* founded by Léon Vanier that same year. This magazine was regarded, according to Verlaine,[10] as a last militant *Parnasse contemporain,* and its contributors included many of those with whom Verlaine had figured in 1866. It was there, however, on November 10, 1882, that the "Art poétique," the "morcel de vers nonipèdes," appeared. Charles Morice, the following month, in an article entitled "Boileau-Verlaine," made fun of the poem, saying that this theory of prosody had as sole characteristic a complete lack of clarity.[11] Verlaine's answer, denying his intentions of being revolutionary but insisting on the right to weep, to dream, or to sing according to his mood, was published in *La Nouvelle Rive gauche* on December 15, 1882, and on January 5, 1883, Verlaine made his first poetic contribution to the same magazine in a sonnet which had first appeared in *Le Hanneton* in 1867. Thus between the publication of *Sagesse* in 1881 (the volume which Laforgue described as "une langue inconsciente ayant tout juste le souci de

9. Kahn has described their meeting and conversations in *Symbolistes et décadents,* pp. 26–29.

10. Paul Verlaine, *Œuvres complètes,* V, 370.

11. Morice's article, signed "Karl Mohr," appeared in the fourth issue of *La Nouvelle Rive gauche* (December 1, 1882). Morice quickly repented of this article and became a good friend of Verlaine. The "Art poétique" was later dedicated to him.

rimer") [12] and the article signed Jean Mario in the *Nouvelle Rive gauche* of February 9, 1883, where Verlaine's influence on some of the young poets is indicated, a complete transformation in reputation was effected. During the same interval the Hydropathes underwent mutation and new groupings appeared.

However frivolous and lacking in taste these literary clubs may have been, they brought together people who were unconservative in outlook and provided an outlet for young poets.[13] The founders of the Hydropathes were both versifiers; they attracted other poets, not only Rollinat and Laurent Tailhade, but Charles Cros and Jean Moréas. Even the brief appearance among them of Bourget, Kahn, and Laforgue is not without some importance. Wit, laughter, and music at least counteracted apathy. Friendships and enmities were formed, ideas were exchanged, and the stage set for the numerous periodicals which were shortly to spring up. About 1881 the Hydropathes were transformed into the Hirsutes; the latter in turn disappeared in the spring of 1893. Meanwhile, however, Rodolphe Salis had established Le Chat noir, a "literary" restaurant with a stage where poets were encouraged to recite their compositions. Often a spirit of hilarity and sarcasm seems to have reigned in the Chat noir, but serious poetic efforts also found expression there.[14] On Thursday evenings Charles Cros, now past forty years of age and famous as the creator of such monologues as the "Hareng saur," with Louis Marsolleau, the future author of *Les Baisers perdus,* presided at recitations of verse in the obscure little bar known as the "Maison de bois." The group of *Lutèce* with the editors Léo Trézenik and Georges Rall, the clients of Salis' Chat noir, the Zutistes of Charles Cros, all aided in the formation of ideas and theories. The practical jokes of Sapeck and Allais, the dandyism of Moréas and Tailhade were a part of this desire to ignore the conventional and exalt the individual. Eccentricity was to be the characteristic of "Adoré Floupette."

In *Lutèce,* especially in 1883 and 1884, appeared poems by Jean Moréas; their publication in *Les Syrtes* (1884), at almost the same time as Verlaine's *Jadis et naguère,* constitutes a date in the history of symbolism, not so much

12. Jules Laforgue, *Lettres à un ami,* p. 48.

13. Ernest Raynaud's *La Mélée symboliste,* Emile Goudeau's *Dix Ans de Bohême,* and André Barre's *Le Symbolisme* give accounts of the literary clubs of the early 1880's.

14. The recitations of poetry in the restaurant were only a part of its activity. Salis published a little sheet called *Le Chat noir* in which were printed poems by his clients. Poems by Moréas appeared at least eight times between September 30, 1882, and April 14, 1883. At the latter date he abandoned the café and did not reprint these poems in his volumes of verse. Samain appeared in the sheet several times in 1884 and 1885. Verlaine first appeared in the *Chat noir* on May 26, 1883; his principal verse contributions came later: in thirteen issues of 1889, in ten numbers of 1890, in seven during 1891, and in five of 1892. While the *Chat noir* never assumed the character of a magazine, it is a curious collection of well known and obscure poets of the period.

by reason of Moréas' originality as by the master he chose to follow. The inspiration of Verlaine is almost too evident at times:

> Hiver: la bise se lamente,
> La neige couvre le verger.
> Dans nos cœurs aussi, pauvre amante,
> Il va neiger, il va neiger.[15]

In the images, so often those of death and anguish, in the liturgical words, and above all in the exasperated despair of the ideas, Moréas also reveals the ascendancy of Baudelaire. He writes: "Je veux un amour plein de sanglots et de pleurs"; he announces that his heart is an empty coffin in a tomb, or a ruined church in which no tapers can be lighted. The atmosphere and diction of Moréas' first poems are well illustrated by "Chimaera," which begins:

> J'allumai la clarté mortuaire des lustres
> Au fond de la crypte où se révulse ton œil,
> Et mon rêve cueillit les fleuraisons palustres
> Pour ennoblir ta chair de pâleur et de deuil.[16]

After the morose melancholy of Rodenbach's Les Tristesses (1881), the mortuary horror of Rollinat's Les Névroses (1883), Moréas' volume stands apart not so much in theme as in the search for strange words and musical effects secured through assonance. The few magazines which spoke of Les Syrtes noted the melodious qualities of the verse, and Gabriel Sarrazin went so far as to say that Moréas' melodic effects surpassed those of Verlaine.[17]

Among the other poets who were contributors to Lutèce were two, Tailhade and Vignier, who were never to enter wholly into the symbolist movement but who were concerned in certain of its manifestations. Laurent Tailhade's first volume of verse, Le Jardin des rêves, had appeared in 1880, after he had come from Toulouse to Paris in order to study law. He was one of the Zutist group of Charles Cros. He was famous for his eccentric costumes and for the ostentatious accumulation of liturgical imagery in his verse. During the years when he published his "Quatorzains" in Lutèce, he affected disdain for alliance with any literary group. Later, a brief association with Baju's Décadent, his part in the composition of poems signed with the name of Arthur Rimbaud, his caustic wit and frequent quarrels with erstwhile friends, his satirical ballades in Au pays du mufle (1891), his collaboration with La Plume and Le Mercure de France, his affiliation with the anarchist movement, his loss of an eye after a mysterious bomb explosion at the Foyot Restaurant in 1894

---

15. Jean Moréas, Premières Poésies, 1883–1886, p. 47.

16. Ibid., p. 67.

17. See La Revue indépendante, II (January, 1885), 263–264 and La Revue contemporaine, Nos. 2 and 3 (1885).

kept his name very much alive in the periodicals of the period. Although some of the current fashion for sumptuous ornament is to be found in his sonnets, his verse, carefully wrought as to form, belongs in general to the tradition of Théodore de Banville, who wrote an enthusiastic preface for *Le Jardin des rêves.* Tailhade has also been known as the exponent of "le symbolisme féroce," because of the violent terms he employed in his satirical verse against the complacency and hypocrisy of middle-class society; it is a convenient expression, but this modern Juvenal has little to do with symbolist doctrine.

Temporarily known as one of the admirers of Verlaine and as one of the frequent contributors to *Lutèce,* Charles Vignier soon abandoned poetry for journalism. He is the author of one of the eight sonnets in the January 8, 1886, issue of the *Revue wagnérienne,* and later was one of the faithful devotees of the Rue de Rome. From his pen we have but a single volume of verse, published in 1887. Its title, *Centon,* is puzzling and might suggest the poetic mosaic of the Latin decadents, but its contents are rather poor imitations of Verlaine's *Fêtes galantes* and *Romances sans paroles. Centon* was not received with any enthusiasm, Wyzewa noting that there was nothing particularly symbolist about it,[18] unless it was in the substitution of one idea for another, and Jules Tellier, after reproving the author for slavish imitation of Verlaine and for lack of clarity, concedes that Vignier might be called a great poet if one compares him with Gustave Kahn.[19]

The verse published in *Lutèce* by Verlaine, Tailhade, Moréas, and Vignier helped to create the impression of a new poetic manner of strange images and diction, but the important directive forces came from the publication of two prose works, the *Poètes maudits* and *A rebours.* During 1883 Verlaine, in order to earn a little money, had published in *Lutèce* some fragments of the *Mémoires d'un veuf.* To the same magazine, between August 28 and December 29, 1883, he contributed his studies on Tristan Corbière, Arthur Rimbaud, and Stéphane Mallarmé.

When these essays were published the next year in book form, the effect was doubly important. At last Verlaine had written something that sold well, thereby increasing his fame and making possible his long and complicated transactions with Léon Vanier. He had revived the names of three almost forgotten poets, and by his quotations had given examples of their art. Rimbaud, with such rare published items as two poems in *La Revue pour tous* and the satirical newspaper *La Charge* in 1870, and "Les Corbeaux" in *La Renaissance artistique et littéraire* in 1872, was but a legendary figure. Only a few copies of the Brussels edition of *Une Saison en enfer* were known to exist and *Les Illuminations* were still in manuscript form. With Verlaine's essay sev-

---

18. *La Revue indépendante,* II, No. 4 (February, 1887).
19. Jules Tellier, *Nos Poètes,* pp. 238–240.

eral important poems became known: the sonnet on the vowels, the "Bateau ivre," the "Oraison du soir," "Les Assis," "Les Effarés," and "Les Chercheuses de poux." [20] In addition Verlaine spoke of other works whose whereabouts he did not know and adjured anyone who possessed manuscripts to communicate with him. His essay was shortly to be most fruitful in the recovery of documents, and even in the hoax of "Mitrophin Crapoussin."

Corbière, who had died in 1875, two years after the publication of *Les Amours jaunes* in a small and expensive edition, was also in complete obscurity. As for Mallarmé, occupied with the edition of *Vathek,* further translations of Poe's poems, an English vocabulary list, and a school text on mythology, there was no collection of his work, and the largest group of verses published in one place had been in the *Parnasse contemporain* of 1871, where it was to be discovered by des Esseintes and given new life.

Huysmans' novel, coming so closely after the publication of the *Poètes maudits,* reached a wide circle of readers, excited much comment, and very likely launched the literary reputation of Mallarmé. Mallarmé's account of the eccentricities of Robert de Montesquiou, Huysmans' utilization of the narration for the creation of des Esseintes, the publication of the "Prose (pour des Esseintes)" in the *Revue indépendante* [21] form a curious chain of events. Even more strange is the destiny of the term "décadent," which had been applied to Baudelaire and which was to envelop, in des Esseintes' preferences in modern literature, not only the author of the *Fleurs du mal,* but Verlaine, Corbière, and Mallarmé.

One of the immediate repercussions of *A rebours* was an essay by a young man who had come to Paris in 1882 from Nancy and who in four numbers of a little magazine, which he composed in its entirety, began a somewhat spectacular rise to fame. His name was Maurice Barrès, and his periodical, published in 1884 and 1885, was called *Les Taches d'encre.* The first sentence of the initial number indicates the trend of his publication: "Le mode du jour sacrifie un peu trop, ce me semble, l'étude des esprits supérieurs à celle de la basse humanité." [22] The superior mind which Barrès chose to study was that of Baudelaire, whose poetry had been the delight of his schooldays. Barrès states that Baudelaire's whole esthetic outlook is derived from Poe. Dreams,

---

20. A curious bibliographical fact is that of the inclusion of two stanzas of "Les Chercheuses de poux" in Félicien Champsaur's *Dinah Samuel* (1882). The author of the lines is called "Arthur Cimber" and is designated as the greatest poet on the earth by "Paul Albreuse." See Arthur Rimbaud, *Œuvres complètes* (Pléiade ed.), pp. 651–653.

21. In the January, 1885, issue, p. 94.

22. *Les Taches d'encre,* November, 1884. The essay on Baudelaire, entitled "La Folie de Charles Baudelaire," was continued in the second issue of the periodical, that of December, 1884. In the third number of his magazine Barrès examines another superior mind, that of Leconte de Lisle. Barrès represents him as faced with the same dilemma which beset Baudelaire, hatred and rejection of realities but finding a solution in Hellenism.

somnambulism, madness, a sense of the mystical relationships between the senses and the phenomena of nature are the heritage left by the American poet to Baudelaire and in those who felt his influence. Even fiction has felt the impact of Baudelairian horror in Mendès, Loti, Poictevin, and the Goncourt brothers. Barrès realizes that Rollinat has none of the depth of Baudelaire, that the poems of *Les Névroses* recited with musical accompaniment in the bars of Montmartre were rather a theatrical than a literary success. Des Esseintes, seeking synthesis in sensations, appears to him not to possess the qualities of soul of Baudelaire. But the followers of Baudelaire, in their reaction against materialism and against the superficial qualities of romanticism, in their revelation of the secret places of the mind, are nevertheless worthy of praise. Above all, they are not content to follow the pattern of their epoch.

Au demeurant, c'est leur effort, la chose à faire plutôt que la chose faite que nous admirons. Tout un monde renouvelé, sourd parfois en nous; des liens secrets nous rattachent aux grands mystiques; la *Vita nuova,* les Primitifs sont plus voisins de nous que les deux siècles derniers.[23]

Barrès suggests abnormal acuteness of the senses as the principal trait which characterizes Baudelaire's followers. In a footnote he cites as an example of this peculiarity a volume of verse shortly to be published and entitled *Rosa mystica.*[24] It is not strange that Barrès should select this book, for its author, Stanislas de Guaita, was one of his closest friends. They had been in school together at Nancy, where both had undergone a crisis similar to that of Paul Bourget. Their anguish resulted from the difficulty of conciliating religious faith with a modern world of scientific claims at variance with the instructions they had received in school. When he was but eighteen years old, Stanislas de Guaita had published a small volume of verse entitled *Oiseaux de passage.* It is, however, after his arrival in Paris, where he came at the same time as Barrès, that the influence of Baudelaire is evident. The themes of *La Muse noire* (1883) and *Rosa mystica* (1885), both published by Lemerre, are the problem of evil and the search for religious faith. The poet's despair at the ignoble, lying world is expressed in nihilism:

> Mon rêve saint—mon rêve infâme,
> C'est de détruire l'Univers,
> Vieux corps qui n'a plus d'âme! [25]

The vanity of human knowledge in "La Prophétie du squelette," the ultimate destruction of all things in "L'Atlantide," a poignant "Mater dolorosa,"

23. *Les Taches d'encre,* No. 2 (December, 1884), p. 40.
24. *Ibid.,* p. 48.
25. *La Muse noire,* p. 16.

and varying aspects of injustice, suffering, and death are the subjects of his poetry. After 1885 he was to abandon verse for investigation into the occult sciences,[26] but was haunted until his death in 1897 by the enigma of evil. His poetic period comes just at the flowering of the decadent movement; some of his poems were published in 1883 and 1884 in *La Jeune France*, which printed at this time some horror poems of Rollinat. That Beauclair, one of the co-authors of the *Déliquescences d'Adoré Floupette*, was a contributor to this magazine is noteworthy. The emergence in a periodical hitherto extremely conservative in its poetic publication of these two disciples of Baudelaire must have impressed him.

Meanwhile a new magazine, under the direction of Félix Fénéon, had emerged. Its name was *La Revue indépendante* and its first series ran from May, 1884 to April, 1885. The periodical, which was later to change its directors and literary allegiances several times, although keeping the same title and format, is permeated at this time with the spirit of introspection, perversity, and dark tragedy which were the forerunners of the symbolist movement.[27] Verlaine's six poems of Sapphic love, "Les Amies," Stanislas de Guaita's "A Charles Baudelaire," Jean Moréas' "Sensualité," Mallarmé's "Prose pour des Esseintes," Charles Morice's "La Mort des papillons," Laurent Tailhade's "Funerei Flores" are among the contributions in verse. These are the authors which *Lutèce* had favored, and the contributions in the *Revue indépendante* are in a sense more daring in theme and diction than those which had previously been published. By their pessimism, their lassitude, their atmosphere of refined suffering, such poems may well have provoked the appelation of decadence. Even in the field of art, attention is directed by the magazine to the most eccentric and satanic of pictorial artists. Camille Lemonnier composed an article on Félicien Rops, while J.-K. Huysmans discussed an album of drawings by Odilon Redon. Moréas accentuated the pessimistic note with an article on Schopenhauer.

With the publication of the *Poètes maudits*, Verlaine had entered into a period of fame. He and his book are the occasion of an article by Louis Desprez,[28] in which analogies are drawn between Baudelaire and the author of *Sagesse*. Desprez cites in the two poets the preference for twilight hours and for liturgical words. In both he finds the mingling of the religious with the voluptuous, a merging of sounds and colors, and a sequence of strange reveries. Of Rimbaud, however, he speaks more harshly:

26. *Essais des sciences maudites* (1886, 1890, 1891, 1897).

27. Marcade wrote of the new magazine in the literary supplement of *Le Figaro*, May 24, 1884. He does not discuss the poetry in the periodical.

28. *La Revue indépendante*, I (July, 1884), 218-234.

M. Rimbaud me semble le produit le plus typique du byzantinisme baudelairien, aboutissant à la folie. De la mystification grave et convaincue, incompréhensibilités psychiques et linguistiques, du rêve biscornu, démential.[29]

Desprez does not impress one as a very good critic; he censures Mallarmé for his taste for "sonorités vides et tintinnabulantes" but agrees with Verlaine that Corbière's poem "La Fin" is personal, energetic, and very picturesque. The article concludes with the statement that Verlaine will be the leader of a small group of poets of distinguished and subtle minds.

In the midst of the new currents stirred up by *Le Chat noir, Lutèce,* and *La Revue indépendante* appeared a volume which pleaded for effacement of the poet's personality from his lyric utterance. Written by Catulle Mendès, *La Légende du Parnasse contemporain* (1884) is a curious blend of anecdote and theory. In the closing words of the volume Mendès gives his estimate of the accomplishment of the group he had helped to form. He contends that Parnassianism set poetry on the right pathway, that excessive sentimentality and carelessness have been corrected, that the necessity of hard work to ennoble inspiration, and the advisability of submission to sacred rules have been amply demonstrated. Now, he says, poetry can develop "sans entraves." This is a curious statement in view of several hindrances he sets up in the course of the volume. If the young generation had taken his judgments as a breviary, their production would have been at best labored and cautious.

First of all, there is the question of the poem as mirror of the individual. Mendès suggests that Lamartine's and Musset's work may not survive, because the personality of the authors is constantly evident in their verse and eternally claims the reader's attention.[30] Although eager to prove that the Parnassians are not impassive, Mendès insists that personal emotion should be subordinated to art. The reservations he makes in speaking of individual poets are indicative of this spirit. After citing Léon Dierx's "Soir d'octobre," Mendès says:

A vrai dire, une entente aussi profonde de la vague rêverie des choses ne va pas toujours chez Léon Dierx sans un peu de vague dans les idées, sans quelque indécision dans les contours de la phrase.[31]

This vagueness, called by others suggestion or delicate shading, was the basis of the new admiration surrounding Verlaine, of whom Mendès speaks quite briefly but, it would seem, with slight distaste. Verlaine is "un poète sinistre," his smiles are almost sincere, and Mendès hopes that his intellectual

29. *Ibid.,* p. 225.
30. *La Légende du Parnasse contemporain,* p. 23.
31. *Ibid.,* p. 253.

health will be improved. To Mallarmé he is more kind, intimating that the strange, subtle art of this most conscientious writer demands only intelligence and attention to be understood. That Mendès should speak well of a poet whose verse is so largely constructed on suggestive power may seem a paradox, but in the author's mind one feels that the sense of artistry, of labored, patient effort, as opposed to the first summons of inspiration, is uppermost.

Soon after the publication of the *Légende du Parnasse contemporain* occurred the banquet given in honor of Lemerre, the publisher who had made the Parnassians famous during the 1870's. During the next two years there was renewed activity in the group. Mendès' *Poésies* (1885) in seven volumes, Armand Silvestre's *Le Chemin des étoiles* (1885), Sully-Prudhomme's *Le Prisme* (1886), François Coppée's *Arrière-saison* (1886), and Léon Valade's *Poésies* (1886) were crowned by the publication of the long-awaited *Poèmes tragiques* of Leconte de Lisle. Mendès' volume and the production of Parnassian poetry served, in so far as literary history is concerned, to accentuate differences in outlook of two schools of poets. The alignment of those who had chosen as masters Baudelaire or Verlaine or Mallarmé becomes increasingly clear.

Another event which played its part in the establishment of literary positions was the death of Victor Hugo in May, 1885. The countless articles praising Hugo as the greatest poet of the nineteenth century or even of French literature filled the newspaper and magazine columns of the year. The dead writer's huge poetic production, which seemed to have run the entire gamut of lyric expression, was so overwhelming that innovation might have appeared unnecessary if not impossible. On the other hand, as Mallarmé and several younger poets later stated, Hugo's death appeared to some as the close of an era. The imposing shadow of the titan was gone and the way was open for new ideas. In the intense poetic activity of 1886, it is advisable to consider the desire of the young for new and rapid growth in the absence of a dominating and awesome figure.

Certainly, after Hugo's death, there was almost immediate evidence of novel poetic expression and the appearance of new names. Among publishers, Vanier was beginning to represent a countercurrent to Lemerre. Jules Laforgue, Henri de Régnier, René Ghil, Ephraïm Mikhaël, and Francis Vielé-Griffin published their first volumes. Verlaine, after *Les Poètes maudits* and *Jadis et naguère* of 1884, not only contributed abundantly to magazines but added to the legend surrounding his name by *Les Mémoires d'un veuf*. By the time *Lutèce* ceased publication in 1886, a whole group of little magazines had sprung up, much more combative in tone, and a battle had been waged about the term "décadent." After des Esseintes had emerged the personage of Adoré Floupette.

Chapter IV: ADORÉ FLOUPETTE, 1885

THE MANNER in which a rather silly literary joke, begun in *Lutèce*,[1] developed into a series of journalistic discussions and helped launch a literary movement is the most interesting event in the poetic history of 1885. More widespread publicity than Verlaine and Huysmans had attained the preceding year followed in the wake of a little pamphlet of parodies. Mockery and hilarious exaggeration became the new weapons of combat and the very concept of decadence was modified.

The followers of Baudelaire, discussed in 1881 by Paul Bourget and in 1884 by Barrès, the publication of Rollinat's *Les Névroses,* Verlaine's poem "Langueur," [2] and the essays of the "Poètes maudits" [3] had tended to continue the ideas expressed by Gautier in the preface to the *Fleurs du mal.* Perhaps of greater importance was the personification given to decadence by des Esseintes. By his thoughts and artistic tastes this unforgettable character had proclaimed vividly his hatred of the commonplace. In the walls covered with rare materials, in the Gothic windowpanes, the period furniture, even in the monastic simplicity of the bedroom the search for the artificial is the keynote. Nature alone must not furnish the stimuli for the senses; therefore Huysmans' hero seeks in floral monstrosities and in strange gustatorial combinations what he believes to be the refinement of sensation. Of all literary creations, des Esseintes seems to be in closest harmony with Mallarmé's Hérodiade. The line, "Oui, c'est pour moi, pour moi, que je fleuris, déserte," with its jealously guarded isolation from worldly contact, would furnish a fitting motto for both characters.

The idea of literary decadence was immediately associated in readers' minds with the theme of *A rebours.* Emile Hennequin, writing a review of the novel in July, 1884,[4] employs the term in reference to Verlaine. Enumerating the favorite books of des Esseintes, Hennequin says that in addition to the ancient authors one finds:

. . . une énumération d'auteurs français dans laquelle se coudoient curieusement des écrivains catholiques qui n'ont d'intérêt que pour les antiquaires en idées et en style, quelques poètes réellement décadents comme Paul Verlaine dont certains

1. February 1, 1885.
2. *Le Chat noir,* May 26, 1883.
3. *Lutèce,* August 24, 31; September 21; October 5, 12, 19; November 2, 10, 17, 24; December 29, 1883.
4. In *La Revue indépendante,* I, 199–216.

volumes ont les subtilités métriques et le niais bavardage des derniers hymno-graphes byzantins, et une bonne partie de ce que la littérature contemporaine a produit de supérieur et de raffiné.[5]

During 1885, in the little magazines, can best be seen the continuity of the idea of decadent literature. Charles Buet's *La Minerve,* which lasted for only six monthly issues and which professed allegiance to no literary school, offers examples. There Laurent Tailhade, reviewing Moréas' *Les Syrtes,*[6] placed the volume in the lineage of Baudelaire through its sadness, its solemnity, its richness of coloration, and its scorn for the crowd. Tailhade detected other influences in the work: Verlainian vagueness, Mallarméan intensity, and Schopenhauerian pessimism. Stanislas de Guaita, writing of Péladan's *Le Vice suprême,*[7] naturally dwells at length on the idea of decadence, since that is the novel's principal theme. Maurice Barrès, reviewing *Rosa mystica,*[8] finds the younger generation divided in admiration between Renan and Baude-laire.

Apart from *Lutèce* and *Le Chat noir,* a newly founded Belgian periodical, *La Basoche,* offers most examples in 1885 of the type of literature which was called decadent. The magazine's founder, Henry de Tombeur, disclaimed, as did Buet, any alliance with a literary school, but he gave hospitality to many of the young French poets. Ghil's first manifesto, with its eloquent praise of Mallarmé, was printed in the Brussels magazine during the last half of 1885. Among the poets whose works appeared in the periodical were Jean Ajalbert, Stanislas de Guaita, André Fontainas, Georges Khnopff, Jean Lorrain, Stuart Merrill, Ephraïm Mikhaël, and Rodolphe Darzens. Each of these writers entertained a special admiration for Baudelaire or Verlaine or Mallarmé. Titles such as "Spleen d'hiver," "A la Morgue," "Fête galante," "Tristesse de septembre," and "Crépuscule pluvieux" reveal the tonality of the poems. In two prose offerings, "La Nyctalope" and "Le Christ du père Séparion," Stuart Merrill seemed to be emulating the macabre tales of Poe. The magazine also reprinted, after an eighteen-year interval, one of Mallarmé's poems from the first *Parnasse contemporain.*

What was accomplished by Beauclair's and Vicaire's parody, *Les Déli-quescences d'Adoré Floupette,* was a closer definition of the word decadent. Floupette offered an example of the decadent writer and gave conservative critics a target because of his eccentricities of style. Literature had been called decadent simply because it presented, as in Péladan's *Le Vice suprême* or Jean

Lorrain's *Modernités,* a picture of a perverted and dying civilization. Even melancholy or pessimism in a literary work seemed to attract the epithet; Jean Ajalbert's little poems, collected under the title *Sur le vif, vers impressionnistes,* were called decadent largely because they presented a picture of misery and poverty. Adoré Floupette had, in addition to an outlook on life as bizarre as that of des Esseintes, the kind of strangeness in syntax and vocabulary which was inspired by Verlaine and Mallarmé.

Before the publication of *Les Déliquescences* in pamphlet form, the introduction and several of the poems had appeared in *Lutèce.* Trézenik and Rall, the editors of this periodical, seem to have adopted during 1885 a jocose if not satiric attitude toward their collaborators. Using the pseudonym of "Mostrailles" they wrote some twenty mocking thumbnail sketches of the contributors to their magazine. At the end of the year, when the periodical's precarious existence was terminating, Ernest Raynaud began to publish his "Carnet d'un décadent."

The immediate sources of *Les Déliquescences,* suggested by a few epigraphs and stylistic evidence, seem to have been the *Poètes maudits* and the "Prose pour des Esseintes." The latter had recently been published in the January issue of the *Revue indépendante.* In the satirical introduction, signed "Marius Tapora," Adoré's masters are indicated as Etienne Arsenal and Bleucoton, easily identified as Mallarmé and Verlaine. The collection of poems and preface are interesting in the dual revelation of the idea of the symbol and of decadence. Floupette, having damned all the previous currents of poetry, is asked, "Mais enfin, que reste-t-il donc?" Gravely he answers, "Il reste le Symbole." A parody, inspired by Mallarmé's "Prose pour des Esseintes," is called "Idylle symbolique," but there are also a "Bal décadent" and a "Liminaire" which encourage the reader after this fashion:

Mais l'Initié épris de la bonne chanson bleue et grise, d'un gris si bleu et d'un bleu si gris, si vaguement obscure et pourtant si claire, le melliflu décadent dont l'intime perversité, comme une vierge enfouie emmi la boue, confine au miracle, celui-là saura bien,—on suppose,—où rafraîchir l'or immaculé de ses Dolences.[9]

According to the introduction, Floupette is wont to recite the death of "La pénultième" and it is easy to see that his prose style has been affected by Mallarmé's example. In some of the poems it is rather the vague and fragile music of *Romances sans paroles* or *Sagesse* which seems the point of departure. Verlaine's "La fuite est verdâtre et rose" may have inspired "L'horizon s'envole, Rose, Orange, et Vert," and "Beauté des femmes, leur faiblesse, et ces mains pâles" may have some part in "La chair de la femme, argile Estatique." When Floupette announces: "Mon cœur est un Corylopsis

9. *Les Déliquescences d'Adoré Floupette,* p. 50.

du Japon," [10] one may be permitted to think of some lines from Moréas'
Les Syrtes:

> Mon cœur, mon cœur est sur l'étang
> Un chaste nénuphar flottant.[11]

and there seems reasonable certainty that the lines from the *Déliquescences:*

> Si l'âcre désir s'en alla,
> C'est que la porte était ouverte.
> Ah! verte, verte, combien verte,
> Etait mon âme ce jour-là! [12]

are combined memories of the "âcre besoin" of Rimbaud's "Oraison du soir"
and Verlaine's "O triste, triste était mon âme." More important than surmises
as to the source of Floupette's eighteen poems is the psychological state which
is represented in them. The mingling of the sensuous and the religious, the
search for odd words, the theme of lassitude, the correspondence between
colors, sounds, and ideas, exaltation, and intoxication in dreams are the
dominant elements in Floupette's verse. Certain eccentricities in form, which
recall Corbière, and lines of an odd number of syllables, probably inspired
by Verlaine's "Art poétique," are the peculiarities in prosody, while the
slightly tormented syntax sometimes makes one think of Mallarmé. How
malicious the work was intended to be is debatable; on the rear cover is an
advertisement for Léon Vanier which includes books by Beauclair, Vicaire,
Verlaine, Moréas, and Corbière. Verlaine never seems to have taken offense
at the satire directed at him. He addressed a sonnet to Gabriel Vicaire in
Dédicaces (1890) and in 1894 praised the same author for *Au bois joli* in an
article [13] where he designated Vicaire as "mon bon ami et l'un de mes
auteurs de chevet."

Gustave Kahn indicates as targets of the *Déliquescences,* in addition to
Mallarmé and Verlaine, Tailhade and Laforgue. The inclusion of this last
name seems dubious. Two of Laforgue's "Complaintes" had appeared in
Lutèce on March 8 and a third on March 22, 1885. They provoked a letter of
protest from Edmond Haraucourt, but the volume of the *Complaintes* did
not appear until July, after the publication of the volume of parodies. The
article, "Les Décadents," by Paul Bourde,[14] destined to provoke a whole series
of commentaries and give names to the poetic currents of the day, does not
name Laforgue. Since 1882 the poet, except for fleeting visits to Paris, had been

---

10. This poem, signed "Etienne Arsenal," had been published in *Lutèce*, February 1, 1885.
11. Jean Moréas, *Premières poésies*, p. 81.
12. *Les Déliquescences d'Adoré Floupette*, p. 63.
13. *La Revue blanche*, May, 1894.
14. *Le Temps*, August 6, 1885.

almost constantly in Germany, composing much but publishing little. During 1886, with collaboration in *La Vogue* and new volumes of poetry, the author of *Les Complaintes* began to be known. His death in 1887, shortly after his marriage and return to Paris, was but the beginning of his fame.

During his brief appearance among the Hydropathes in 1879 and 1880 and the five years in Germany as reader for the Empress Augusta, Laforgue had meditated much on the nature of poetry. In December, 1881, admitting the influence that Kahn and Mallarmé have in his ideas of poetic form, he writes:

Je songe à une poésie qui serait de la psychologie dans une forme de rêve, avec des fleurs, du vent, des senteurs. D'inextricables symphonies avec une phrase (un sujet) mélodique, dont le dessein reparaît de temps en temps.[15]

Already at that time a devotee of the subconscious, thanks to Hartmann's text, passionately fond of painting and music, Laforgue had a profound conception of dream and recurrent melodic theme as the basis of verse. The expression of this idea in *Les Complaintes* is conditioned by a long period of homesickness for Paris, money difficulties, an innate pessimism, and an ironic temperament. In Laforgue's poetry it is not a question of choosing the most fitting poetic material and language but rather of the presentation of the thoughts as they appear at the surface of the mind. Unabashed by neologisms, preferring a great variety of rhythms to a staid procession of quatrains, using a colloquial turn of speech to express a tragic idea, Laforgue's contribution is one of the most original in French poetic history. A part of his genius lay in the choice of a simple but telling image:

> On voudrait saigner le Silence,
> Secouer l'exil des causeries;
> Et non! ces dames sont aigries
> Par des questions de préséance.[16]

The rather bitter humor of the poet against human nature and the blows of destiny creates a type of irony rarely found in French verse but recalls certain lines of Villon and Tristan Corbière. Considering the selfishness of the individual human being, who in truth seldom allows his emotion to transcend the boundaries of self, Laforgue indicates the reason for our forgetfulness of the dead:

> Les Morts
> C'est sous terre;
> Ça n'en sort
> Guère.[17]

15. Jules Laforgue, *Exil, poésie, spleen*, pp. 61–62.
16. Jules Laforgue, *Les Complaintes:* "Complainte sur certains ennuis."
17. *Ibid.*, "Complainte de l'oubli des morts."

The year 1885 also marks the first volume of a poet twenty years of age who had published a few poems in *Lutèce,* who is dreamy and melancholy, but whose expression in this first volume recalls rather the sentimentality of the Parnassians. The poet, Henri de Régnier, was to have a long and honorable career and indeed was to be called the only great poet of the second generation of the symbolists, but *Les Lendemains* (1885) give little promise of originality.

The fortunes of Mallarmé changed utterly after the publication of the *Poètes maudits* and *A rebours.* The writer, whom Huysmans described as living apart from the world in order to pursue the analysis of fantasy and intelligence, was within a few months after the publication of *A rebours* the center of an admiring group. In the fall of 1884 the evening receptions of the Rue de Rome assumed the importance they were to have for a full decade. Yet however great may have been the influence exerted by Mallarmé's conversation on his visitors, it remains true that they sometimes caused their host to change the direction of his thought. This is particularly true in 1885, when an ardent young Wagnerian, Edouard Dujardin, took Mallarmé to one of the Lamoureux concerts. With Téodor de Wyzewa, Dujardin had founded the *Revue wagnérienne* at the beginning of 1885, and gradually those who gathered at Mallarmé's apartment came to be collaborators of the magazine.

In August, 1885, Mallarmé who had been attending the Lamoureux concerts with great regularity and who found in Wagner the most interesting of composers, published in the *Revue wagnérienne* an essay, "Richard Wagner, rêverie d'un poète français." The idea of the synthesis of music and verse there enunciated not only is important for the esthetic concepts of the *Divagations* but also for the story of René Ghil's "instrumentation verbale." Perhaps the crowning literary event of the *Revue wagnérienne* was the publication in January, 1886, of eight sonnets of homage to Wagner. The authors were Mallarmé, Verlaine, Ghil, Merrill, Morice, Vignier, Wyzewa, and Dujardin. In the course of the year Wyzewa's articles contributed not only to the glory of Wagner but to that of Mallarmé.

The name of Mallarmé was given new publicity, not only by Dujardin's periodical in 1885, but by the first volume of René Ghil, *Légende d'âmes et de sangs.* The preface of this book, in which Ghil makes the startling assertions that Zola is a poet and Mallarmé a realist, gives the plan for Ghil's life work. He will sing the history of mankind's life, from primordial times to a prophecy of the future ages. It is for the expression of this idea that he seeks a fitting language, not that which narrates but that which gives an impression of the "frémissement de la vie," a music of colors, sounds, odors, and moods. Only one poet, says Ghil, has given expression to this desired idiom; that poet is Stéphane Mallarmé.

In the *Légende* Ghil has recourse to certain peculiarities of typography; he prints in capitals the words "HAUT," "TOUT," and the forms of the verb "MONTER," "VIVRE," and "ALLER," as well as certain present participles which he wishes to emphasize. Initial capital letters sometimes serve to indicate alliterative sounds but are rather capriciously distributed. A few lines from the last poem of the volume will illustrate this peculiarity:

> Tous les Troupeaux, quand ils s'en VONT, et, de leurs queues
> TUANT les Taons, les Roux, les Noirs, les Taureaux grands:
> Au Travail de la grange, eux, las de vieilles lieues,
> Ils VONT, les deux longs Vieux,—et d'odeurs du vieux Temps
> Un doux revenez-Y grise un peu leurs vieux sangs.[18]

Ghil professes to have become acquainted with the poetry of Mallarmé only a few months before the publication of his volume, and his admiration is not necessarily influence. Indeed it was during the following year, in some sonnets, that a real indication of Mallarmé's direct inspiration is evident in Ghil's verse.[19]

Meanwhile eccentricity of art continued to be associated with oddness of personality. Paul Bourde's article, "Les Décadents," published in *Le Temps* on August 6, 1885, was evidently inspired by the satire of Adoré Floupette. Bourde ascribes to the decadent the characteristics that Beauclair and Vicaire had noted in their preface: perverted mysticism, satanism, the use of morphine to attain the desired morbid state. Not very important in itself, this journalistic item is chiefly remembered as the inspiration of another piece of writing in which the new poetic currents received the name of symbolism.

Moréas, the frequent contributor to *Lutèce*, the ardent defender of Paul Verlaine, and recent author of *Les Syrtes,* made an immediate rebuttal of Bourde's article.[20] He protested that the young and original poets are not neurotic; at worst they can be called melancholy. They are but seeking to create beauty and their art is the pursuit of "le pur Concept" and "l'éternel Symbole." Moréas proposes the name of "symbolistes" instead of "décadents" for the group.

The idea of the symbol in verse was very much in the air. Moréas' article appeared only a. few days after the publication of Mallarmé's meditation on Richard Wagner and René Ghil was already elaborating his theories in *La Basoche.* Nor must it be forgotten that in the *Déliquescences* the arrival of the new poetry is hailed as the advent of the symbol:

18. *Légende d'âmes et de sangs,* p. 173.

19. Mallarmé replied courteously to Ghil's praise, making a gentle reproach that Ghil seemed to be attacking the problem of verse rather as a composer than as a poet. See *Les Dates et les œuvres,* p. 17.

20. In *Le XIXᵉ Siècle,* August 11, 1885.

Le symbole est venu. Très hilares, d'abord
Ont été les clameurs des brises démonées.
Tristes, aussi, leurs attitudes, tant ridées
Par la volonté rude et l'incessant effort.[21]

The name chosen by Moréas, disseminated through a manifesto he published the following year and through the title of a little magazine he helped found, has remained. That it is not a particularly good term was recognized by many and first of all by the man who, through his conversations, had probably given currency to the word:

Symboliste, Décadente ou Mystique, les écoles se déclarant ou étiquetées en hâte par notre presse d'information, adoptent, comme rencontre, le point d'un Idéalisme qui (pareillement aux fugues, aux sonates) refuse les matériaux naturels et, comme brutale, une pensée directe les ordonnant: pour ne garder de rien que la suggestion.[22]

The decadent phase of symbolism, with its anguish, nihilism, and its pursuit of the eccentric, represented in 1885 more a state of mind and a deformation of the language than a valid artistic concept. But the two who were recognized as leaders had already indicated the more important elements of the new lyric expression. Both Mallarmé and Verlaine had published enough verse, in which the elements of suggestion and music were paramount, to give a definite clue of the significance of their style. But in 1885 very few of their admirers had yet published volumes of poetry. The new school in truth received the name of "décadent" and "symboliste" before it was really constituted. To build a literary school around *Les Syrtes* of Moréas, *La Légende d'âmes et de sangs* of Ghil, and *Les Complaintes* of Laforgue was both presumptuous and premature.

On the other hand, the fanfare and publicity which ushered in the age of symbolism was most fecund in its results.[23] Never was there a year like 1886 for the appearance of new talents, for the ferment of activity in poetic circles, for the founding of new magazines, and for the creation of new manners in expression. The individual talent, so long the docile follower of what had been done, was no longer afraid to embark upon the new. Verlaine's revela-

21. *Les Déliquescences d'Adoré Floupette*, p. 62.
22. Stéphane Mallarmé, *Divagation première: Relativement au vers.* This is the title in the *Vers et prose* of 1894. Mallarmé published "Divagation" in the *Ecrits pour l'art*, February, 1887.
23. After the article by Bourde and Moréas' reply, the press reacted immediately. The literary supplement of the *Figaro*, which had scarcely mentioned contemporary verse during 1885 except to commemorate the death of Victor Hugo (issue of May 23, 1885), began a campaign against the new currents in October. Félicien Champsaur in "Poètes décadenticulets" (October 3, 1885) allied the young generation with the pessimism of the romantic school and attacked Barbey d'Aurevilly, Bloy, Hello, Péladan, and Charles Buet in an article, "Les Ecrivains sacrilèges" (October 17, 1885). Champsaur admits, however, the beauty of Mallarmé's "Apparition."

tion of Corbière, Mallarmé, and the glimpse he had given of Rimbaud, Moréas' proclamation of the genius of Verlaine, Huysmans' novel—the very creation of the legend of the "décadent" were about to bear rich fruit. Sincere admiration for Mallarmé and Verlaine, eagerness to explore the mystery of Rimbaud, the deification of the once neglected Baudelaire, great as were these influences they did not prevent the expression of many individual and personal ideas. The importance of the movement termed symbolism is not perhaps greatest as a collective and unified expression but rather as a demonstration of personal independence. After a lapse of fifteen years the desire penned by the hand of a boy genius was to find fulfillment:

En attendant, demandons au *poëte* du *nouveau,*—idées et formes. Tous les habiles croiraient bientôt avoir satisfait à cette demande:—ce n'est pas cela! [24]

By the close of 1885 the magazines which had given the first impulse toward a poetic renascence had done their work. *Lutèce,* since its founding in November, 1882, had printed not only items by Verlaine but poems by Moréas, Charles Morice, Ernest Raynaud, Laurent Tailhade, Jean Ajalbert, Jules Laforgue, and some of the first poems of Vielé-Griffin and Henri de Régnier. The Saturday issues of *Le Chat noir* had published not only poetry by Verlaine, Tailhade, Moréas, Morice, and Rollinat, but also early writings of poets who were later to be associated with the *Mercure de France:* Albert Samain, Louis Denise, Louis le Cardonnel, and Edouard Dubus. Reprints of Mallarmé's prose had appeared in two issues. Some prose poems of Marie Krysinska, later to be offered by her as evidence of her part in the invention of free verse, had also been printed in Salis' periodical. From time to time Léon Bloy, temporarily a favorite of the young writers because of his admiration for Baudelaire and his bitter hatred of the journalistic world,[25] had contributed articles. Dubus and Denise continued their collaboration with *Le Chat noir* through 1886, but after that date the periodical offers very little of interest save for publications of Verlaine's work.

Belgium did not yet have a publication of its own for the new poetic expression. Picard's *L'Art moderne,* thanks to the pen of Emile Verhaeren, had published some laudatory words on Baudelaire. In 1885 there appeared a series of eight unsigned articles, probably written by Picard himself, entitled "Essai de pathologie littéraire." Again the point of departure was *Les Déliquescences,* and in the course of discussing Adoré Floupette the author said many unkind things about Baudelaire, Mallarmé, Verlaine, and the writers of *Lutèce.* The articles provoked a letter, printed in the magazine,[26]

24. Arthur Rimbaud's letter to Paul Demeny, May 15, 1871.
25. Bloy vented his spleen against journalists in four issues of a magazine, *Le Pal,* which he published in March and April, 1885.
26. *L'Art moderne,* V (September 27, 1885), 312–314.

from Georges Khnopff. Defending the authors who had been attacked, offering quotations from their work to substantiate his remarks, Khnopff expressed
his disgust at the attention bestowed on the pamphlet of parodies.

Although *La Basoche,* during 1885, had appeared a promising vehicle for
the publication of new verse, the little magazine terminated its brief career
in April, 1886. Stuart Merrill, Jean Lorrain, and Pierre Quillard continued
as its collaborators until the end, and the magazine did, before its demise,
publish reviews of Laforgue's *Complaintes* and *Imitation de Notre-Dame la
lune.*

Chapter V: THE FLOWERING OF
SYMBOLISM IN 1886

THE LARGE NUMBER of periodicals which sprang up during 1886 is both a source of confusion and a proof of tremendous activity. A long-drawn quarrel between the "décadents" and the "symbolistes," rather futile and none too clear, agitated at length not only the question of personal talents but that of whether the poet should set down the direct impressions of the senses or should transmute them into a symbolical form. In practice, however, the poets who debated these problems were eclectic; their work is seldom confined to any one theory. Even René Ghil, the most individualistic of all, recognized several spiritual ancestors.

Before 1886 only *Lutèce,* the first series of the *Revue indépendante,* and the *Revue wagnérienne* represent the leadership of Verlaine and Mallarmé. Beginning with the first issue of *Le Scapin,* in December, 1885; the founding in the early part of 1886 of *Le Décadent, La Vogue,* and *La Pléiade;* and the appearance in October of *La Décadence* and *Le Symboliste*—indications of new ambitions and rivalries, as well as allegiances to Verlaine and Mallarmé, assume definite form. Anatole Baju, Jean Moréas, and René Ghil propound questions of theory, insult one another, and establish poetic groupings.

The new magazines were unequal in value and ephemeral. In 1889, three years after their founding, Charles Morice spoke of them with considerable scorn: *La Vogue* was a "charmant vide-tiroir," *Le Scapin* was juvenile, *Le Décadent* was simply grotesque, and the four numbers of *Le Symboliste* contained nonsense signed with the names of Moréas and Paul Adam. Morice is rather more kind to the *Revue wagnérienne,* which he compliments on having set itself just limits—the exposition of Wagner's esthetics.[1]

Certainly most of the critical material in these periodicals is of small value and often resolves itself into personal attacks. But the publications of verse are more interesting. *Le Scapin* offered many poems by two newcomers, Edouard Dubus and Louis le Cardonnel; in the same magazine René Ghil published sonnets which seem at times like parodies of Mallarmé but in which the search for a new and musical idiom is apparent:

Ma Triste, les oiseaux de rire
Même l'été ne volent pas

1. Charles Morice, *La Littérature de tout à l'heure,* pp. 297–300.

45

Au Mutisme de mort de glas
Qui vint aux grands rameaux élire,

Tragique d'un passé d'empire,
Un seul néant dans les amas,
Plus ne songeant au vain soulas
Vers qui la ramille soupire.[2]

Le Scapin, like the other new magazines,[3] sought to enroll Verlaine among its contributors and obtained the poem "Agnus Dei"; Léo d'Orfer and Alfred Vallette wrote in it their judgments of the "école du Symbole." [4] The future director of the *Mercure de France,* admitting that the general tendency in poetry seems to be toward symbolism, observes that never have poets been less regimented. Denying Moréas' assertion that the movement is necessary and inevitable, he predicts that symbolism will remain but a subterranean stream in the great currents of French poetry.[5]

La Pléiade, of which the first issue appeared in March, 1886, owed its contributors to a group which often assembled at the Brasserie Pousset, in the Montmartre district. Two graduates of the Lycée Condorcet, Ephraïm Mikhaël and Pierre Quillard, after having published some verse in the Brussels periodical *La Basoche,* were contemplating establishing a magazine with the help of two of their friends, Paul Roux and Rodolphe Darzens. It happened that at this time two school friends from Ghent, Maurice Maeterlinck and Grégoire le Roy, spent several months in Paris. They gladly agreed to join in the enterprise and even added the name of another Belgian, Charles van Lerberghe, to the list of collaborators. The seven numbers of the magazine present many poems with no innovations in form and diction and which, if it were not for the vague and dreamy quality which is dominant, would seem the continuation of the Parnassian tradition. The *Pléiade* does not speak of symbolism or decadence; it criticizes Jean Moréas, not for freeing himself from narrow poetic rules, but for a slight deformation of the language and for false rhymes. It published René Ghil's "Traité du verbe," with its words of praise for Baudelaire, Mallarmé, Verlaine, and Rimbaud; it gave especial honor to the works of Villiers de l'Isle-Adam. Pacific and quiet, it did not enter the quarrels of the period and appears rather a friendly grouping of young writers than a magazine with a definite literary program. In that it marks the

2. *Le Scapin,* October 1886, p. 44.

3. Verlaine contributed poems to *Lutèce, La Revue wagnérienne, La Vogue, Le Décadent,* and *Le Symboliste* as well as to *Le Scapin,* in 1886. His reputation gained perhaps as much by the reprinting of some of his verses from the earlier volumes as from his current writings. *Le Scapin* offered to its readers "Les Ingénus" and "Colloque sentimental" from *Fêtes galantes,* and *La Décadence* printed "L'Allée" from the same volume.

4. *Le Scapin,* September, 1886, pp. 1–7.

5. *Ibid.,* October 16, 1886, pp. 73–81.

literary beginnings of Maeterlinck, van Lerberghe, Saint-Pol-Roux,[6] and early poems of Grégoire le Roy the magazine is a landmark.

The serenity of the *Pléiade,* a melancholy, dreamy serenity expressed in verse and prose poems, is counterbalanced by the aggressive *Le Décadent,* founded by Anatole Baju in April, 1886. First printed in newspaper form, the periodical published verse by Verlaine in seven different issues during 1886.[7] During the summer of that year a group of visitors who had gathered in the hospital to visit Verlaine met Baju and his friend Maurice du Plessys and formed projects for changing the badly printed little sheet into a magazine.[8] Baju, whose brain was constantly inventing new projects and whose enthusiasm was greater than his critical sense, had constantly published little manifestoes, and in June, 1886, won Verlaine's approval by inventing the term "décadisme." In vigorous but empty eloquence, Baju announced that the decadents were not exactly a literary school but a group which was to destroy the outmoded literary patterns and prepare the "éléments fœtusiens" of a new national literature. He spoke of indicating the greatest number of sensations in the fewest possible words, noting the most delicate shadings, and exploring the rare, intimate, and hidden parts of reality. The newly found collaborators of Baju, Ernest Raynaud and Laurent Tailhade, seem not to have had very much respect for the critical faculties of their editor in chief and to have used the periodical for the perpetration of a literary hoax by composing poems and ascribing them to Arthur Rimbaud.[9] In the thirty-fourth number of the *Décadent,* on November 29, 1886, appeared "Sonnet," which contained such expressions as "fort miel des doctes confitures" and "le concombre inclément de leur vierge abdomen." It was signed with Rimbaud's name. In 1888, when the *Décadent* resumed publication after a hiatus of several months, the farce was to be resumed.

The socialistic diatribes of Baju and his veneration of Paul Verlaine largely filled the *Décadent's* first year of existence.

In April, within a few days of the first issue of the *Décadent,* appeared a new magazine, destined to last only for the remainder of 1886 but far more important in its contents than any of its contemporaries. Its name was banal enough, *La Vogue;* its founder, Léo d'Orfer, almost immediately left all

6. Maeterlinck contributed a short story, "Le Massacre des innocents" to the issue of May, 1886; poems by Charles van Lerberghe appeared in the two following months; four poems by Grégoire le Roy had been published in the April number.

7. Verlaine has given a flattering portrait of Baju in "Les Hommes d'aujourd'hui." See the *Œuvres complètes,* V, 376–383.

8. Ernest Raynaud, *La Mêlée symboliste,* I, 63–71.

9. Raynaud, in *La Mêlée symboliste,* says that the Rimbaud parodies were composed to excite the curiosity of the public and make the decadent doctrine understood. Rimbaud was to become the ideal decadent; Tailhade, according to Raynaud, wished to exasperate the conservative middle classes through this verse.

problems of policy in the hands of Gustave Kahn. Kahn, after a brief appearance among the Hydropathes in 1880, had spent several years in military service in Africa and had returned to Paris shortly after the *Poètes maudits* and *A rebours* had set in motion new literary activity. He immediately established friendly relations with Mallarmé and Verlaine, whom Léo d'Orfer had known for some time. Thanks to these acquaintanceships, the new periodical was able to offer in its first number three prose poems of Mallarmé, Verlaine's "Ecrit en 1875," and Rimbaud's "Les Premières Communions." The first two items were not hitherto unpublished, Mallarmé's contribution having appeared in *La République des lettres* on December 20, 1875, and Verlaine's poem in *Le Zig-Zag* on June 14, 1885; the Rimbaud item was furnished by Verlaine and because of its numerous variants from an earlier manuscript is commonly supposed to have been set down from memory.[10] But *La Vogue* had only begun its work of publicizing the three masters.

For Mallarmé there was the essay by Téodor de Wyzewa entitled (in a pamphlet published by the magazine) "Notes sur Mallarmé," in which some of the more difficult sonnets were analyzed. The sonnet "M'introduire dans ton histoire" also appeared in the periodical. Verlaine published the studies of Marceline Desbordes-Valmore and of himself which were to become a part of the new edition of the *Poètes maudits,* as well as a few poems and prose passages. An essay by Léo d'Orfer, in the second number of the periodical, praised Verlaine.

But the crowning achievement of *La Vogue* was the recovery and publication of the elusive manuscript of *Les Illuminations* [11] and of poems which Rimbaud composed in 1872. Later in the year the reprinting of the almost unknown *Une saison en enfer* gave at last the bulk of Rimbaud's creative writing, known before only through the six poems and fragments of *Les Poètes maudits.*

The managing editor of the magazine, whose dominant trait was not modesty, was the chief contributor of poetry. But if a large part of the verse that was to become *Les Palais nomades* was printed by Kahn, it is also true that he did not forget his friend Jules Laforgue, who was in Germany until the fall of 1886. Poems which Laforgue had composed for his projected *Fleurs de bonne volonté,* aphorisms called "Dragées," prose poems, "Le Concile féerique," [12] the stories of the *Moralités légendaires,* and translations from

10. See Bouillane de Lacoste's article, "Verlaine éditeur de Rimbaud," *Mercure de France,* June 15, 1937. See also his *Rimbaud et le problème des Illuminations,* published in 1949.

11. The story of this manuscript, which apparently passed through the hands of Charles de Sivry, Louis le Cardonnel, and Louis Fière before Kahn and Fénéon obtained it, is told in the Pléiade edition of Rimbaud's *Œuvres complètes,* pp. 693–696. Kahn gives his account in *Symbolistes et décadents,* p. 56.

12. Printed in pamphlet form by the *Vogue.*

Walt Whitman are among his contributions to the periodical. From his answers to Kahn's letters one gathers that he was urged to send copy. Certainly the material he offered was expeditiously printed.

Among the contents of the magazine the "Souvenirs occultes" of Villiers de l'Isle-Adam, some rondels by Edouard Dujardin, contributions in prose and verse by Charles Morice and Charles Vignier are worthy of mention. In the second issue, while Léo d'Orfer was still a voice in the management, René Ghil published two sonnets. A few pages away appeared the name of his imminent pet aversion, Jean Moréas. In 1886, with Paul Adam, Moréas was attempting some innovations in impressionistic prose style. A sample of this unfortunate collaboration, taken from *Le Thé chez Miranda*,[13] was published by *La Vogue* in this April issue and toward the end of the year Moréas contributed some verse. It is interesting to note that Paul Bourget has not entirely given up poetry in 1886; he is a collaborator of *La Vogue*, perhaps as a kind of token of friendship for Laforgue.

This indication of the magazine's contents, to which might be added "Les Calvaires," one of Verhaeren's earliest contributions to Parisian periodicals, makes it easy to see how much worth while poetry and prose was printed in *La Vogue* and how superior it was to other little magazines of the period. The review attempted to broaden its interests by printing scientific articles by Charles Henry, an intimate friend of Gustave Kahn.

The *Vogue* of 1886 contains, in addition, almost all the important documents relating to the beginnings of free verse. Edouard Dujardin has listed [14] the seven items from the magazine which can be called free verse: the two sections from *Les Illuminations,* published in May and June; Laforgue's translations from Whitman; a portion of Gustave Kahn's "Intermède"; an extract of Moréas' and Adam's *Les Demoiselles Goubert;* and finally another poem by Moréas, published in November. In the first number of the new series of *La Revue indépendante,* that same month, Laforgue published "Sur une défunte."

The question of who first invented free verse has been much debated; Gustave Kahn has constantly said that he had the idea as early as 1880; Marie Krysinska makes a claim for the prose poems she published in *Le Chat noir* and *La Vie moderne* in 1882–83. Some critics, such as Paul Fort and Louis Mandin, refuse to recognize not only these but even Rimbaud's "Mouvement" and "Marine" as free verse.[15] Saint-Georges de Bouhélier advances the theory that Marie Krysinska may have invented free verse unwittingly:

---

13. Moréas and Adam also collaborated in *Les Demoiselles Goubert* (1887).

14. Edouard Dujardin, *Mallarmé par un des siens,* pp. 134–140; his chapter, "Les Premiers Poètes du vers libre," gives the necessary documentation on the subject.

15. *Histoire de la poésie française depuis 1850,* p. 148.

D'origine polonaise, et ignorant tout de la prosodie, elle avait dû en transgresser les règles et, d'abord, sans s'en douter. La théorie n'était venue qu'après.[16]

As for questions of influence, the conclusions cannot be definitive because Kahn had in his hands the manuscripts of Les Illuminations before any of his free verse appeared. The translations from Whitman may have inspired Laforgue. Baudelaire's prose poems suggest themselves as influences. Kahn, in a veiled reference,[17] implies that his theories were the point of departure of Marie Krysinska's publications of 1882–83. When one adds to these considerations those of liberties taken by Verlaine and the vague problem of the Peruvian exile, della Rocca de Vergalo,[18] the points of departure are too diverse and numerous to make definite conclusions.

In October, 1886, appeared two other magazines not so important for their literary content as for marking rivalries between two poets, Jean Moréas and René Ghil. Both of these reviews date from Moréas' manifesto in Le Figaro on September 18, 1886. According to Paul Adam,[19] the newspaper asked Moréas to elucidate the movement represented by the writers of La Vogue; according to Gustave Kahn,[20] the joint authors of Le Thé chez Miranda and Les Demoiselles Goubert went to see Marcade of Le Figaro and obtained the insertion of the manifesto in order to depict symbolism according to their own ideas and to constitute themselves as leaders. When Moréas had replied to Paul Bourde's article in 1885, suggesting the name "symbolistes" instead of "décadents," he was somewhat justified since the critic of Le Temps was attacking the contributors of Lutèce, specifically Moréas, Morice, Tailhade, and Vignier.

But in 1886, Ghil having launched his Traité du verbe, a loyal group having

16. Le Printemps d'une génération, p. 198.
17. Symbolistes et décadents, pp. 28–29.
18. Le Livre des Incas, published in 1879 by Lemerre, including poems both in Spanish and in French, with many dedications to poets of the Parnassian school, contains curious rhythms which at times are close to the fluidity of Verlaine. "La Ville aux amandiers," for example, uses this stanza form of three and four syllables (pp. 114–115):

Importun,
Qu'on exile,
Ce parc est un
Charmant asyle.

La blancheur
De vos marbres
Et la fraîcheur
De vos grands arbres,

Ont calmé
Ma souffrance,
Vous dont j'aimai
La tolérance!

19. La Vogue, October 4, 1886; Adam's article is entitled "Le Symbolisme."
20. Symbolistes et décadents, p. 46.

gathered around Mallarmé, Kahn and Laforgue having given expression to free verse, the signature of Moréas to the principles of the whole movement seemed somewhat presumptuous. *Le Scapin* immediately contested his claims as leader,[21] and its director, Raymond, offered Ghil the post of managing editor of a new magazine he was intending to found.[22] Ghil, accepting the offer, composed an article for the first number of this magazine which bore the name *La Décadence artistique et littéraire.* This essay, "Notre école," accused the group of decadents of trying to steal the honor of having found the symbol, the doctrine which Ghil claimed to have elucidated in his *Traité du verbe.* A week later the first number of *Le Symboliste* printed a reply by Paul Adam, who spoke of some very young people, doubtless well-intentioned but without talent, united under the name of "décadents." He laments that the press has seized upon the "diaboliques naïvetés" of *Le Scapin* and *Le Décadent* instead of recognizing the real personalities of innovation. The editors of *Le Symboliste* rallied around the name of Verlaine, securing for one of their four issues the poem "Un Conte." [23] On the other hand, René Ghil's *Traité du verbe* was published in October with a foreword by Mallarmé. This celebrated preface, from the pen of a man who had meditated for over two decades on the mysteries of language, resumed succinctly the possibilities of connotation and evocation of the word, and opened new horizons on the magic overtones which follow the original sonority:

Je dis: une fleur! et, hors de l'oubli où ma voix relègue aucun contour, en tant que quelque chose d'autre que les calices sus, musicalement se lève, idée rieuse ou altière, l'absente de tous bouquets.

Verlaine's attitude toward this polemic activity was characteristic. He tried to evade the issue, first of all by praising Moréas on the *Cantilènes* and by writing a laudatory essay on René Ghil in the collection of "Les Hommes d'aujourd'hui." [24] The exasperation of his poem "Jean-René" was to come later, as well as quarrels with both authors, but in 1886, beset with many monetary troubles and by illness, he kept an air of detached amusement. Shortly after the brief lives of *La Décadence* and *Le Symboliste* had come to an end, he wrote in a letter to Jules Tellier:

Dieu merci, la querelle entre les Symbolistes, Décadents, et autres enphuistes est apaisée.—Tant tués que blessés, personne de mort—sômatiquement.[25]

21. In the issue of October 1, 1886.

22. Henri Mondor, *Vie de Mallarmé,* II, 491.

23. *Le Symboliste,* October 15, 1886, with the title of "Bouquet à Marie." The poem utilizes the thirteen-syllable line, employed by Verlaine in four poems, of which the first was the "Sonnet boiteux."

24. A letter to Moréas, dated June 12, 1886, is in the *Correspondance de Paul Verlaine,* III, 248. The essay on Ghil was composed in February, 1887.

25. *Correspondance de Paul Verlaine,* III, 334. The letter is dated November 22, 1886.

Thus of the magazines of 1886, four are chiefly of interest as publicity agents for personalities and for rather unsuccessful attempts to define poetic doctrine. The sensational methods of Baju, the pretensions of Moréas and Ghil brought into public notice the names of Verlaine and Mallarmé, and Moréas' manifesto in *Le Figaro* did at least oppose symbolism to the kind of verse which had triumphed during the 1870's:

Ennemie de l'enseignement, la déclamation, la fausse sensibilité, la description objective, la poésie symboliste cherche à vêtir l'idée d'une forme sensible qui néanmoins ne serait un but à elle-même, mais tout en servant à exprimer l'idée demeurerait sujet.[26]

His indications on metrical matters are perhaps not those which would represent the entire group; but the "skillfully arranged disorder," the multiple pauses, the verses of an odd number of syllables, even the "fluidités absconses" of which he speaks are indications of the dominance of Verlaine's "art poétique." Members of the press, as Paul Adam says,[27] may have commented on the article with their usual insincerity and ignorance (Adam excepts Anatole France and Sutter Laumann), but at least they did comment. During the year recognition of a vital resurgence of poetry was accomplished.

The moment is also that of the entrance, into the French movement, of Belgian poets who had been accomplishing since 1880 a poetic renascence [28] in which the chief link with symbolism was admiration for Baudelaire. Not only the participation of Maeterlinck, van Lerberghe, and Grégoire le Roy in *La Pléiade,* but the publication of Verhaeren's second volume of verse by Lemerre, and the founding of *La Wallonie* by Albert Mockel (then but twenty years of age) occurred in 1886. The rapid growth of relationships among the literary groups in Paris and those in Belgium, begun by *La Basoche* in 1885 and continued by Gaston Dubedat's (really René Ghil's) *Ecrits pour l'art,* received its most powerful impulsion from *La Wallonie.*[29]

In published volumes of poetry the year is very rich. Moréas, Laforgue, and Henri de Régnier presented their second volumes. From the group of *La Pléiade* appeared Mikhaël's *L'Automne;* Pierre Quillard's mystery play in verse, *La Fille aux mains coupées;* and Paul Roux's *Lazare.* One of the Belgian collaborators of the magazine also published his first volume.[30] Vielé-Griffin, after contributing a few poems to *Lutèce,* gave his first collection the title of *Cueille d'Avril.* Louis Marsolleau, one of the leaders of the Hydro-

26. *Les Premières Armes du symbolisme,* prepared by Moréas, contains this text.

27. *La Vogue,* October 4, 1886.

28. The Belgian renaissance in poetry, with its varied French allegiances, is described in Guy Michaud's *Message poétique du symbolisme,* II, 236–241.

29. For a study of this important periodical, see A. J. Mathews' *La Wallonie 1886–1892.*

30. Grégoire Le Roy, *La Chanson d'un soir.*

pathes and the Zutistes, was the author of *Les Baisers perdus*. Georges Roden-bach, suppressing from his list of published works the anterior volumes, of-fered a new collection, *La Jeunesse blanche,* and shortly afterward came from Belgium to reside in France.

Among all these collections of verse that of Laforgue was certainly the most original. The conversations of Pierrot, which are addressed to the moon, con-tain the irony and the skepticism revealed in *Les Complaintes*. But *L'Imita-tion de Notre-Dame la lune* reaches farther into the world of the unconscious. What was the boredom of Sundays, of days of rain and wind, what had been the melancholy of poverty and homesickness now transcends time and space and becomes cosmic:

> Les.dieux s'en vont; plus que des hures;
> Ah! ça devient tous les jours pis;
> J'ai fait mon temps, je déguerpis
> Vers l'Inclusive Sinécure.[31]

Laforgue's friend and admirer, Gustave Kahn, underlines the intuitive and suggestive elements of the volume and senses the curious reflection that emanates from the moon to the mind of the observer, who in turn sends his meditation toward the strange, deserted planet:

L'Imitation de Notre-Dame la Lune est une multiforme élégie cosmogonique. C'est l'étude des reflets de la Lune à la Terre dans l'âme d'un songeur. C'est l'étude de sentiments modernes semblables, quoique diminués, à ceux pour Phœbé ou Tanit.[32]

Laforgue did not live to see the rapid spread of his fame. His two volumes of poetry and the contributions he had made to the *Vogue* made his pub-lished work seem extensive for so young a writer. It was only after his death, however, that the importance of his *Moralités légendaires,* called by Mallarmé the "contes de Voltaire du Symbolisme," and that of his experiments in free verse were recognized.

The extraordinary gifts of this writer are manifest in the critical judgments in his letters and in the brief notes he penned for studies on Baudelaire and Corbière, in his projects for writing the story of a soul, in his artistic acute-ness, and in his mingling of fantasy and irony. These are some of the facets of a personality whose death, on August 20, 1887, is almost as important as Rimbaud's forsaking of literature. Among his contemporaries he left the memory of a man of genius whose talent had been only partly revealed. Henri de Régnier, Remy de Gourmont, and Camille Mauclair do not measure their

---

31. Jules Laforgue, *Poésies,* p. 239.
32. Gustave Kahn, *Symbolistes et décadents,* p. 184. First published in *La Revue blanche,* February, 1896, pp. 122–126.

praise for his work,[33] and immediately after his death Kahn and Wyzewa devoted themselves to perpetuating his fame.[34]

Moréas, on the other hand, loud in theory, is somewhat disappointing in deed. Innovation in technique and conscious literary artistry are offset by an instinct for imitation. His first volume had been a reflection of decadent fashion; in 1886, with *Les Cantilènes,* the memory of German ballads, of the Victor Hugo of 1828, and perhaps of the narrative poems of Greece dominates many of his poems. He uses refrains, assonance, multiple distribution of pauses, and at times rare or antiquated words. Gustave Kahn, with some justice, speaks of the great importance Moréas attached to the form rather than to the idea,[35] and Laforgue, after reading *Les Syrtes,* comments: "Rhétorique à la dernière mode, mais pure rhétorique." [36] They might have added that he had a sense of rhythm and that his experiments with the suppression of rhyme are not altogether unsuccessful. Particularly when he sought to give a kind of artlessness and antique flavor to his ballads, he accomplished his purpose:

> —Mon mari fait la guerre,
> Voilà sept ans à Pâques.
> J'attends encore un an
> Et puis j'entre au couvent.
>
> —Votre mari, la belle,
> Est mort l'hiver dernier,
> Et j'ai payé les chantres,
> Les chantres et le prêtre.[37]

But when he attempts to create the "Pur concept," when he leaves the imitative realm, Moréas is usually pedantic and cold. The last poem of *Les Cantilènes* contains this stanza:

> L'Anacampsérote au suc vermeil
> Est éclose: au cœur las panacée;
> Au flux de son aile cadencée
> L'Iynge berce l'amer sommeil.[38]

Mikhaël, like the other poets of the *Pléiade,* made no innovations in form, yet *L'Automne,* with its mingling of colors and sentiment, its twilight melan-

---

33. See Henri de Régnier's *Nos Rencontres,* pp. 87–96; Remy de Gourmont's *Le Livre des masques,* pp. 205–209; Mauclair's *Jules Laforgue.*

34. *La Revue indépendante,* during 1887 and 1888, was the periodical which publicized Laforgue's name and art.

35. *Symbolistes et décadents,* p. 48.

36. *Lettres à un ami,* p. 91.

37. Jean Moréas, *Premières poésies, 1883–1886,* p. 169.

38. *Ibid.,* p. 231.

choly, its languor, seems more in the tradition of Baudelaire. In 1886 Mikhaël
was but twenty years old; he died at the age of twenty-four. From the work
which he left one could surmise that he would have remained outside of
any grouping into schools, that the elegiac note of Lamartine was attuned
to his temperament, that the theme of boredom and synthesis of sensations
would at times seem to ally him with Baudelaire, and that the structure of
his verse would remain strictly Parnassian.[39] The atmosphere and the diction
of most of his verse closely resemble those of "Crépuscule pluvieux":

> Et pourtant, maintenant, dans l'horreur languissante
> D'un soir de pluie et dans la lente obscurité,
> Je sens mon cœur que nul amour n'a déserté
> Mélancolique ainsi qu'une chambre d'absente.

Mikhaël's verse serves to measure the evolution that had taken place in
poetry during a decade. In 1875 his verse would have been striking and would
probably have provoked from the Parnassians the accusation of vagueness.
In 1885 he seems rather conservative, but the transfer of the landscape to
the mind, the evocative imagery proclaim his alliance with the new poetic
art. In the lines just quoted, while he does not use the ellipsis in thought which
one finds in "Il pleure dans mon cœur" of similar theme, the image of the
deserted room, the note of absence so dear to Mallarmé, open the way for
dream and meditation. With this poet as with many another, the frontiers
of symbolism assume a broader meaning than adherence to any doctrine.
The role of suggestion, the invitation for the reader's active participation in
the reverie of the poet become important contributions to the movement.

It is also by the incursion of the dream world that Henri de Régnier's second volume, *Apaisement,* belongs to symbolism. The title does not convey
the evening twilight, weariness, and suffering expressed in many of the
poems. Régnier, the friend of Sully-Prudhomme, Verlaine, and Mallarmé
after the publication of *Lendemains,* and of José-Maria de Heredia, whom
he visited first in 1888, refused to ally himself with any group; and while
his long poetic career offers in turn examples of free verse, poetry in the
current symbolist imagery, and sonnets of purely classic style, he did not enter
the quarrels which provoked so much rancor during the period. To one of
the issues of *Lutèce* he contributed a humorous account of a young man who
had read *A rebours* and who became a decadent.[40] This appeared at the time
the magazine, shortly to expire, was publishing the equally ironic "Carnet
d'un décadent" by Ernest Raynaud. Generally, however, he appears as a
reserved writer, inclined by nature to dreams and remembrance, and eclectic

39. Remy de Gourmont (*Le IIᵐᵉ Livre des masques*, p. 238) thinks that Mikhaël's last verses
may indicate liberation from severe rules of prosody.
40. Quoted in full by Raynaud in *La Mêlée symboliste*, I, 32–34.

in his allegiance. In 1890, when he embraced free verse for a time, he was reproached by Sully-Prudhomme, but he says that he refused to sacrifice his poetic expression for friendship.[41]

Verhaeren, who had published his first volume of verse, *Les Flamandes*, in Brussels in 1883, was almost unknown in France before 1886. At that time the publication of *Les Moines* by Lemerre gained the admiration of some poets, among them Rodolphe Darzens. Darzens was impressed by the harmony, the richness and unusual quality of the images, and the able expression of complicated sensations.[42] These are indeed elements which change the poems from mere descriptions into the world of the mind. Written in a monastery to which Verhaeren had retired for their composition, these mystical memories of the solitaries of Bornhem brought into play all the art of music for the creation of atmosphere. The poem "Soir religieux" reveals in its opening lines the importance of sound, not the codified system of René Ghil, but the natural selection of a sensitive and talented poet:

> Des peupliers penchant, pâles, leur profil triste
> Nimbé de lune, au bord des mares sans remous,
> Avec un va-et-vient de balancement doux,
> Font trembler leurs reflets dans les eaux d'améthyste.[43]

The note of silence, meditation, and twilight, more uncommon with Verhaeren than sudden flashes and violence, is characteristic of *Les Moines*. That his artistic competence extended to many themes and varied tones is revealed by the epic note of "Les Crucifères" and that of horror in "Moine sauvage" and "Vision." Even the silence of the monastery is broken by the clanging of the bells; at such moments Verhaeren shows the close relationship he feels between theme and sound:

> Brusque, résonne au loin un tintement de cloche,
> Qui casse du silence à coups de battant clair
> Par-dessus les hameaux, et jette à travers l'air
> Un long appel, qui long, parmi l'écho, ricoche.[44]

After the publication of *Les Moines*, Verhaeren's literary activity was for some years concentrated in Belgium, and even his trips out of his native country were largely to London. In France he remained relatively obscure. In 1888 Jules Tellier, whose volume *Nos poètes* is a strange mixture of prejudice and omissions, grants Verhaeren two lines: "M. Emile Verhaeren (*les*

---

41. Henri de Régnier, *Nos Rencontres*, pp. 15–19.

42. *La Pléiade*, June, 1886, p. 128.

43. Emile Verhaeren, *Poèmes* (Mercure de France, 1895), p. 184.

44. This is the version of 1886. In the edition just cited there are slight revisions, Verhaeren preferring to make the "tintement" plural, changing "résonne" to "sonnent" and "et jette" to "jetant." See *Poèmes*, p. 228.

Moines) est Belge comme M. Rodenbach. Je goûte moins son talent." [45] Even in 1896, when Mallarmé and Moréas were elected as those most worthy to succeed Verlaine in the admiration and affection of the poets, Verhaeren is mentioned only eight times. Sully-Prudhomme, Henri de Régnier, Léon Dierx, and José-Maria de Heredia received more praise and more votes than he. Yet he had published by that time the trilogy of *Les Soirs, Les Débâcles,* and *Les Flambeaux noirs,* as well as *Les Apparus dans mes chemins, Les Campagnes hallucinées, Les Villages illusoires,* and *Les Villes tentaculaires.* The *Mercure de France* had begun a reprinting of his work the preceding year.

Vielé-Griffin, who had been from time to time a contributor to *Lutèce,* was the author of a first volume of verse, *Cueille d'avril,* in 1886. Shortly to become an advocate of free verse, both in essays and in works, the author remains traditional in this first effort. His inspiration is the landscape of Touraine, a landscape transformed into fugitive images of amatory and idealistic yearnings. Already the poet of the forest and sea, but in a different sense from Theuriet and Richepin (since his verse is evocative rather than descriptive), he merits the comment of Remy de Gourmont that "il y a, par Francis Vielé-Griffin, quelque chose de nouveau dans la poésie française." [46] In writing those lines the author is not thinking merely of the form but the idea of Vielé-Griffin's verse, the enthusiasm, the sumptuous imagery perhaps inspired in part by reading of Swinburne, and the adroit use of refrains from traditional songs.

Although the journalistic press did not trouble itself with the criticism of poetic volumes of the decadents and symbolists, it did print many hostile echoes to the theories which Moréas and Ghil announced during 1886. [47] Universal condemnation of the obscurity, of the desire to be isolated from the crowd, and especially of the diction and syntax are followed by the suggestion that the school of the Decadents is on the road to insanity. Even Sutter Laumann, whose article in *La Justice* is noteworthy in that it is not sarcastic, questions whether the new school can really innovate, since the poets are turning their backs on reality and making an alien realm of modern life.

The pompous and tortured style of the *Traité du verbe,* which Sutter Laumann called "le sublime du baroque," did no great service to the better under-

45. Jules Tellier, *Nos poètes,* p. 180.

46. Remy de Gourmont, *Le Livre des masques,* p. 53.

47. Moréas' manifesto was printed on September 18. On September 20 appeared an unsigned article in *Le Temps* and Sutter Laumann's article in *La Justice;* on September 22 "Quisait" wrote a withering criticism of Moréas and Ghil in *Le Gaulois.* Anatole France's ironic examination of the manifesto appeared in *Le Temps* on September 26. On October 2 Henri Fouquier in *Le XIXᵉ Siècle* and on October 24 "Mermeix" in *La France* were equally denunciatory of the movement.

standing of poetic reforms, but by the publicity it aroused brought several names into prominence. The supplement of the *Figaro*, on November 27, printed an article by Auguste Marcade concerning the little magazines in which one could find manifestations of the "inquiétante tournure d'esprit à notre époque." He mentions *Le Scapin, La Vogue,* and *La Revue indépendante,* and gives as prophets of the new poetry Verlaine, Mallarmé, and René Ghil. He merely lists the names of collaborators he has noticed in the periodicals, designating Rimbaud as one of "les plus farouches décadents." No profundity or critical evaluation of the poetry itself concerned the journalists, who in general utilized the quarrels and most sensational proclamations for their articles.

Yet the year had seen not only in books but in magazines much excellent publication. In *Le Scapin* and *La Décadence,* which represent almost an identical list of contributors, Stuart Merrill and Edouard Dubus had printed many good poems. Each of the four numbers of *La Décadence* contained something by Mallarmé, and *Le Scapin* reprinted "Hérodiade," "Le Spectacle interrompu," "Cette nuit," and "Apparition." [48] Le Cardonnel, Samain, and Henri de Régnier are among the poets who appeared in the same magazine during the course of the year. In *La Vogue* the verses of Kahn, Laforgue, and Moréas were frequent. That jealousy and ambitions prevented more unified action may seem regrettable, but the character of the new poetry, tending always toward liberation, was so definitely individualistic that clashes of personalities seem almost logical in its evolution.

48. No. 3 (January 1), No. 17 (September 1), No. 19 (October 16), No. 20 (November 1).

Chapter VI: THE YEARS OF
STRUGGLE, 1887–88

THE GREAT ACTIVITY of 1886 in poetic circles had restored lyric art to a place it had not known for many decades. Even if the general public, after reading the newspaper articles, thought of symbolism as mad and eccentric, it was true that poetry had ceased to be an almost forgotten realm of current literature. But the champions of suggestion and music, of introspection and personal lyricism had unfortunately divided into rival camps which threatened chaos and disorder rather than triumph. More or less united in recognition of Baudelaire as forerunner and of Mallarmé and Verlaine as leaders, the younger generation had failed to find a valid guide within their own group. The manifesto of Moréas had been fairly clear in its general outlines, but what he proposed for the future development of poetry was scarcely acceptable. His "impollués vocables," his "période qui s'arcboute alternant avec la période aux défaillances ondulées," and his preaching the restoration of the older French language were immediate cause for criticism. Ghil's even more curious theories were not in general acceptable, and neither Moréas nor Ghil appeared to be of the stature necessary for a literary leader.

Rivalries had been aroused. Not content with a broad and eclectic view, several ambitious poets were striving to impose their favorite ideas on fellow writers. Others, like Henri de Régnier and Emile Verhaeren, were pursuing their own paths and were writing poetry which was the more important in that it did not try to limit itself by theory.

The poetic future now held the important factors for its development. In form, the possibilities of free verse or of combinations of regular and liberated meters had been proposed. The use of assonance and alliteration to give a new musical quality to poetry had been put into practice. Especially had the realm of poetic subject matter been established as that of the interior world. A form of expression in which the reader could complete the thought by his own imaginative powers was a tenet of the new poetry. Given these general traits, verse might have pursued a more or less calm evolution. But difficulties, some purely material and others psychological, were to be the immediate problems of the movement.

The periodicals of 1886, having lived their brief and impecunious existences, and even *Lutèce* having disappeared, the year 1887 opens with perhaps only two important periodicals in the realm of poetry. These are the *Ecrits pour l'art* with Gaston Dubedat [1] as director and Edouard Dujardin's new series of the *Revue indépendante*. The former was the outlet for René Ghil's scientific and instrumentalist theories of verse; the latter represents the dual continuation of Wyzewa and Kahn, with the implications of loyalty toward Mallarmé and Laforgue.

The *Revue indépendante* began its new existence with two numbers in the last months of 1886. Huysmans and Villiers de l'Isle-Adam, as well as Mallarmé, were collaborators from the beginning; but Kahn, still occupied with the final numbers of *La Vogue,* the monetary difficulties arising out of the magazine's temerarious entry into the publishing field,[2] and the publication of his own first volume, did not join the editorial staff until 1888.

Meanwhile, between November, 1886, and July, 1887, Mallarmé wrote the extraordinary series "Sur le Théâtre," in which he talked of the dance, music, and other esthetic questions but in which he skillfully avoided comment on the current stage. To the January issue of the magazine Mallarmé also contributed four poems,[3] now among his most famous, in which a smoldering fireplace, a vase without a flower, a lace curtain at a window, and a meditation after reading a book were the points of departure for complicated and delicate dreaming. Wyzewa contributed a commentary on these sonnets,[4] persisting in his idea that Mallarmé is not so interested in the symbol itself as in the expressive harmony of syllables and the elevation of thought. In this Wyzewa was repeating his essay of *La Vogue* in 1886 and continuing the Wagnerian analogy of relationship between words and music. For Wyzewa the accomplishment of the younger poets had been in the perfecting of the musical vocabulary of literature and in the destruction of the old rules of caesura, regular rhymes, and fixed rhythms. He sees, however, a danger in the pursuit of these harmonies, the loss of precision and meaning as well as the effacement of sincerity. But neither Laforgue nor Mallarmé is, to his way of thinking, guilty of such faults. As an example of definiteness in scene and emotions, he cites "L'Après-midi d'un faune." Wyzewa is probably most insistent on originality; imitation, even of the authors he admires, seems to him inadvisable. Rimbaud is "un maître sans émule"; Ghil is imitating Mallarmé in *Le Geste ingénu* to the point of parody; even Vielé-Griffin seems to be too much a follower of Leconte de Lisle.

1. Dubedat was an ardent Wagnerian, and had written some musical criticism for *Le Scapin*. He died, still a young man, on May 4, 1890. René Ghil tells of his role in *Les Ecrits pour l'art* in *Les Dates et les œuvres,* pp. 76–78.

2. *La Vogue* had published Rimbaud's *Illuminations;* Laforgue's *Le Concile féerique,* Félix Fénéon's *Les Impressionnistes en 1886* and Wyzewa's *Notes sur Mallarmé. La Revue indépendante* secured the unsold copies of these and of *La Vogue,* which it placed on sale in July, 1887.

3. *La Revue indépendante,* No. 3 (January, 1887), pp. 61–64.

4. *Ibid.,* No. 4 (February, 1887), pp. 152–155.

Among those who represent a really personal and unimitative manner of thought and expression, not only Mallarmé but Villiers de l'Isle-Adam and Jules Laforgue come frequently to Wyzewa's mind. He laments the indifference of the public toward all three authors and compares the destinies of Stendhal and Baudelaire to theirs. He mentions an article by Bergerat in *Le Figaro* which has at last revealed the name of Villiers to the public and resulted in the sale of a few copies of the *Eve future;* he notes that the first serious, intelligent study on Mallarmé has been published by Vittorio Pica in the *Gazzetta letteraria* of Milan.[5]

The *Revue indépendante,* like the *Vogue* of the preceding year, undertook to give these favored authors a trifle less obscurity by publishing their work. In 1887 appeared from its press the so-called *Poésies complètes* of Mallarmé, photographed from manuscripts and with a design by Félicien Rops. A small number of copies was printed, and the only object gained was the placing in the hands of a few admirers a more nearly complete collection of verse scattered here and there in periodicals. On the other hand, an edition of five hundred copies of Laforgue's six *Moralités légendaires* gave new life to the stories which had been published in *La Vogue.*

Wyzewa is not kind to the Parnassians in his critical articles of 1887. He finds Plessis grave and sententious; Coppée's *Arrière-Saison* is a poor collection of anecdotes; Theuriet's verse recalls a Latin manual for school use. If the initials "T.W.," signed to an imaginary speech receiving Leconte de Lisle into the Academy, stand for Téodor de Wyzewa, he is equally unfriendly to the poetic production of the leader of the school. The supposed academician compliments the author of the *Poèmes barbares* on the solid monument he has built, but adds that all the stones of that edifice have been taken from the quarries of Victor Hugo. With the words, "Vous n'avez pas imité l'œuvre de M. Hugo: vous l'avez utilisée," he concludes a series of politely phrased shafts.[6]

Toward Gustave Kahn, who was to take over his place as literary critic of the *Revue indépendante* in 1888, Wyzewa is much more enthusiastic than toward Henri de Régnier, Stuart Merrill, or Vielé-Griffin, all of whom published volumes of poetry during 1887. *Les Palais nomades,* a series of emotional moments, each introduced by a kind of prose poem, appeal especially to Wyzewa for their sudden inundation of images, and for the rhythm which obeys only the feeling of the author: "Voici la forme poétique enfin libérée de

---

5. It was not until February and March, 1891, that Pica's study of Mallarmé, under the title "Les Modernes Byzantins" was published in *La Revue indépendante.* By that time François de Nion and Georges Bonnamour were the editors of the magazine. Wyzewa's reference is inexact. The *Gazzetta letteraria* of Turin published Pica's article on November 20, November 22, and December 4, 1886, pp. 377–379, 387–390, 393–396, respectively.

6. *La Revue indépendante,* No. 6 (April, 1887).

ces rimes régulières, et de ces rythmes imposés que nos poètes subissent douloureusement." [7]

Les Palais nomades offer verses in which the rhyme and syllabic count are the basis of the music; in contrast there are poems in which both considerations have been cast away and only the elements of tonic accent and assonance remain. At the beginning of the volume one finds:

> Bon chevalier, la route est sombre,
> Crains-tu donc pas les assassins?
> Les âmes mortes, par essaims,
> Larmoyant aux émois de l'ombre? [8]

Sometimes the metrical count breaks down but the rhyme is kept:

> Boire et puis disparaître aux remous
> Résonner et disparaître en cycles mous
> Courir vers la fin seule de la faim
> Dormir enfin.[9]

Finally extreme liberty is achieved in a stanza such as:

> A l'ombre de l'arbre des désirs
> Endormez vos inquiétudes, endormez
> Vos chansons et vos frissons des antans
> Et les pennons brodés d'Orient, glacés de lacs, les pennons mauves
> Dômeront en flots d'apothéoses, dômeront vos vallaces, vos visionnaires
> trêves.[10]

Kahn, like almost all of the early exponents of free verse, did not wish utterly to discard the alexandrine and the usual poetic meters. He desired to admit a sort of rhythmic measurement other than the syllabic, a measurement based upon the phrase, the stress, the sonority of the voice, and the pauses in the thought. This form of poetic line, which he felt could reign concurrently with the traditional ones, he defines: "L'unité du vers peut se définir encore: un fragment le plus court possible figurant un arrêt de voix et un arrêt de sens." [11]

In order to give coherence and unity to the line, Kahn counsels the use of assonance and alliteration, musical elements he obviously prefers to the regular recurrence of rhyme. Many of the poems of the *Palais nomades* use the insistent repetition of a word as the basis of unity:

7. *Ibid.*, No. 7 (May, 1887).
8. Gustave Kahn, *Premiers poèmes*, p. 42.
9. *Ibid.*, p. 85.
10. *Ibid.*, p. 112.
11. *Ibid.*, p. 26. The principal ideas of Kahn's prosody are contained in this preface, which he wrote for the 1897 edition of his early verse.

> Tes yeux luisaient violets dans l'ombre de la route
> De la route sans issues ni voies, la bonne route.[12]

Other problems which interest Kahn are those of tonic accent and of the mute "e." The former, to his way of thinking, is not a matter of the individual word but of the stress given to some part of a phrase by reason of the emotion expressed. This he calls the "accent d'impulsion," [13] and he underlines its importance in the initial verse of a stanza for setting the pattern of the following lines. He neither discards nor accepts the mute "e"; it becomes a pause, a kind of grace note between surrounding syllables. Probably Kahn's most dubious usage is that of long lines in poetry, fortunately not adopted by many of the early adepts of free verse.[14] Not always made melodic by inner rhyme, these seem at times heavy and dragging. Their author defends such usage by contending that the groupings of several phrases represent a single burst of inspiration, but it is questionable whether the unity of construction is not impaired by a succession of three lines such as the following:

> Tes bras sont l'asyle
> Et tes lèvres le parvis
> Où s'éventairent les parfums et les couleurs de fleurs et des fruits.[15]

Admired by Wyzewa, *Les Palais nomades* were very harshly denounced by Jules Tellier. He describes the volume as boring and unintelligible, and he adds that there are perhaps a thousand ways to write bad poetic lines, all of which Kahn knows and practices.[16]

Whatever may be the faults in the composition of the *Palais nomades,* the volume marks a point in French versification since in it were grouped for the first time several examples of free meters. Albert Mockel, whose first attempts in free verse appeared in August, 1887, admits that the influence of Kahn's volume was decisive in his own writing.[17] Verlaine, on the contrary, considered as the apostle of freedom in versification and certainly an important influence in the liberation of verse from narrow rules, took an extremely conservative attitude toward the innovations of Kahn and Moréas. In March, 1888, he published "Un Mot sur la rime," [18] an essay in which he says that the weak accentuation of the French language does not admit of blank verse, and that

---

12. *Ibid.*, p. 129.
13. Mockel and Robert de Souza use "accent oratoire" in much the same sense.
14. Vielé-Griffin used the twelve-syllable line as a basis of his verse. Adolphe Retté is one of the poets who followed Kahn's example with lines of fifteen or eighteen syllables.
15. Gustave Kahn, *Premiers poèmes*, p. 117.
16. Jules Tellier, *Nos poètes*, pp. 240–244.
17. Edouard Dujardin, *Mallarmé par un des siens*, p. 172.
18. In *Le Décadent*, March 1, 1888.

he prefers regular lines. He specifically cites a recent poem of Kahn, "Eventails," of which the last three lines are alexandrines and suggests that the reader may regret that the rest of the poem does not utilize this regularity. Citing his own use of assonance in "Cécile" and "faucille," he requests that this liberty not serve as a model. It is not until 1894, when many poets had adopted the medium of free verse, that Verlaine wrote the poems of *Epigrammes* which speak in a more direct fashion of the innovators:

> Que l'ambition du Vers Libre hante
> De jeunes cerveaux épris de hasards!
> C'est l'ardeur d'une illusion touchante.
> On ne peut que sourire à leurs écarts.[19]

René Ghil both in the *Ecrits pour l'art* and in the new edition of his *Traité du verbe* proclaimed his theories of "instrumentation verbale" during 1887. For a time he appeared to have a kindred spirit in Stuart Merrill, whose first volume of poetry, *Les Gammes,* was dedicated to him. Merrill's admiration and friendship for Ghil date back to their schooldays together in the Lycée Fontanes, perhaps to the moment when Merrill showed the slightly older boy some of his verses and received encouragement.[20] During 1883 they had collaborated on a little lithographed sheet, *Le Fou,* with their fellow students Quillard, Mikhaël, Darzens, and Fontainas. In 1884 Merrill, obliged by the sudden blindness of his father to leave France with his family, was separated from the group. He was in New York from 1884 to 1889 as a student in the law school of Columbia University and did not return permanently to Paris until 1892.

Thus Merrill, during the period when decadence and symbolism were taking form, was not in the midst of such activity. But, like Laforgue during the years in Germany, he kept in close contact with literary developments in Paris and even in Brussels.[21] His first publications appeared in *La Basoche,* which also printed offerings from his other friends of the Lycée Fontanes and notably the first version of the *Traité du verbe* under the title "Sous Mon Cachet." An ardent Wagnerian, Merrill was one of the seven authors whose sonnets appeared in the January 8, 1886, issue of the *Revue wagnérienne,* and in 1887 he wrote two articles on Wagner's music for the *New York Evening Post.*

From New York Merrill sent the manuscript of *Les Gammes* to Ghil, who corrected the proofs. The volume appeared the same month as *Le Geste*

19. Paul Verlaine, *Œuvres complètes,* III, 222.

20. René Ghil, *Les Dates et les œuvres,* p. 85.

21. For a list of some contributions made by Merrill to *La Basoche,* as well as to American newspapers, see M. L. Henry's *Stuart Merrill,* pp. 275–276.

ingénu (February, 1887). A month later,[22] in the *Ecrits pour l'art,* Ghil jubilantly announced that *Les Gammes* constituted a conclusive and victorious achievement for poetry composed according to the instrumentalist theory.

Ghil's certainty of having won a disciple is not entirely unwarranted. Merrill was primarily interested in the musical effects of poetry; even as late as 1889 he wrote to Ghil: "Je répète formellement que j'adopte tes théories, tout en les interprétant d'une manière large et personnelle." [23]. In the *Gammes* some of the first poems, in particular "La Flûte" and "Nocturne," contain alliterations and vowel sequences of definite artifice. That these musical effects lack delicacy and are perhaps the most labored of Merrill's production is undeniable. Unlike Ghil, their author is perfectly clear and untroubled in his syntax. The nightingale "module en mal d'amour sa molle mélodie" and the wind has "frous-frous frêles," but these excesses in alliteration may well have come as much from the inspiration of Swinburne as of Ghil. Others of the seventeen poems of the little volume suggest in theme or in form Verlaine or Baudelaire.

A great diversity of admirations and influences such as these, an incomplete acceptance of the orchestration theories, and above all a much simpler and more natural style made some critics, such as Wyzewa, find diversities rather than similarities between Ghil and Merrill. Both writers were interested in social reform, but whereas the author of the *Traité du verbe* saw in poetry a legitimate expression for such ideas, Merrill tended to keep the domain of verse free of didacticism. While Ghil progressively made his doctrine more and more complex by speaking of the role of science, evolution, the necessity of a unified work, in addition to the orchestration of sounds and the symbols of ideas, Merrill adhered to the simplicity of a program he had announced to Vielé-Griffin about 1886 or 1887.[24] He wished to give the French alexandrine some of the musical qualities of English verse and to express emotion by means of words. Slow in adopting free verse, he was interested in the prose poem at an early date. This literary form furnished the contents of a volume of translations, *Pastels in Prose,* published by Harper and Brothers in 1890. Here Merrill chose selections from the past, from Bertrand and Banville, as well as from his contemporaries, especially his school friends from the Lycée Fontanes. Among his own early writings is a prose poem entitled "La Princesse qui attend" and published in *La Wallonie* in 1887.[25]

Despite quite a different turn of mind from that of Ghil, Merrill remained

22. In the issue of March 7, 1887.
23. M. L. Henry, *Stuart Merrill,* p. 76.
24. *Ibid.,* p. 58.
25. Merrill had the intention of publishing a book of his own prose poems, probably under the title *Merveilles.* Some of these are included in the posthumous volume *Prose et vers.*

one of the loyal adherents of the *Ecrits pour l'art,* not only in its six issues of 1887, but in its later revivals. Ghil's two cofounders, Vielé-Griffin and Henri de Régnier,[26] were already separated from the periodical and from the theories of scientific verse by the third number, that of May, 1887. Lack of funds and perhaps their departure brought an end to the first series in June. Then Albert Mockel, though announcing that his *Wallonie* would remain eclectic, offered to give space in his magazine to the collaborators of the defunct periodical.

Actually in France, by the middle of 1887, there was a dearth of periodicals favorable to the symbolists. After the death of the *Ecrits pour l'art* the only important magazine of poetry which continued uninterruptedly for the rest of the year was the *Revue indépendante.* Even in the two or three following years, despite attempts to found new publications, the center of activity shifts somewhat to Belgium, and specifically to Liége, where *La Wallonie* published many poems of French symbolists and gave critical judgment on their work.

By this time the importance of the Belgian school of poets was beginning to be recognized by the French symbolists. In June, 1887, Octave Maus contributed an article to the *Revue indépendante* in which he discussed the verse of Rodenbach, Verhaeren, and Khnopff. Poems by these three representatives of the literary group of Brussels followed the essay.[27] While this is but a prelude to the more complete integration which would be accomplished after the founding of *La Plume* and the *Mercure de France,* together with the transfer of *La Revue blanche* to Paris in 1891, it carries on the work begun by *La Basoche* in 1884–85 and *La Pléiade* in 1886. From 1887 to 1890 chief credit for bringing together the parallel movements in the two countries should go to Albert Mockel, for not only Ghil, Merrill, Vielé-Griffin, Moréas, Quillard, and Henri de Régnier were received into the company of Verhaeren, Le Roy, and Van Lerberghe,[28] but later arrivals, such as Retté, Louÿs, and Gide were welcomed by the eclectic but progressive *Wallonie.*

In 1887 Verlaine published little verse in magazines. Vanier had issued a new edition of the *Fêtes galantes* in 1886 and of the *Romances sans paroles* in 1887, but Verlaine, passing from one hospital to another, writing the biographies of *Les Hommes d'aujourd'hui,* preparing the publication of *Amour,* was quite poverty-stricken and certainly would not have been reluc-

---

26. Ghil says that Henri de Régnier broke with the *Ecrits pour l'art* because he did not approve inclusion of unknown writers in the magazine. Like many statements in *Les Dates et les œuvres,* this one seems subject to caution. Ghil is always rather bitter about those whom he thought to have won to his theories and who refused to accept him as mentor.

27. *La Revue indépendante,* No. 8, pp. 372–389.

28. Other Belgians who became known in France partly through the *Wallonie* were Max Elskamp and André Fontainas.

tant to making a little pocket money by publication of his verse.[29] But the *Revue indépendante,* to which he did contribute poems on two occasions in 1887, was apparently slow in making remuneration, for Verlaine complains repeatedly in his letters of money promised him by Edouard Dujardin but not forthcoming. Verlaine's appearance in three issues of *Les Chroniques* during the year may be directly traced to his friendship with Jules Tellier, who was one of the contributors to the periodical. At the end of 1887 Verlaine accepted collaboration with the new series of Baju's *Le Décadent,* his "Ballade pour les Décadents" appearing in the first number of the revived publication [30] and a letter he wrote Baju being the leading feature of the January 1, 1888, issue.

It might seem strange that Baju, whose *Décadent* of 1886 had existed at a time when the name for the new poetic school was the burning question, should wish to revive the periodical. In truth he had never abandoned championship of his chosen term, and during 1887 had published a pamphlet entitled *L'Ecole décadente.* Full of inane repetitions of what had already been said much more effectively, the little book, together with its author, was not taken very seriously.[31] But Verlaine, unlike most of his contemporaries, praised Baju for having attempted to knit together the diverse and uncertain poetic currents of the epoch.

In the eyes of the public and of the critics of the press, those writers who looked upon the exterior world as a vain semblance of truth and who arrogated to themselves the right to express the inner reality according to their own whim constituted a group bearing the double name of decadents and symbolists. Such an opinion is voiced by Maurice Peyrot in *La Nouvelle Revue,* in November, 1887. In turn Peyrot takes the names of Moréas, Ghil, Laforgue, and Mallarmé in order to hold them up to ridicule. Even Mallarmé's most fervent disciples, he says, are utterly unable to agree as to the meaning of the master's verse. Ghil's three volumes of poetry are not only incomprehensible but hopelessly dull. Laforgue, who had died a few months before Peyrot's article appeared, is described as a master in linking disorder of words with incoherence in ideas. The conclusions of the article, while denying that Ghil's theories will last, seem to credit them with some influence:

De tout ce mouvement littéraire, il ne restera donc à notre avis, que certaines locutions archaïques heureusement rajeunies, un arrangement plus harmonieux et

---

29. Verlaine's activities and his poverty are best revealed through the voluminous correspondence with Léon Vanier.

30. The issue of December, 1887.

31. Wyzewa, for instance, thinks of the ironic smile which reading of Baju's pamphlet would have produced on the face of Laforgue (*La Revue indépendante,* October, 1887). In November Maurice Peyrot is amused by Baju's description of Maurice de Plessys as "Quasiment vierge de toutes sortes de productions" (*La Nouvelle Revue,* XLIX, 141–142).

plus musical de la phrase, une recherche plus attentive de la forme, qui rendra au style de nos écrivains quelque peu lâché en ces derniers temps, sa souplesse et sa précision d'autrefois.[32]

Peyrot's article, confused and not well informed, is indicative of the general curiosity concerning the decadents and the symbolists which was shortly to provoke articles from Jules Lemaître [33] and Brunetière.[34] The critical comments in the more important magazines and newspapers during 1887 and 1888 have often been labeled as masterpieces of ignorance and incomprehension, but it must be admitted that the symbolists themselves did very little to aid the commentators. The articles by Moréas and Adam, as well as those by Ghil, were not models of clarity, and the little essays which appeared in *Le Scapin* or *Le Décadent* were generally elucidations of personal ambition and jealousy rather than doctrine. Laurent Tailhade and some of his friends further confused the issue during 1888 by their publication in the *Décadent* of a number of compositions which they ascribed to Rimbaud. The sonnet "Instrumentation" appeared in the January issue, "Les Cornues" in February, "Le Limaçon" in May, "Doctrine" in July, and "Oméga blasphématoire" in September. Tailhade and Raynaud even invented a professor in Germany and a wealthy baron from South America to explain the discovery of this "glane d'après-midi, si pleine de Vomissures et d'Azur."

The numerous articles by Baju during 1888 on the characteristics of the decadent, his place in society, his esthetic outlook, and his influence on his age are of small importance. Baju was principally concerned with indicating that those who called themselves symbolists, particularly Ghil and Moréas, had merely usurped titles which logically belonged to others. The great service which the magazine rendered in 1888, as in 1886, was the support it gave Verlaine. Ernest Raynaud, who wrote a reply to Lemaître's attack in *La Revue bleue* and two articles on *Les Poètes maudits*,[35] and Louis Villatte, who contributed a criticism of *Amour,* are among the admirers of Verlaine, whose "Un Mot sur la rime" and several poems were the chief contributions to the periodical.

It is not in the *Décadent* but in *La Revue indépendante* that one can find a valid defense of the symbolist school in 1888. Gustave Kahn had taken over the department of literary criticism from Wyzewa and in February answered Lemaître's article on Verlaine. Kahn announces that he is weary of hearing commentary on imitation of Baudelaire, on alcoholism, and on noctambulism.

32. *Ibid.*, p. 146.

33. *La Revue bleue,* 3ᵉ série, XV (January 7, 1888), 2–14.

34. *La Revue des deux mondes,* XC (November 1, 1888), 213–226.

35. *Le Décadent,* No. 5 (February 15, 1888), No. 20 (October 1, 1888), No. 21 (October 15, 1888).

Of greater moment, he feels, is the recording of the idea at the moment it emerges from the subconscious. He insists that it is Verlaine's spontaneous statement of the specific thought or sensation which gives life to his verse. Throughout the year, in his critical articles,[36] Kahn defends what is personal and intuitive. He attacks Sully-Prudhomme's *Le Bonheur* as being composed of alexandrines which are descriptive, philosophical, and above all boring, and Maurice Bouchor's *Les Symboles* as totally lacking in poetic qualities. Kahn does not even spare Victor Hugo, whose greatness is generally unquestioned by the symbolists. The posthumous publication of *Toute la lyre* inspired Kahn to say that the sonority, the exterior decoration, and the preaching of such a volume are inacceptable to those who wish to understand the origin of their ideas. Admitting that poetry which expresses this immediate state may not have superficial brilliance, Kahn insists that it is really more profound.

Clearly this is but a defense of the *Palais nomades,* in which Kahn had sought to follow the sinuosities of ideas. Some of Mallarmé's verse has no other goal, but through a clever blending of the specific sensorial impression with the ensuing meditation, through a learned use of ellipsis and a constant attention to form, Mallarmé avoided the vague and wandering patterns which are Kahn's chief defect. Kahn's ideas of setting down the immediate presence of the poetic idea are diametrically opposed to the elaborate craftsmanship of sounds and arrangement proposed by Ghil and offer similarities with other theorists of his period only in the domain of suggestion, freedom in prosody, and musical effect.

Kahn, unlike René Ghil, is not so preoccupied with his own theories that he cannot accord some measure of praise and understanding to others. The publication of an enlarged edition of Verlaine's *Poètes maudits* and of Mallarmé's translation of Poe's poems elicits many eulogies, not only for these authors and the poets treated in the Verlaine volume, but for Baudelaire, Gérard de Nerval, and Laforgue.

Laforgue, a great friend of two of the editors of *La Revue indépendante,* Fénéon and Kahn, had died on August 20, 1887, only a few months after his return from Germany. The magazine carried on the work it had begun the previous year in publishing the *Moralités légendaires* by printing such poems of the manuscript "Des Fleurs de bonne volonté" as had not been published.[37] This was a considerable addition to the work of the poet, comprising over forty items, which were finally collected in a book of *Derniers vers* in 1890.[38]

36. Kahn's articles of 1888, almost in their entirety, are printed in his *Symbolistes et décadents,* pp. 75–171.

37. *La Revue indépendante,* VII, 5–53; IX, 466–480 (April and December, 1888).

38. A limited edition prepared by Félix Fénéon and Edouard Dujardin.

An increasing interest in foreign literature, some of which was close to symbolist art, is evident in *La Revue indépendante*. Kahn, writing on Dostoevski's *Crime and Punishment,* notes the anguished search for understanding of the inner soul that characterizes Russian writers such as Dostoevski and Tolstoy. Vielé-Griffin contributed translations of Swinburne's "Laus Veneris" and of a poem by Walt Whitman. A portion of Prozor's translation of *A Doll's House* appeared in the October issue and Mallarmé's "Le Ten O'clock de M. Whistler" [39] in May. Contributions by Verlaine, both in prose and verse, an important essay on Gérard de Nerval, and some free verse offerings by Kahn also make the year 1888 an important one in the history of the periodical.

An attempt to found a little magazine, not for purposes of combat but in order to publish the poetry of symbolist poets, occurred in 1888. The instigators, Georges Lecomte and Adolphe Retté, were young men who were quite unknown at the time and who were not allied with any group. Both admirers of Verlaine, they enlisted his sympathies for a new publication and secured promises of adhesion from the poets of *La Revue indépendante*. As usual, Félix Fénéon, who seems during this period to have taken upon himself the double duty of finding subscribers for the little magazines and of defending the painting of Seurat and Pissarro, proved an energetic lieutenant. The title of the new periodical was *La Cravache,* taken from that of a weekly newspaper which had gone into bankruptcy. Impecunious and almost unknown, the little sheet struggled for a year and is known today only through several bibliographical items in the work of Verlaine and for the description given of its vicissitudes in Retté's *Le Symbolisme*.

The volumes of poetry published during 1888 are not striking for innovations in form, although a few lines of free verse appeared in Vielé-Griffin's dramatic poem *Ancæus*. Henri de Régnier in *Sites* (1887) and *Episodes* (1888) is still the rather strict craftsman of the sonnet, the quatrain, the quintain, and the *terza rima*. In both collections the constant presence of exterior description, the images of gardens, fountains, the sea, prows of ships, vintages, orchards, and birds might seem to be an exteriorization of thought. In truth, however, few poets have so insistently proclaimed that the sensations experienced, the landscapes observed are but the matter of dream. The visual images are fictitiously created by the poet to describe his state of mind, an almost reverse process to that of Verhaeren, who uses reality as a starting point for the evocation of the mysterious and the terrible. With Régnier one is present at the process of an artificially constructed landscape; with Verhaeren the process is that of a transmutation through the mind. The paradoxical element in the reading of such verse is that many readers will feel the sincerity of the

39. Published in pamphlet form in 1888 by *La Revue indépendante*.

Belgian's distorted images and sense a kind of artistic insincerity in the less startling settings evoked by Régnier.

Yet both methods are valid in the realm of symbolist verse, for both are built on the idea of suggestion of mood through imagery. The broad and exquisite genius of Baudelaire seems to have encompassed the two procedures and given contrasting masterpieces—such as the poems of "Spleen" and the "Invitation au voyage." In 1888 Régnier's art is limited to evocation of the scene, as in the poem "Le Verger":

> Je vis de la fenêtre ouverte sur le Rêve,
> Au cadre fabuleux d'un vieux site écarté,
> Un verger merveilleux de rosée et de sève
> Apparaître à travers l'aurorale clarté
> De l'heure où l'aube naît dans la nuit qui s'achève.[40]

At the time Régnier's *Sites* and *Episodes* were published in France, Verhaeren appeared with two volumes of poetry in which his hallucinatory faculty, desperately tragic, seemed almost to approach madness. Printed in Brussels in small editions with illustrations by Odilon Redon, *Les Soirs* and *Les Débâcles* were not well known in France. Kahn, however, commenting on the first of the volumes, praises Verhaeren for his truly poetic qualities. It seems strange that the very violence of the personification in Verhaeren's poetry did not elicit more comment. No poet has used the device more frequently and, in a sense, more rashly. A group of huts and a windmill become a cluster of beggars watching the sufferings of the dying:

> Et dans la plaine immense au bord du flot dormeur
> Elles fixent—les très souffreteuses bicoques!
> Avec les pauvres yeux de leurs carreaux en loques,
> Le vieux moulin qui tourne et, las, qui tourne et meurt.[41]

Meanwhile Verlaine and Léon Vanier were engaged in multiple projects of publication. Although after *Jadis et naguère* of 1884, no new volume of verse by Verlaine appeared until *Amour* of 1888, Vanier's second editions of *Fêtes galantes* (1886) and *Romances sans paroles* (1887), together with the *Mémoires d'un veuf* (1886) and the enlarged edition of the *Poètes maudits* (1888), kept Verlaine's name more or less before the public. Vanier, who was

40. Henri de Régnier, *Premiers poèmes*, p. 191.
41. Emile Verhaeren, *Poèmes* (nouvelle série), p. 48. It is interesting to compare an image from the *Sites* of Régnier in which the windmill calls forth violence which would not seem unusual in Verhaeren but which seems an isolated case in Régnier:

> Mais la route dévie et dans le crépuscule,
> Avec un bruit sinistre d'ailes, on entend
> Un moulin qui se désespère et gesticule.

> *Premiers poèmes*, p. 121

extremely cautious, did not hesitate to print six hundred copies of the second editions of verse, and was collecting the poems for future volumes: *Bonheur, Parallèlement,* and *Dédicaces.*

Verlaine's own adjectives for describing *Amour* were "catholique, pas clérical, bien que très orthodoxe." He hoped that the tone of the volume, more varied than that of *Sagesse,* would make it successful and give him openings for other lucrative ventures.[42] This very tone, that of ingenuous simplicity, together with the long series of poems dedicated to Lucien Létinois as his adopted son, have won for their author many accusations of insincerity. But to certain of Verlaine's contemporaries the protestations of paternal affection and of repentance for past misdeeds seemed quite acceptable. Lepelletier wrote a favorable review for the *Echo de Paris,* Théodore de Banville sent a laudatory letter to Verlaine,[43] and Gustave Kahn, after an analysis of the volume, concluded with this general appreciation:

Toutes ces choses écrites dans une forme classique, aux défaillantes douceurs, qui fait penser aux méditations de quelque solitaire grave et depuis si longtemps triste, errant en quelque Port-Royal plein de douceur et de vague, et s'asseyant le soir pour rêver aux effigies disparues, avec la résignation d'un Job doux.[44]

Verlaine's addition of the essay on Villiers de l'Isle-Adam to the *Poètes maudits* of 1888 suggests the part that writers of prose were playing in a movement which, though primarily poetic, embraced broader views of literary art and even of outlook on life. Verlaine gives as principal reason for including the author of *Axel* in his augmented volume the fact that l'Isle-Adam, though well known, is not appreciated at his full value. In his essay on the same author for *Les Hommes d'aujourd'hui,* Verlaine further explains that Villiers de l'Isle-Adam has an essentially poetic nature, both by reason of his sensitivity and of his magnificent use of language.[45]

The whole generation of symbolists admired Villiers de l'Isle-Adam for many other reasons. They knew him as a poet, a dramatist, and a short story writer whose published work in no way flattered public taste. Villiers de l'Isle-Adam saw the exterior world as a series of false and deceptive images and constantly sought out the inner reality. The evocation of this magic world, the satire of progress and pursuit of money, the language which suggested but did not state, the note of revolt against the traditional, the use of symbols in a concrete sense, and above all the strange mingling of irony, idealism, and mystery were reasons for spiritual alliance with the symbolist poets.

42. See the letter to Edmond Lepelletier, dated October 26, 1887, in *Correspondance de Paul Verlaine,* I, 214–215.
43. See Paul Verlaine, *Œuvres poétiques* (Pléiade ed.), p. 958.
44. *La Revue indépendante,* VII (May, 1888), 350–351.
45. Paul Verlaine, *Œuvres complètes,* V, 309.

In his manifesto of 1886 Moréas had stated that prose, in novels and short stories, was undergoing an evolution analogous to that of poetry. He suggested as disparate sources the analysis of Stendhal, the vision of Balzac, the sentence cadence of Flaubert, and the impressionism of Edmond de Goncourt.[46] Out of a complicated series of phrases, clear idea emerges: Moréas believes that the novel tends to be more subjective than objective; inner reality is triumphing over the world of the senses. Moréas, with Paul Adam, had experimented with a form of symbolist prose in *Le Thé chez Miranda* (1886) and *Les Demoiselles Goubert* (1887), but neither volume had awakened either interest or admiration. But other novelists, who did not yield to popular taste and in whom the symbolists discerned an aversion for idealism, held their sympathies.

Among these novelists, besides Villiers and Huysmans of the older generation, two younger men were often named in symbolist groups. After his collaboration with Moréas and his critical articles in *Le Symboliste*, Paul Adam became a prolific writer of fiction. In 1888 he was the author of a *Petit glossaire pour servir à l'intelligence des auteurs décadents et symbolistes*, which appeared under the name of Jacques Plowert,[47] and of a novel *Etre*. Another novelist who remained associated with the symbolist movement was Francis Poictevin. Both Adam and Poictevin appeared in Gustave Kahn's critical articles of 1888 in *La Revue indépendante* and both were later treated in Remy de Gourmont's *Le Livre des masques*, where Adam's gifts of observation and style were compared with those of Balzac and where Poictevin was credited with the invention of a style which could treat the immaterial and the seemingly ineffable. What chiefly allied these writers with the group of the symbolists was the quality that was apparent in some of the Russian novelists, the search for comprehension of the inner self, the questing after the meaning of individual existence, and the abandonment of the exterior for inner realms of consciousness. Theirs was only a parallel path to that of poetry, but current criticism often enveloped them in the same pronouncements of anathema. Auguste Marcade, writing in the supplement of the *Figaro* in 1888, grouped together in his ridicule the contributors to *La Revue indépendante*: Barrès, Henri de Régnier, Paul Adam, and Gustave Kahn: "Tous ces messieurs ont le même objectif: une incohérence raffinée, maladive, qui ferait craindre pour leur raison s'ils s'attardaient dans leurs voies."[48]

By 1888 there is a tendency for symbolism to attempt broadening of its chosen realm of dream and mystery. Paul Adam in *Etre*, using a fifteenth-century setting, devoted a whole novel to the efforts of the Countess Mahaud

---

46. Jean Moréas, *Les Premières Armes du symbolisme*, pp. 38–39.

47. Gustave Kahn speaks of the origins and publication of this curious pamphlet in *Symbolistes et décadents*, pp. 59–62.

48. *Le Figaro* (supplément littéraire), September 8, 1888.

to understand her own nature. Poictevin in *Paysages* and *Nouveaux songes* gave an impressionistic reflection of sensations as a series of dreams. Forgotten today, he is the writer whose mind Verlaine described as:

> Mystérieux comme la Lune,
> Clair et sinueux comme l'Eau.[49]

In *Ancæus,* Vielé-Griffin attempted the form of the dramatic poem and, with a mythological background, preached the importance of dreams. Maeterlinck was already working on *La Princesse Maleine,* which was published in 1889. The message of these art forms had been given many times by Villiers de l'Isle-Adam and notably in his drama *Axel.* Thanks to his ironic and fantastic genius the ideal as opposed to the real had been rather more effectively presented than in the vague reveries of the writers of 1888. Not greatly important as literary achievements, such volumes as *Etre, Paysages,* and *Ancæus* do represent the strength of the poetic impulse which ventured beyond verse into prose writing and drama.

During 1887 and 1888 Ferdinand Brunetière twice deigned to reprove the activity of the young writers. The first of his essays, entitled "Charles Baudelaire," [50] was occasioned by Eugène Crépet's edition of the *Œuvres posthumes.* Brunetière is distressed, even as had been Edmond Scherer in 1882, at the influence exerted by Baudelaire on writers. He gives some derogatory commentary on those whom he calls Baudelairian imitators: in verse, Mallarmé and Verlaine; in prose, Huysmans and Poictevin. Then more definitely attacking Moréas, Verhaeren, Vielé-Griffin, and Wyzewa, he caustically remarks that young Greeks, Belgians, Americans, and Poles are currently intent upon explaining to the French the mysteries of the Gallic tongue. His chief reproach against the followers of Baudelaire is that they do not make imitation of nature the goal of art.

Then toward the end of 1888 Brunetière launched a second protest entitled "Symbolistes et décadens." [51] This time his article was well documented with names and titles, for the critic wished to make it plain that he had earnestly and conscientiously studied symbolist volumes and magazines in search of a masterpiece. His essay mentions *Fêtes galantes, Hérodiade, Les Complaintes, Les Cantilènes, Les Palais nomades, Les Cygnes, Ancæus, Le Thé chez Miranda,* and *Derniers songes* and regretfully announces that such reading has not revealed a writer of talent. Brunetière's conclusion is that the symbolists and decadents have but one merit, that of being utterly incomprehensible.

---

49. Paul Verlaine, *Œuvres complètes,* V, 482.
50. *Revue des deux mondes,* LXXXI (June 1, 1887), 695–706.
51. *Ibid.,* XC (November 1, 1888), 213–226.

The cruel and condescending tone of these articles left its memory for many years in symbolist publications, where Brunetière was often held up to ridicule or cited as a kind of archfiend. His judgments, as well as those of Lemaître and the journalists, seem to have whetted the ambitions and combative ardor of the young writers, unable to agree among themselves but united in abhorrence of conservatism.

Chapter VII: BEGINNINGS OF CRITICAL SYMBOLIST LITERATURE, 1889

DURING 1888 it seemed that the symbolists, after the energetic manifestations of 1886, were losing ground. Except for the *Revue indépendante,* with the critical columns of Gustave Kahn, they no longer possessed a medium in which to defend their interests. *La Cravache* was a struggling, poorly printed little sheet; the enormities of Baju in *Le Décadent* barely offset some acceptable poetry by Verlaine, Raynaud, and Tailhade. René Ghil, after the *Ecrits pour l'art* had ceased publication in the summer of 1887, had left France to accept in Belgium the hospitality of Mockel's *La Wallonie.*[1] Although the *Ecrits pour l'art* resumed publication, printing two numbers in July and December, 1888, Ghil's formal break with *La Wallonie* did not occur until June, 1889. The activities of this theorist, probably better known in Belgium than in France, became more and more a personal rather than a collective action. Ghil, not content with the inspiration of Helmholtz in his instrumentalist poetry, added the ideas of scientific synthesis and of Darwinian evolution to his *Traité du verbe.* Even though Dubedat and Merrill remained his friends and gave him financial aid, he could hardly be said to have a following.

La Wallonie, after Henri de Régnier became a member of its staff in 1890, was to become an important periodical for the French symbolists. It ceased being regionalistic from the moment it invited the collaborators of *Ecrits pour l'art* to contribute to its pages. Henri de Régnier, at Mockel's invitation, sent the periodical two poems, which appeared in the issue of October, 1887. Stuart Merrill, still in New York, was an occasional contributor. Verhaeren and Khnopff,[2] who had been collaborators of *Ecrits pour l'art* and who, like Mockel, were fervent Wagnerians, embraced almost all the ideas of the French symbolist movement. Mockel wrote a laudatory review of Mallarmé's translations of Poe's poetry in the November, 1888, issue of *La Wallonie.* Mallarmé contributed a sonnet to the January, 1889, number of the magazine. These are but preludes to *La Wallonie's* final three years of existence (1890–92), when

---

1. Baju gleefully exclaimed that Ghil's retreat beyond the French frontier was a wise choice. *Le Figaro,* August 31, 1887.

2. After 1887 Georges Khnopff disappears from the literary scene. A campaign launched against him by Max Waller of *La Jeune Belgique* and charging him with plagiarizing Verlaine is supposed to have been the cause of his abandoning writing for music. See A. J. Mathews' *La Wallonie, 1886–1892,* p. 65.

Vielé-Griffin, A.-F. Hérold, Quillard, Fontainas, Retté, Moréas, and Verlaine were among the contributors, but Mockel had already in 1888 begun his attacks against poetry which he found too traditional and imitative. He championed the symbol as the realization of ideas through imagery, as the bond between the material and the immaterial; he proclaimed music as the basis of poetic art.

While Mockel was defending symbolism in Belgium, there appeared in Paris the volume *Nos poètes* by Jules Tellier. In it the symbolists, with the exception of Verlaine, are scathingly treated. Beginning his book with long essays on four masters, Leconte de Lisle, Théodore de Banville, Sully-Prudhomme, and Coppée, the author devotes most of his pages to comments, for the most part favorable, on minor Parnassian poets. Two sections, one entitled "Les Baudelairiens" and the other "Décadents et symbolistes," are devoted to poets of the symbolist group.

Tellier's judgment of Baudelaire, whom he sees as a threefold being—partly mystical, partly "fumiste," and lastly somewhat a charlatan—explains why one finds as "Baudelairiens" such diverse personalities as Rollinat, Rodenbach, and Richepin, along with Louis le Cardonnel, Raoul Ponchon, and Emile Goudeau in a single grouping. There is more than a grain of truth in what Tellier says concerning the influence of exterior aspects of Baudelaire's poetry on certain of the later poets, but since the name of the great precursor is not once mentioned in the section which treats of the symbolists, the worth of such criticism would appear vitiated.

Verlaine described *Nos poètes* as a volume with which he had little fault to find and as not much inferior to the criticism of Sainte-Beuve.[3] He urged Edmond Lepelletier to speak well of the book in the *Echo de Paris*.[4] One can understand that Verlaine might have enjoyed Tellier's withering comments on Ghil and Kahn, but it is with difficulty that one imagines his subscribing to this judgment on Mallarmé:

Il écrivit jadis, au temps du Parnasse, des vers très clairs et très banals. Il en écrit maintenant qui sont dépourvus de sens autant que d'harmonie, absurdes également pour l'oreille et pour l'esprit; et il se rencontre des gens qui le considèrent comme un grand penseur et comme un grand musicien.[5]

Tellier does not mention the work of Rimbaud, although there is doubtless a reference to him in the "Génie méchant et subtil" who taught Verlaine wickedness.[6] Neither does Laforgue's name occur in the volume. In truth all that Tellier attempts to do is to portray Charles Vignier as imitator of Verlaine,

3. Paul Verlaine, *Œuvres posthumes*, III, 93–95.
4. *Correspondance de Paul Verlaine*, I, 226.
5. Jules Tellier, *Nos poètes*, p. 230.
6. *Ibid.*, p. 216.

Kahn as aper of Moréas, and Ghil as an abominable derivative of Mallarmé.
It seems only too clear that Verlaine, in his praise of *Nos poètes,* was blinded
by his affection for Tellier, an affection revealed by letters, by two sonnets of
Dédicaces, and by the long discussion Tellier accorded his work.[7]

If Tellier's volume were to be taken as a true picture of current French
poetry, symbolism and decadence had become dead issues in 1888. The following year, however, criticism of symbolism really began with the publication
of Moréas' *Les Premières Armes du symbolisme,* Georges Vanor's *L'Art
symboliste,* and Charles Morice's *La Littérature de tout à l'heure.* The first
two are merely pamphlets probably intended by Vanier to publicize the school
of which he was the accredited publisher. The documents which Moréas collected in his pamphlet are chiefly intended to emphasize his part in naming
the new movement and in taking up the challenge offered by Bourde's and
France's articles of 1885 and 1886, but in the preface Moréas intimates that he
no longer believes many of the things he preached three years before. In poetry
he feels that henceforth the influence of Baudelaire may prove an obstacle and
he demands that symbolism rid itself of obscurity and of dilettantism. He asks
that the movement be understood as a protest against vulgar and mediocre
literature which, for sensation and material description, had rejected idealism
and the presentation of the soul.

Moréas does not mention by name any of his contemporaries nor does he
make any judgments of their work in his preface. Even in his manifesto of
1886 he had mentioned only Mallarmé as venturing into a new and mysterious
realm and Verlaine as having completed the liberation of verse begun by
Théodore de Banville. It seems curious that he does not remember the poets
who had appeared since the article of Paul Bourde and among whom could
be counted, besides his enemy René Ghil, Vielé-Griffin, Henri de Régnier,
Laforgue, Stuart Merrill, Verhaeren, not to mention the publication of Rimbaud's work or the periodical contributions of Albert Samain and Edouard
Dubus. The *Premières Armes du symbolisme* has the weakness of being the
personal impression of a single writer who does not choose to discuss the part
of others in a collective literary action.

Georges Vanor probably wished to accomplish this. *L'Art symboliste* is far
from being a good critical volume, but in it is some attempt to make distinc-
tions in the fortunate and unfortunate influences which had entered the movement. Vanor believes that Baju and Ghil have compromised the names of several good writers who had produced an important intuitive literature, both in

---

7. Verlaine also dedicated the sonnet "Parsifal," first published in *La Revue wagnérienne,* to
Tellier. After the latter's death from typhoid fever in 1889, at the age of twenty-six, the publication of much of his work the following year and the complete edition of 1925, edited by Raymond de la Tailhède, have revealed a talented poet.

poetry and prose. Stating that the Parnassians have not attained the sublime expression of Mallarmé and Verlaine, he contends that unrestricted praise is due Rimbaud and Laforgue. It is true that Vanor, unsparing in the use of the superlative, gives the impression of a poor critic; he thought that Kahn's *Les Palais nomades* would greatly influence future poetic expression; he found profound psychology in Paul Adam's novel *Soi*. Yet his prognostications of future fictional form were not without some perspicacity, for he foresees a novel built solely around the soul of a single character or about the fortunes of a philosophical idea issuing from one mind and effecting the destinies of a group. Poictevin, mingling humanity and nature, or Maurice Barrès, observing the struggle of ideas in his own mind, appear to Vanor in sympathy with the ideology of symbolism.

Among the poets discussed in *L'Art symboliste* are Moréas, Vielé-Griffin, Henri de Régnier, and Gustave Kahn. Vanor says that Moréas has reacted against Parnassian aridity, that Vielé-Griffin has revealed the mysterious qualities of material things (even as did Poe in "The Fall of the House of Usher"), that Henri de Régnier has created an imaginary world of dream, and that Kahn has suggested important technical and musical elements in poetry.[8] Vanor, like Félix Fénéon, is also conscious of an affinity in art with symbolist suggestiveness, mentioning Pissarro, Seurat, Signac, Puvis de Chavannes, Whistler, and others as masters of a symbolic tonality and form. In music he sees Vincent d'Indy as a follower of Wagnerian synthesis in theme and melody.

Paul Adam wrote the preface for the little volume. He praises somewhat extravagantly Vanor's *Les Paradis* and agrees with the author that the future age will be that of mysticism. In the last pages of *L'Art symboliste* is to be found a contention of the importance of religious symbolism as the basis of literary inspiration.

Both Vanor and Adam seem to have used the term mysticism in the sense of idealism which turns away from materialism and unbelief to religious faith and God. Vanor speaks of "le glorieux et mystique Verlaine" and opines that the consoling promises of the Church would have solved Laforgue's pessimism. Adam groups together Barbey d'Aurevilly, Verlaine, Léon Bloy, and Villiers de l'Isle-Adam as unknown but glorious apostles of beauty. In their company he places Huysmans, who in 1889 had not yet accomplished the pilgrimage through occultism to religious faith. One can easily understand

8. Vanor also mentions Jean Ajalbert, author of several volumes of verse in which the visible landscape is often translated into a picture of pessimism and despair. Ajalbert is the author of *Mémoires en vrac*, the memories of a man seventy-five years of age concerning his part in the literary movement of 1880–90. Like many other accounts, this volume tends to be merely a series of anecdotes. Yet in it there are many references to writers who were of some importance in that decade and who are unknown today.

how, in a literary trend which proclaimed mystery, dream, and idealism, and in which was the implicit renunciation of materialism and science, the idea of mysticism found its way. The publication of Verlaine's *Sagesse* and *Amour,* the liturgical terms in Laurent Tailhade's poems of *Lutèce,* Louis le Cardonnel's sojourn in a religious seminary in 1888 are foretastes of a certain turn of spirit, which would be later manifested by a series of conversions.

Yet the term mysticism as an integral element of symbolism seems inexact, especially as the occult and esoteric are perhaps more noticeable in members of the group. The whole period presents the large problem of conflict or of attempts at reconciliation between modern science and religious faith, and Vanor's pamphlet comes at a time when the problem was beginning to be closely studied. Edouard Schuré, whose Wagnerianism had been important in the 1870's, published in 1889 a volume entitled *Les Grands Initiés,* which he announced by a preface expressing hope for reconciliation of the spiritual and scientific factors in modern civilization. Coldly received in the year of publication, these studies of great idealistic leaders who were also founders of religious cults became increasingly well known and the book went through many editions. In his preface Schuré states that current literature shows a profound desire to know the invisible and spiritual world. But like Schuré most of the literary figures during the symbolist period were interested in the esoteric philosophies of the Orient or in the arcana of magic. Stanislas de Guaita, Péladan, V.-E. Michelet, and Papus represent this form of what was called mysticism. Even those who proclaimed themselves apostles of Catholicism: Bloy, Villiers de l'Isle-Adam, Ernest Hello, who had died in 1885, and Barbey d'Aurevilly, whose death occurred in 1889, appear to have been regarded with suspicion by the Church.

Symbolism, in its search for the soul of things, in its constant preoccupation with the mysterious, seems to have affinities with the mystic tradition, begun with Swedenborg, Catherine Théot, Montfaucon de Villars, J.-B. Boyer, Martinez Pasqualis, brought to the threshold of the nineteenth century with Saint-Martin, and continued in such works as Gérard de Nerval's *Les Illuminés* or Balzac's *Séraphita.* But in 1889, despite the example of Verlaine, mysticism seems only a secondary and vague influence in symbolist poetry. The concept of the oriental religions had entered much more profoundly into the poetry of Leconte de Lisle and his Parnassian followers, for in the symbolists are usually present only the symbols of the liturgy, the exterior trappings of religion.[9]

9. Charles Morice is conscious of this profanation of religious symbols. In *La Littérature de tout à l'heure* (1889), he speaks of Laurent Tailhade as a "païen mystique, un sensuel spiritualisant." What he says of this poet could be applied to much of the liturgical imagery of the poetry of the period (p. 304):

On the other hand, poetry in 1889 among the symbolists is almost entirely a reflection of the mind, the repudiation of realities. Three poets published their first volumes that year and in all three the realm of the senses is made increasingly subservient to the interior world of the mind. Adolphe Retté, in *Cloches en la nuit,* seems clearly to have been inspired by the poet to whom his volume is dedicated, Gustave Kahn. Using as images the clanging of bells and the raging waves of the ocean, he endeavored to give a picture of his despair. André Fontainas, in *Le Sang des fleurs,*[10] represents an almost opposite state of mind, in which the dominant mood is that of gentle melancholy; and Maurice Maeterlinck, in *Serres chaudes,* sings in a series of poems the themes of desire, regret, and boredom. But in the vehement disorder of Retté, in the dreamy sadness of Fontainas, or the personal evocations of mood of Maeterlinck, the poetic purpose is to suggest the innermost part of the author's nature. Living and sensory impression are only the pretext of the dream, and it is this, perhaps more than questions of form or outlook on life, which gives the maturing movement its character.

Charles Morice, at almost the same time that Vanor and Moréas published their pamphlets, attempted in a long volume to study the more general aspects of his age. His *La Littérature de tout à l'heure* is indeed the first serious effort to understand the currents of the symbolist period in relation to the past and to indicate its trends. Morice, in 1882, had protested against Verlaine's "Art poétique" but had soon become the friend and champion of that poet. One of the group who had contributed a sonnet in praise of Wagner to Dujardin's periodical, he was also a faithful visitor to the Rue de Rome. Already the author of a short study of Verlaine, he began a broader defense of symbolism in 1888. The occasion was furnished by Anatole France, who had complained that the young generation of poets was not content to write poems unless they expressed some hidden meaning and that in so doing they had lost clarity and simplicity.[11]

Morice's compendious volume belies its title by a curious survey of French literature over a period of three centuries; it is commendable rather for its attempts to make synthetic judgments and for its indications of forces which entered into the composition of symbolist verse than for the sanity of its conclusions. Morice at least was not attempting to defend a narrow group; an admirer of Verlaine and Mallarmé, he was yet willing to grant the Parnassians

---

"Des mysticités douteuses et trop parées, une madone telle que l'eût priée Baudelaire, mais combien plus sombre d'avoir oublié de l'être, combien plus triste de sourire ainsi! Une sorte de piété sacrilège. Le rêve du poëte ne sait guère que se jouer avec des instruments sacrés, s'accouder à des missels, vêtir des chapes sur des surplis."

10. Fontainas' book was published in Belgium and his name was little known in France in 1889, except to his old schoolmates of the Lycée Fontanes.

11. *Le Temps,* August 5, 1888.

some praise and attempt to explain the currents of the 1880's as part of an evolutionary process. He names as the great literary forces of the second half of the century Wagner and Balzac; the latter because he had tried to catch the hidden sense of the society of his time and to demonstrate in what ways his age supported or deviated from the true and the beautiful, the former because of his concept of the union of the arts.

Although only a portion of *La Littérature de tout à l'heure* is devoted to poetry, the author is enough the disciple of Mallarmé to regard that literary form as the most lofty form of expression.[12] He indicates Baudelaire as opening the secret pathways of the soul's depths, Villiers de l'Isle-Adam as opposing the sense of mystery to the pretensions of science, Huysmans as having revealed the conflict between dream and life, Verlaine as having probed the essence of things, and Rimbaud as the master of the intense and metaphysical meaning of existence. In Mallarmé he discovers the living consciousness of art, the search for the absolute beauty of prose and verse which had been incompletely accomplished by Rimbaud.

In a discussion of poets of lesser stature who followed the traditions of the Parnassian school, Grandmougin, Bergerat, Blémont, the author's comments resume the contention that the literary artist should not be content merely to do well what had been done before but should be an independent creator. It is this, the concept of originality, preached by Rimbaud nearly two decades before, that Morice uses as principal argument in favor of the symbolists. The problem of literary evolution became for him a series of combining influences, of attempts to unite scientific and spiritual elements into art forms.

In a section entitled "Formules nouvelles," Morice speaks of many of his contemporaries. The ornate, religious imagery of Laurent Tailhade, the combinations of color and music in the poetry of Moréas, Laforgue's ironic and penetrating outlook on life, and Gustave Kahn's technical innovations are all passed in review. Morice calls Louis Dumur's speculations concerning the scansion of lines according to tonic accent an interesting but dubious innovation, and considers Ghil's theories of instrumentation absurd. Disclaiming any intention of giving a complete list of modern poets, the author chooses some lesser known figures, Vignier, Morhardt, Jean Court, Ernest Jaubert, Dubus, and Fernand Mazade for brief comment. Under the impression that Louis le Cardonnel had already become a priest, he quotes "Le Rêve de la reine"[13] as testimony of the poet's talent. Many others of the young generation receive no critical comment from Morice: Henri de Régnier is complimented

12. Morice gives Flaubert, the Goncourts, and Barbey d'Aurevilly important places in development of prose. He considers Hugo as the recipient of many influences but as no innovator.

13. This poem had appeared in *Le Scapin*, January 10, 1886. A volume of le Cardonnel's poetry was not published until 1904. The author excluded from it many of the poems which had been printed in *Le Chat noir* and other magazines of the period.

on his grace and fluidity and rebuked for repetitious diction; Stuart Merrill and Vielé-Griffin appear only in a footnote; the Belgian poets are not discussed.

On the contrary, Morice devotes several pages to Albert Jounet, whose *Les Lys noirs* [14] had appeared in 1888 and who represents the occult spirit in poetry. Far from blaming the author's preoccupations with the supernatural, Morice sees in him a mind searching for the absolute and finding the answer in the hermetic cults of antiquity. In noting this obscure poet, Morice shows some sagacity, for the full flowering of spiritualism, magic, and occultism was shortly to occur in 1891 with Péladan, Michelet, Stanislas de Guaita, the founding of the "Salon de la Rose-Croix" and of such magazines as *Psyché*.

Meanwhile, in 1889, while the critics of poetry were busy discovering the mystic aspects of lyric art, the poet whom they all mention as an example of spiritual exaltation appeared with a volume which was sensuous, often gross, and certainly realistic. The title of Verlaine's *Parallèlement* was peculiarly apt since his *Amour* had appeared in 1888 and Vanier produced a second printing of *Sagesse* in 1889. Having written of his candor of mind, of his innocence and religious aspiration, Verlaine now chose to describe his fleshly desires with an audacity and wealth of detail which excluded delicacy.[15] As in the composition of *Jadis et naguère,* Verlaine drew heavily on his past work. "Sappho" and "Allégorie" had appeared in *Le Hanneton* in 1867, and other poems are known to have been composed long before their publication in the volume.

Verlaine had prepared in 1888 an item designed to give publicity to his forthcoming collection of poems, and in it he had compared his intentions to the "douloureux programme" of Baudelaire.[16] But if Verlaine thought that critics would compliment him on revealing another facet of the secret corners of the heart, he was somewhat mistaken. George Bonnamour announced *Parallèlement* and suggested the discussions it might incite, but passed rapidly to an essay on Verlaine as a prose writer.[17] J.-H. Rosny avoided the problem of the message of the volume by speaking in a general way of Verlaine's sincerity, love of liberty, and of the subtleties of his diction.[18] The Verlaine legend

14. In 1913 Adolphe Retté, after his conversion to Catholicism, wrote a book describing the errors of the symbolist age. He called it *Au Pays des lys noirs,* probably finding his title in Jounet's volume.

15. The matter of delicacy is of course relative. At the time when *Parallèlement* appeared, Verlaine was preparing an even more sensational collection, *Femmes,* which appeared "sous le manteau" in 1890.

16. This advertisement of the volume appeared in *La Cravache* on September 29, 1888. The same magazine printed "Ballade de la mauvaise réputation" (May 19, 1888), "L'Impudent" (August 4, 1888), and "Laeti et errabundi," "Mains," and "A Mademoiselle . . ." later in the year. On February 2, 1889, appeared "Ces Passions qu'eux seuls nomment encore amours," one of Verlaine's most frank confessions of abnormality.

17. *La Plume,* No. 4 (June 1, 1889).

18. *La Revue indépendante,* No. 39 (August, 1889).

was already created, and although the author of *Romances sans paroles* had now little to offer except the alternation of religious and sensuous verse, his reputation was made and he could bask somewhat on past performance. If *Parallèlement* is the best of the volumes in which Verlaine celebrated carnal desire, its qualities come as much from the poetry composed many years before as from Verlaine's more recent creations. The volume gained some admirers, as was shown by the questionnaire sent to writers after Verlaine's death. Although *Sagesse, Fêtes galantes, Amour, Romances sans paroles* and *La Bonne Chanson* are the favorite collections, there are numerous mentions of *Parallèlement*.[19]

Free verse won an important adherent in 1889 with the publication of Vielé-Griffin's *Joies*. Gustave Kahn, in *Les Palais nomades* of 1888, and Adolphe Retté, in *Cloches en la nuit* of the following year, had combined regular and free verse in volumes where the rhythm of the line was intended to convey the sinuosities of thought. In his preface to *Joies* Vielé-Griffin did little more than try to explain that poetry should no longer be cast into exact molds but should be the expression of the poet's own mind. His accomplishment in the poems of *Joies* was original enough, however, to give a new importance to free metrical art. Instead of the confused and involved syntax of Kahn and Retté, the reader could discover a clear and simple melodic line which had the artlessness of a child's refrain:

> Derrière chez mon père, un oiseau chantait,
> De l'aube jusqu'en la nuit:
> Et dans les soirs de solitaire ennui
> Sa chanson me hantait;[20]

Vielé-Griffin, avoiding the formless and overly long lines with which Kahn and Retté had experimented, created free verse in which the rhymes, the clear and bright imagery, the refrains from old songs, and his own sense of music gave lightness and charm. During the years following the publication of *Joies* he wrote many essays on the theory of free verse and on poetry. He found in Thomas Carlyle's *Sartor Resartus* perhaps a more satisfying statement of the role of the symbol than any which his generation had proposed,[21] and he ably defended symbolism as a way of revealing the infinite. Vielé-Griffin, in connecting symbolism with the idealistic opinions of Professor Teufelsdroeckh, was following a pattern of his time. The symbolists by 1889 were eager to find their spiritual ancestors and Georges Vanor had gone back to Saint Cyril of Alexandria and Saint Augustine to support his definition: "L'art

19. *La Plume*, Nos. 163–164 (February, 1896).
20. Vielé-Griffin, *Poèmes et poésies*, p. 110.
21. *Entretiens politiques et littéraires*, No. 1 (April 1, 1890).

est l'œuvre d'inscrire un dogme dans un symbole humain et de le développer par le moyen de perpétuelles variations harmoniques." [22]

It is not strange that in their searching the critics of symbolism discovered what was a self-evident truth, but one which several people declaimed during the Huret questionnaire of 1891; the symbol had always existed in literature. The fact remains that the symbolists of the nineteenth century went beyond the crude form of allegory and made of analogy a key to hidden relationships of the mind. Baudelaire and Rimbaud had been among the immediate inspirations of these correlations; and their work, together with the intellectual disquisitions of Mallarmé, had powerfully contributed to those two great formulas of symbolist art, mystery and suggestion. To these ideas must of course be added the phenomenon of music, with the influences of Wagnerianism, Verlaine's genius, and the several influences which led to free verse.

Vielé-Griffin, with essentially the same doctrine as others of his generation, gave a different cast to poetry in that he chose the beauty of nature to suggest his idealism and his acceptance of the world rather than the imagery of horror and despair which had been so prevalent during the decadent period of symbolism, and where too servile an imitation of Baudelaire had its part. Among so many pessimistic volumes, and perhaps one of the striking examples was *Cloches en la nuit* which appeared only a short time before *Joies,* Vielé-Griffin appears as the apostle of joy. Such he seemed to Remy de Gourmont, who comments on the calm acceptance of beauty and nature, rare among the symbolists, which is combined in the poet's work with the usual dreaminess of the period.[23]

In giving this triumphant note to his verse, Vielé-Griffin often utilizes the very imagery which had produced the atmosphere of melancholy in poems of his contemporaries. One of these images is that of the rain, which almost every symbolist poet, following the example of Baudelaire, Verlaine, and Laforgue, employed to suggest boredom, lassitude, and regret. But in *Joies* the raindrops are emblems of passion and feeling:

> J'ai pris de la pluie dans mes mains tendues
> —De la pluie chaude comme des larmes—
> Je l'ai bue comme un philtre, défendu
> A cause d'un charme;
> Afin que mon âme en ton âme dorme.[24]

This is a strong countercurrent to the melancholy lyricism of the period, in which even such figures as springtime and the variety of the seasons emerge as monotony:

22. Georges Vanor, *L'Art symboliste*, p. 35.
23. Remy de Gourmont, *Le Livre des masques*, p. 47.
24. Francis Vielé-Griffin, *Poèmes et poésies*, p. 177.

Et les printemps, et les étés, phénomènes,
phénomènes vagues, où tout fuit lié
à je ne sais quels fatidiques hiers.
Les lèvres saignent à d'identiques piliers
d'inextricables cryptes du phénomène.[25]

If *Joies* sounded a new acceptance of life among the symbolists, it is still
true that pessimism and terror were important ingredients in much of the
poetry of 1889. Retté's *Cloches en la nuit* represents almost the extreme limits
of hopelessness and despair and his mood seems that of the decadents of 1885,
when many poets attempted through an accumulation of melancholy phrases
to create an impression of complete anguish. Judging by the utter silence which
greeted his volume, one can imagine that Retté had arrived a trifle late with
a type of lyricism which was already outmoded. Rollinat, having run the
gamut in evocation of the macabre, was already the author of numerous
"Poèmes rustiques," which the supplement of the *Figaro* did not hesitate to
print; Moréas, after the sadness of the *Syrtes,* had produced the *Cantilènes;*
Louis le Cardonnel had largely abandoned the excesses in diction which he
had used in his poems of *Le Chat noir* in 1885 and which are not unsimilar
to images in *Cloches en la nuit.*[26] The volume is chiefly interesting as a manifestation of influences from the immediate past. The combinations of regular
and free verse suggest Gustave Kahn; the poems contain many of the words
given in Jacques Plowert's dictionary; the syntax is tortured and may have
been influenced by Mallarmé; the images are the usual ones of the school,
swans and lilies to suggest the search for the ideal; the sea and bells to indicate
anguish of spirit; liturgical terms used to produce a mystical atmosphere; the
whole background to suggest a state of mind.

Ernest Raynaud, one of the contributors to *Lutèce* and *Le Décadent,* and
shortly to become one of the followers of Jean Moréas, was the author of a
volume of verse, *Chairs profanes,* in 1889. Two years before he had published
Le Signe from the press of Baju, and *Le Décadent* had announced the volume
in its usual extravagant language. But neither the descriptive evocations of
Raynaud's first volume nor the sensuous poems of the second were impressive
or original. The admiration for Verlaine, which was the bond that held together the editorial personnel of *Le Décadent,* is visible in Raynaud's verse.
He likes to imagine past centuries as he wanders through Versailles; in *Chairs
profanes* he speaks of his amatory passions. His most successful poems are
in sonnet form, and in 1889 he was known as much for his parodies of Coppée
and Rimbaud as for serious verse. It was not until the publication of *Les*

25. Gustave Kahn, *Premiers poèmes,* p. 133.
26. Le Cardonnel's "Vêpres de semaine" (*Le Chat noir,* October 17, 1885) and "Le Piano"
(*ibid.,* November 14, 1885) are examples of this tragic diction.

Cornes du faune in 1890 that his poetry attracted much attention, although Baju described *Chairs profanes* as "d'une plastique qui eût étonné Gautier et Baudelaire, si achevée qu'elle laissait croire que l'auteur, ayant épuisé toutes les ressources de la langue, n'irait plus loin." [27]

The year assumes importance not only by reason of the beginnings of critical literature on symbolism, the emergence of more sensual and aggressive states of mind in verse, and the development of a new technique of free verse in Vielé-Griffin, but also by the endeavors to create new periodicals. Although only one of the new magazines was destined to have a long or important career, and although most of the efforts tended to produce isolated literary sets, the activity of the period is considerable. Baju attempted to found *La France littéraire* and collected together some of the old group of *Le Décadent,* among whom were du Plessys and Louis Villatte. René Ghil continued his *Ecrits pour l'art* with his friends Stuart Merrill, Mario Varvara, and for a time Achille Delaroche.[28] *La Pléiade* enjoyed a passing rebirth, with some of its former members, Mikhaël, Quillard, Saint-Pol-Roux, and Jean Ajalbert, to whom were added Alfred Vallette, Dumur, Dubus, Albert Aurier, and Gabriel Randon. In 1890 it was this same group, under the direction of Vallette, which was to found the *Mercure de France. Le Chat noir* printed fourteen poems from Verlaine's forthcoming volume *Dédicaces* as well as "La Neige à travers la brume" from *Bonheur.*

La Cravache had to discontinue existence in 1889. One of its editors, Adolphe Retté, sought out Gustave Kahn, who had been dispossessed of his post as critic of *La Revue indépendante* when François de Nion became director of the magazine in January, 1889. The two united their efforts in attempting to found a new series of *La Vogue* and secured as collaborators Henri de Régnier, Vielé-Griffin, and Félix Fénéon.[29] Despite this relatively important group the magazine did not at all succeed and after the third issue the printer had gone into bankruptcy and had disappeared. Dujardin indicates that the magazine's importance lay in printing free verse by Retté, Kahn, and Vielé-Griffin.[30] If the periodical had enjoyed a larger reading public, Kahn's judgment in the second issue on Maurice Maeterlinck's *Serres chaudes* would have been note-

27. For quotations of Baju's comments on Raynaud see *La Plume,* No. 33, p. 163 and No. 202, p. 576.

28. After Delaroche left the *Ecrits pour l'art,* Eugène Thébault and A. Lantoine became part of its staff. Ghil published his revision of poetic theory during 1889, under the title of "Méthode évolutive-instrumentaliste d'une poésie rationnelle."

29. Retté has told the story of *La Cravache* and the second *Vogue* in *Le Symbolisme.*

30. Copies of the *Vogue* of 1889 are very rare. Retté states that he destroyed unsold copies when he found that the printer had left Paris. The two articles which Retté quotes in *Le Symbolisme* are not calculated to make one regret the magazine's brief existence (July–September, 1889).

worthy. The author of the *Palais nomades* is extremely harsh toward the Belgian poet. He taxes him with lack of originality, with repeating themes of Mallarmé, Rimbaud, and Laforgue. Kahn's criticism concludes with the dictum that it is the duty of every symbolist poet to recall no other writer. Sixteen of his own poems, under the title "Eventails tristes," follow this essay.

La Revue indépendante had been, under Dujardin's guidance, a semiofficial organ of symbolism. Through the critical articles of Wyzewa (1887) and Kahn (1888), and by the cult rendered to Rimbaud, Verlaine, and Laforgue it had espoused the new poetic outlook. Its staff was completely changed, however, in 1889, and a new editorial policy made its appearance. It is true that the January number seemed almost entirely a symbolist one. Rodolphe Darzens contributed an article on Rimbaud and printed four unpublished poems by that author; the issue contained poetry by Verlaine, Vielé-Griffin, Henri de Régnier, Jean Ajalbert, Edouard Dujardin, Gustave Kahn, and René Ghil. But during the remainder of the year poetry occupied relatively little space, and J.-H. Rosny having become literary critic, it was prose rather than verse which received his attention.

The principal event in the world of periodicals in 1889 was the founding of *La Plume* on April 15. The director, Léon Deschamps, announced that the magazine would be favorable to the younger writers and would consider literary merit rather than established reputations. An unpublished poem by Tristan Corbière and a short essay on Emile Goudeau of the Hydropathes and the Chat noir in the first issue, poems by Verlaine, Dubus, Tailhade, Raynaud, and Stuart Merrill later in the year, publication of a letter from René Ghil, critical articles on Charles Morice and Paul Verlaine, and two entire numbers devoted respectively to the Chat noir and to publications of Léon Vanier were sufficient to show that the promise was not an idle one. The magazine often lacked taste and perhaps for that reason never won the friendship of some of the more sedate poets, such as Vielé-Griffin and Henri de Régnier, yet it accomplished the purpose which Deschamps had set himself —the creation of a friendly and gay atmosphere among writers, artists, and humorists.[31] The manner in which the casual gatherings at the "Café du Soleil d'or" developed into large meetings in which cabaret songs were sung, poetry recited, and conversation exchanged between painters and men of letters is the story of the whole decade of the 1890's. In literary value the periodical was soon outstripped by the *Mercure de France,* founded in 1890, but as a living and picturesque record of some of the most interesting currents of the period it is unequaled.

The year is marked by the death of a writer whom the symbolists knew and admired and who had been selected by Verlaine for one of his *Poètes*

31. See the chapter on *La Plume* in Raynaud's *La Mêlée symboliste* I, 129–149.

maudits. Villiers de l'Isle-Adam was a symbolist by virtue of his admiration for Wagner and Poe, his idealism, his refusal of materialism, and his championship of the dream. He was regarded as a symbolist because of his friendship with Stéphane Mallarmé, who was to read a lecture two and one half hours in length before a somewhat mystified audience in Brussels, on February 11, 1890, a lecture which was a threnody offered to the memory of the author of *Axël.* After the death of Villiers de l'Isle-Adam, a new altar was created among the symbolists for a great dreamer, one whom many of them had known personally and whose work came to be admired by the younger generation.[32]

32. Immediately after his death, Villiers' reputation began to rise; he died on August 18 and in the *Revue bleue* on September 21 appeared a laudatory article by Henri Laujol, one of the early tributes to a man of genius. Many of the symbolists have written about Villiers, one of the best portraits being that by Henri de Régnier in *Nos rencontres.*

IN SPITE of internal quarrels, of excesses such as Baju's championship of deca-
dence and Ghil's theories of instrumentation, poetry had gained in prestige
between 1886 and 1889. Vanier could count among his poets Verlaine, Moréas,
Laforgue, Vignier, Henri de Régnier, Vielé-Griffin, Stuart Merrill, Kahn,
Ghil, Raynaud, and among his prose writers Paul Adam and Francis Poictevin.
Vanier had also published numerous small biographical pamphlets called *Les
Hommes d'aujourd'hui,* of which Verlaine was often the author. The interest
in free verse was ever-increasing; despite financial handicaps and jealousies,
the attempts to found periodicals had continued and were shortly to have
success in magazines which were less partisan in their outlook than those of
1886. Symbolism never became a completely unified movement, but the trend
seemed to be away from the narrow to a more comprehensive outlook.

During 1889 *La Plume* had been successful enough to warrant some expansion of its interests and at the beginning of 1890 it announced that it would
enter the publishing field with the "Bibliothèque artistique et littéraire." The
first volume of the series was to be a limited edition of Verlaine's *Dédicaces,*
of which the profits were to go to the author. Verlaine had quarreled with
Vanier [1] and had tried to obtain a favorable contract with Savine before Deschamps came to his aid. The edition of three hundred fifty copies quite quickly
found subscribers, and *Dédicaces,* though not a very good volume, could be
considered a success. Continuing its policy of special numbers, begun by the
issues on "Le Chat noir" and on the "Modernes" of Léon Vanier, *La Plume*
published "Les Décadents" and "Les Catholiques-Mystiques." [2]

The chief fault of *La Plume* was its tendency to be cheap and sensational.
It reprinted, with errors, Baudelaire's "Pièces condamnées" and the censored
portions of Richepin's *Chanson des gueux;* it offered its readers from time
to time the "Chansons zutiques" which had been given at Rodolphe Salis'
restaurant, and among the prose contributions were such titles as "Virginité
perdue," "Impuissant," and "Le Dépucelage d'Albert." George Bonnamour,
writing under the name of "Nachette," indulged in invective against Léon
Vanier and Charles Morice. Léon Bloy was a regular contributor during 1890,

---

1. *Dédicaces* contains a poem dedicated to Vanier, by the tone of which one can see that
Verlaine was already proposing reconciliation with his publisher.

2. *La Plume* No. 34 (September 15, 1890); No. 35 (October 1, 1890).

but a parody of his style was published in the magazine; Stuart Merrill wrote an article praising his friend René Ghil and the latter was the author of published fragments from *Le Geste ingénu* and *La Preuve égoïste,* but Edmond Porcher offered in the poem "Mon Œil" a devastating satire of Ghil's style. The magazine could honestly say that it stood for absolute liberty in expression for the artist and that it favored no particular group, yet its methods were quite often vulgar.

The more serious aspects of the magazine (articles on Rimbaud, Laurent Tailhade, Maurice Maeterlinck, J.-K. Huysmans; poetry by Abadie, Dubus, Verlaine, Mallarmé, Signoret, Louis le Cardonnel, and Stuart Merrill among others) often disappeared in the midst of humorous and satirical writing. Fortunately the year 1890 saw the founding of other periodicals of which the tone more nearly corresponded to that of serious magazines but which nevertheless fought for some of the same artistic principles as *La Plume.* These newcomers were the *Entretiens politiques et littéraires* and *Le Mercure de France.*

Unlike the director of *La Plume,* who admitted hundreds of names among his contributors in a single year, Vallette chose only a limited number of writers for the *Mercure de France.* Among his favored poets were Albert Samain, Saint-Pol-Roux, Ernest Raynaud, Edouard Dubus, Jean Court, Louis Dumur, Louis Denise, and Albert Aurier; Ephraïm Mikhaël's death on May 12 was the first loss suffered by the closely knit group of founders. In Remy de Gourmont the magazine possessed a critic favorable to all forms of idealistic literature. Alfred Vallette, friendly toward the young Belgian writers, wrote for the October issue a penetrating article on Maurice Maeterlinck [3] and Charles van Lerberghe. The tone of the magazine is generally serious and mature, but humor and satire played their part in the short stories of Jules Renard and in the "Ballades pour exaspérer le mufle" of Laurent Tailhade.

Tailhade's new poetic manner, first revealed in the *Mercure de France* of 1890, is that of crude violence. The poet who had been one of the Hydropathes, one of the contributors to *Lutèce* in the early 1880's, a collaborator of Baju's *Décadent,* had always had two poetic natures: one which gloried in mystical and dreamy ornamentation and another which found its expression in parodies. In 1890 a third Tailhade emerges; he becomes a modern Juvenal, intent on castigating the society in which he lives. His hatreds are manifold, and his epithets are bold and often obscene.[4] He directs his satirical verse against the mystical pretensions of Péladan and the esoteric poetry of Jounet, against journalists and established literary reputations, but chiefly against hypocrisies

---

3. Octave Mirbeau's article in *Le Figaro* (August 14, 1890) had given sudden publicity to the author of *La Princesse Maleine.*

4. The influence of Lautréamont is possible here. The Genonceaux edition of *Les Chants de Maldoror* had just appeared and Tailhade was acquainted with the work. But Tailhade was also a classical scholar and well versed in the Latin satirists.

of the materialistic Third Republic. This form of writing has been called "le symbolisme féroce," the justification of the title being in the wave of anarchism which swept over France in the early 1890's and which enlisted the sympathies of many of the symbolist poets. Remy de Gourmont's explanation of the poet of *Le Jardin des rêves* and *Vitraux,* who was also the author of *Au pays du mufle,* is perhaps the right one, for the exasperation of the idealist sometimes (as with Léon Bloy) turns to invective:

L'ignominie du siècle exaspère le Latin épris de soleil et de parfums, de belles phrases et de beaux gestes et pour qui l'argent est la joie qu'on jette, comme des fleurs, sous les pas des femmes, et non de la productive graine qu'on enterre pour qu'elle germe.[5]

The problem of prosody which occupies the *Mercure de France* during its first year of existence is not that of free verse but measurement of French poetry according to tonic accents, a system proposed by Louis Dumur and which suggests the scansions proposed in the sixteenth century at the time of the Pléiade. Dumur, whose volume *La Néva* illustrated the principles of iambs and anapests as the measurement of the line, was not destined to produce any important change in French versification. Poets recognized too well that the weak tonic accent of French lent itself very badly to such procedure, but the problem was discussed. Edouard Dubus undertook to refute Dumur's theories,[6] but a few critical articles admitted that the lines of poems in *La Néva,* often of fourteen and fifteen syllables, had produced a strange and interesting pattern in rhythms.

Free verse found its champion in 1890 in a series of articles by Vielé-Griffin. These were published in a magazine which he organized with Paul Adam and Henri de Régnier in May, 1890, and which was called *Entretiens politiques et littéraires.* The political articles are noteworthy as examples of the trend of writers toward liberalism in politics, an attitude which gradually led toward the preaching of anarchistic doctrines, but during 1890 Vielé-Griffin's essays are the principal items of interest. In them the author of *Joies* defends verse which does not depend upon numerical count of syllables but upon the musical cadence determined by the inner emotions of the poet.

Vielé-Griffin is capable of bitter irony when he speaks of the poets of the Parnassian school; he uses such expressions as "la sensibilité attendrie de M. Leconte de Lisle, le sens aristocratique de M. Coppée, la fougue de M. Sully-Prudhomme." He attacks too the journalists who appear outraged because young poets dare to attempt poetic rejuvenation after the death of Victor Hugo. Edison's phonograph furnishes him with a point of departure

5. Remy de Gourmont, *Le Livre des masques,* p. 101.
6. *Mercure de France,* I (May, 1890), 145–150.

for a discussion of man's great reluctance to accept the new, and his seemingly instinctive need to hear repeated what has often been said. Against this polemic tone is set the author's faith in his own generation, which he praises for its comprehension of Mallarmé and Verlaine. He mentions especially Kahn, Dujardin, Maeterlinck, Henri de Régnier, Moréas, Verhaeren, Mikhaël, Adam, and Barrès as being sufficient for the fame of the epoch.

While *Le Mercure de France* and *Les Entretiens politiques et littéraires* were struggling through their first year of existence and each in its own way accomplishing the defense of symbolist poetry, the *Revue indépendante* continued its program of representing no school. The rather small attention shown to poetry by the magazine, after the years when Edouard Dujardin had caused so much space to be devoted to it, gives a distinct impression of a change of attitude. Remy de Gourmont, however, was one of the contributors to the periodical and wrote articles on Stéphane Mallarmé and the *Dernière Mode* of 1874, and on some variants of l'Isle-Adam's *Axël*. Toward the end of the year appeared poems by Moréas, Valéry, Merrill, and Raynaud. Neither does the first year of *L'Ermitage*, later one of the important magazines in the symbolist movement, present much interesting verse. Its poets included Auguste Dorchain, Marc Legrand, Pierre Quillard, and Laurent Tailhade, poets who were not directly in the main poetic current of innovation in form but who were more or less friendly to the groups of *La Plume* and *Le Mercure de France*.

In Belgium the influence of French poetry was increasingly felt. *La Jeune Belgique,* which in 1886 had been very cool to the first efforts of the French symbolists, had by 1890 somewhat reversed its position and was publishing contributions by Mallarmé, Henri de Régnier, Vielé-Griffin, as well as its old contributors, André Fontainas and Maeterlinck; in 1890 Valère Gille wrote a critical article on Mallarmé for the magazine. But the chief link between French and Belgian poetry continued to be *La Wallonie*. After Mallarmé had made his lecture tour in February, 1890, and had spoken before the artists who called themselves "Les Vingt," *La Wallonie* devoted its April issue to this same artistic group, the champions of Van Gogh, Gauguin, Seurat, and Whistler, the group admired by Mallarmé and defended in France particularly by Félix Fénéon. In May the magazine began the practice of devoting a whole issue to individual poets, choosing for this issue the chief Belgian glory among its collaborators, Emile Verhaeren. In August it honored in like manner Adolphe Retté, a poet little known in France except as one of the editors of *La Cravache* and the second *Vogue,* and who had published a strange volume of verse, *Cloches en la nuit,* in 1889. In *La Wallonie* Retté published some fragments of poetic prose which were to become part of his volume *Thulé des brumes* (1891). The book was to be dedicated to Albert Mockel, the editor of *La Wallonie,* who was particularly interested in the alliance between music and writing and whose enthusiasms usually went toward what was contrary to the traditional. The third special issue of 1890 contained prose and poetry by Pierre Quillard, certainly no great innovator in form but one of the group from the Lycée Fontanes who had in 1886 welcomed Maeterlinck, Grégoire le Roy, and Charles van Lerberghe into the company of *La Pléiade.* A part of Quillard's contribution to the special number was a tribute to the memory of his friend Ephraïm Mikhaël. Both Quillard and Mikhaël represent the middle ground between symbolism and Parnassianism. Strict in their observance of traditional form, they were yet to such a degree influenced by the subjective and evocative influences of the time that they are usually included among the poets of the movement. Mikhaël died at the age of twenty-four, and thanks to the efforts of several of his friends (among them Quillard and Catulle Mendès) his work was collected and published posthumously by Lemerre.[7] Many years later when that same publishing house issued *Les Symbolistes: Choix de poésies,* the description of Mikhaël's poetry given in the foreword emphasized the symbolist atmosphere of his work:

Cette poésie qui flotte, pour ainsi dire, entre ciel et terre ressemble à la Dame en deuil que Mikhaël nous dépeint, errant languissament parmi les glycines dans les longues allées, et qui a choisi de vivre "parmi ses mondaines corolles," avec la hantise des paradis inaccessibles, car elle est, dit-elle, malade d'espérance.[8]

In addition to these contributions by French poets, the year 1890 also offered in *La Wallonie* six poems by Moréas which were to become part of *Le Pèlerin passionné* and one sonnet by Heredia. Stuart Merrill, Achille Delaroche, and Albert Saint-Paul continued their collaboration with the periodical. Forgotten today, Delaroche and Saint-Paul were rather frequent contributors to *La Wallonie,* the former being known for his "Sonnets symphoniques" and the latter for experimentations with meters, notably the fifteen-syllable line.

While the bonds between the Belgian and French poets were being drawn tighter, the movement was beginning to be known in other countries. In April, 1890, the English poet Arthur Symons, who was later to write the *Symbolist Movement in Literature,* came to Paris and was introduced by Charles Morice to Verlaine. This began a friendship which later brought about Verlaine's lecture tour in England [9] and an exchange of translations of the two writers' poems.[10] In 1890 appeared in Portugal *Oaristos* by Eugénio de Castro, who had made a trip to Paris and had been impressed by the poetry of Verlaine

---

7. Ephraïm Mikhaël *Œuvres* (1890).

8. *Les Symbolistes: Choix de poésies* (notices par Maxime Formont), p. 230.

9. In November, 1893.

10. Verlaine made prose translations of some of the poems of Symons' *London Nights* (1895). This volume contained verse translations of several of Verlaine's poems.

and Mallarmé. De Castro's preface to his book of poetry denounced the traditional forms of Portuguese verse and called for innovation in meter and vocabulary. Rich imagery, unusual words, and musical effects were some of the aspects of his lyric art, and like René Ghil he did not hesitate to use typographical peculiarities to emphasize his melodic innovations. The poetry of the Portuguese poet and that of his followers, deemed obscure, was soon the object of much criticism and the group came to be known as the "nefelibatas" or "cloud-treaders."

In Germany and Austria the influence of French symbolism also began to be felt about 1890. Stefan George, introduced by Albert Saint-Paul to Mallarmé, carried back to Germany the essentials of symbolist doctrine and by his *Hymnen* began a form of poetry which was the antithesis of the objective and which sought to suggest rather than to state. The *Blätter für die Kunst* did not begin publication until 1892, but in June, 1890, Paul Remer wrote two articles on French symbolism in *Die Gegenwart*.[11] In Vienna the precocious Hugo von Hoffmannsthal was publishing his first verse and assuming leadership over a group that turned away from naturalism to a new kind of romanticism in which French currents had their part. On March 15, 1890, in the *Gazzetta letteraria*,[12] an article by Federico Musso entitled "La letteratura all'ospedale" gave a biographical summary of Verlaine's life and work.

While the fame of Verlaine and of Mallarmé was spreading beyond the frontiers of France, the destinies of the two leaders in their own country were strange and diverse. Mallarmé was publishing little, although a small edition of his lecture on Villiers de l'Isle-Adam was issued by the "Librairie de l'art indépendant," and in November "Le Wirlwind" [13] appeared in *La Wallonie*. But the Tuesday gatherings had taken on almost the appearance of a religious rite and numerous poets gathered around Mallarmé as around an oracle. Verlaine, ill, poverty-stricken, and often under the influence of drink, had his following, but one can see from the names of *Dédicaces* that those for whom he felt any real friendship were painters, journalists, or young poets, often obscure, who accepted his Bohemian mode of life.

The year 1890, in published volumes of poetry, is of little importance in contrast to 1891, when almost all the symbolist group added to the bibliography of the movement. It was, however, probably a year of great activity in the preparation of these works, and many of the collections of poetry were announced as soon to appear. In March, 1890, a corrected version of Villiers de l'Isle-Adam's *Axël* was printed by Quantin and brought the name of the

---

11. "Die Symbolisten" in *Die Gegenwart* (1890), pp. 375–378, 394–397.

12. This is the Turin periodical in which Vittorio Pica, in 1887, published a series of articles on Mallarmé which were much more complete than any which had been published in France.

13. Better known as the "Billet à Whistler."

venerated master into the critical columns. Another posthumous volume of the year was the *Œuvres* of Ephraïm Mikhaël, published with a short biographical introduction. The volume contained both prose and poetry as well as *Le Cor fleuri,* a one-act *féerie* which had been given at the Théâtre libre in 1888.[14]

Perhaps the only important poetic volume published in Paris in 1890 was Henri de Régnier's *Poèmes anciens et romanesques.* His four earlier collections, published between 1885 and 1888, had been good but not too original. Now he had definitely found themes which suited his art, the vague and dreamy forests of legend but made vivid through sumptuous images of jewels. This gemlike adornment of the verse, with its pearls, sapphires, onyxes, and rubies was so marked that Jean Court suggests the immediate inspiration of Gustave Moreau's paintings.[15] The great novelty of the work is the adoption at times of a modified form of free verse. Among his alexandrines Régnier scatters a few short lines which relieve the monotony of his rhythms, and he often uses measures of odd numbers of syllables. The liberties in versification brought their author reproaches and eventually hostility from Sully-Prudhomme, who had admired Régnier's earlier volumes. Rhymes between singulars and plurals, sequences of feminine endings, hiatus, and alliteration were all subjects of the Parnassian's disapproval; free verse he considered an abomination. Although the author of the *Poèmes anciens et romanesques* soon returned to severe classical form, his liberties of 1890 caused Sully-Prudhomme to cease seeing him.[16]

Certainly of all the volumes written by Henri de Régnier this is the one which in form and imagery most closely approaches the manner of the contemporary symbolists. Sometimes the poetry seems attuned to that of Kahn and Retté:

> "La fange des étangs où nous nous enlisâmes
> A nos armures d'or sécha glauque et livide,
> Et nous allions comme vêtus de squames,
> Errants hybrides,
> Etant nous-mêmes l'hydre
> Qu'il aurait fallu vaincre aux étangs de nos âmes." [17]

At other times, regular in meter, the poetry is attuned to that of almost all poets of Régnier's generation in its revelation of a state of mind through suggestive imagery:

14. The volume also included "Florimond," a poem which had won the 1889 prize offered by the *Echo de Paris.* Mallarmé was one of the judges in the contest.

15. *Mercure de France,* I (May, 1890), 173.

16. Henri de Régnier, *Nos rencontres,* pp. 15–19.

17. Henri de Régnier, *Poèmes 1887–1892,* p. 107.

> Et comme un-fruit tombé dont le sang les enivre,
> Voici mordre à mon cœur automnal et mûri
> D'avoir vécu la joie et la douleur de vivre,
> Les oiseaux éperdus parmi le vent fleuri.[18]

But in the *Poèmes anciens et romanesques* perhaps the most important element in relation to the times is the use of the legendary. Moréas had told the ancient stories in the form of ballads, but with Vielé-Griffin and Henri de Régnier the atmosphere becomes an enchanted forest, somewhat the setting of medieval romance but in truth out of time and space. What might have become simply neoromanticism assumes more original aspect by reason of a series of superimposed meanings. These poets were not primarily interested in telling a story after the manner of Victor Hugo but in giving a setting appropriate to their dream. Occasionally this use of legend produces an allegorical poem, but fortunately an allegory in which suggestion rather than didacticism is the dominant note.

An example of this is Mathias Morhardt's dramatic poem *Hénor,* published in 1890, two years after Vielé-Griffin's *Ancæus.* In the latter work Vielé-Griffin had used remembrances of Greek mythology, but Morhardt creates his own myth. His hero is rather a soul in quest of the absolute than a living being; the vast, deserted palace which is the setting is the mind of Hénor. The plot is simply the attempt of Hénor to conquer his melancholy through sensuous love, the realization that the senses are lying and mutable, and the slaying of the woman whose soul the hero has tried vainly to possess.[19] Morhardt is not a great poet and he abandoned poetry almost immediately for the theater and for political writing. His style in *Hénor* is more in the eloquent manner of Victor Hugo than of the symbolists. But by his ideas he seems to belong to the last years of the century: the denial of the material world, the cult of the mind, the funeral oration of Hénor who, having killed Liliane, proclaims: "J'aimais ta Beauté seule et ta Beauté persiste."

The subtitle of Remy de Gourmont's novel *Sixtine,* also published in 1890, conveys the same message of the importance of the mind and its dreams in relation to reality. This "roman de la vie cérébrale" lives up to its name, for the exterior world is almost nonexistent. The entire work is concentrated on the inner reality, the thoughts of the curious protagonist, Hubert d'Entragues. Remy de Gourmont's style, with its multiple images and attempts to convey the synthesis of sensory perception after it has entered the mind, creates a unique form of fiction, perhaps one not to be followed but one beside which

18. *Ibid.,* p. 41.

19. For an analysis of the work see Dumur's article in the *Mercure de France,* I (August, 1890), 288–292. Camille de Sainte-Croix, in one of his articles in *La Bataille,* also noted the conflict between reality and dream in the poem.

the usual psychological novel appears more dependent on material rather than spiritual detail. The obvious fault of such an effort is that the novel as a literary form is too long for such delicate shadings; what seems proper to the poem or prose poem in refinement of sensation becomes monotonous in a longer work. The reader of *Sixtine* is likely to demand some more tangible background and alliance of events than that accorded by Gourmont. The novel preaches its own lesson; Hubert's intellectual idealism is not sufficient to gain Sixtine, who prefers the sensuous to the sensitive.

Although symbolism failed in this novel—and in French literature there are few successful long narratives where suggestion and dream are not supported by much realism—Remy de Gourmont's idea in more expert hands becomes the stream of consciousness so ably handled by Schnitzler and Joyce. Symbolism's direct contribution to fiction is difficult to estimate but the alliance between poetry and drama is much more evident. Maeterlinck and Charles van Lerberghe opened new theatrical possibilities in 1889 and 1890 with *La Princesse Maleine, L'Intruse, Les Aveugles,* and *Les Flaireurs.* During 1890 occurred the first efforts of Paul Fort, then only seventeen years of age, to found a theater. First known as "Le Théâtre mixte," his company of actors, many of whom were as young as he, gave a program on October 5. The plays presented were Grandmougin's *Caïn,* Fort's *La Petite Bête,* and Louis Germain's *François Villon.* A new name, "Le Théâtre d'art," was assumed in November with a program of plays by Rachilde, Emile Bergerat, and Alexis Martin. The tendency of the new group, not clearly evident in these first attempts, was to oppose the Théâtre libre of Antoine which, after having done excellent service in introducing Ibsen, Tolstoy, and other foreign dramatists to the French public, had become more and more realistic. During the next few years, with the presentation of plays by Maeterlinck, Laforgue, and other symbolists, and recitations of poems by Mallarmé and Rimbaud, the theater became associated with the poetic movement.

In the last months of 1890 the "Bibliothèque artistique et littéraire" issued the limited edition of Ernest Raynaud's *Les Cornes du faune,* a volume of sonnets which with Moréas' *Le Pèlerin passionné* was to constitute a document in a new poetic grouping. At the same time appeared Marie Krysinska's *Rythmes pittoresques,* in which the free meters, described by some critics as prose poems with peculiar typographical arrangement, reopened the question as to who had first invented free verse.

The publication of a volume of poetry by the Polish musician and poetess is not significant, but her name on the title page of a book in 1890 with Lemerre as the publisher is rich in memories of the decade. Marie Krysinska had been a Zutiste and a Hydropathe, one of the early clients of Le Chat noir, and a contributor to the little magazine *Lutèce* in the early 1880's. She had set to music poems by Charles Cros and Icres and later those of the new generation. In 1890, having followed the fortunes of symbolism through its career, she is present at evening gatherings organized by the director of *La Plume* and her verse is still occasionally found in the little magazines.[20]

The traditions of the decadent phase of symbolism, the noisy gatherings of writers, artists, and musicians with recitations of both serious and humorous verse were to be carried on somewhat by the "Soirées de *La Plume*"; but symbolism, now provided with such vehicles as *Le Mercure de France* and *La Wallonie* and soon to gain further very good periodicals in *La Revue blanche* and *L'Ermitage*, was on the point of assuming a new existence. If some of its absurdities were soon to be discarded, if the venom and eccentricity of Baju had ceased to confuse the issues, it is nevertheless true that Moréas was about to create a diversion which would cause new rifts and René Ghil had not ceased to be a factor in poetic theory.

But coincident with the new decade is a new kind of recognition accorded the movement. Ferdinand Brunetière's article "Le Symbolisme contemporain," published in *La Revue des deux mondes* on April 1, 1891, and two articles by Anatole France in *Le Temps* later in the year are indicative of a new importance. This realization is also shown in the answers, however confusing they may have been, to the 1891 Huret questionnaire. During the seven years since the publication of *Les Poètes maudits* every year had seen a recruiting of poets eager to cast off the principles of the Parnassians, and even the most timid seemed to have espoused a more personal and intuitive inspiration. Sully-Prudhomme, enthroned in the Academy since 1881, François Coppée since 1884, and Leconte de Lisle, finally elected in 1886, represented a literary fashion which had few adepts of importance among the younger generation.

It is true that the wave of idealism represented by symbolism seems at times more significant as a revolt against naturalism than against any form of poetry; most of the younger generation admired the particular form of Heredia's genius and many of them were conscious of the personal tenderness in poems by Sully-Prudhomme. But their real affections went to Verlaine and Mallarmé; and it was in relation to these poets, with implications of the debt to Baudelaire, that they interpreted lyric qualities. Thus when *L'Appel des voix* by the Belgian poet Charles Sluyts reached the critical columns of the *Mercure de France,* its author was appreciated as follows:

On peut lui reprocher un peu de monotonie, due à l'uniformité de sa facture rythmique, et au retour des mêmes images; mais on ne serait lui dénier une

20. "Le Calvaire" and "Effet de soir," *La Revue indépendante*, June, 1889; "Horizons," *La Plume*, September 15, 1890.

douceur pénétrante et le charme de la demi-teinte: c'est bien là la chanson grise voulue par Verlaine. Il y règne aussi un parfum de mysticisme que les vrais poètes, ceux qui sont doués du sens des correspondances, savent seuls évoquer.[21]

The immense accomplishment of the decade was twofold: the poem, fallen into neglect and obscured by the rising importance of fiction, had been given new life; this new existence implied for the symbolists a search in form and expression which could constitute the realm of lyricism. The creation of melodies and sonorities which would best express the intimate thought of the poet, the novelties in diction which would not give the impression of what had already been said, the incursion of the poetic world in other forms of literature—these were the strong and vital currents which, though not by any means always successful, had constituted a revolution in literature. The impulsion was not yet spent but it is on the threshold of the 1890's that it began to impose its part of validity on a larger public. Its message was that expressed in the preface of Remy de Gourmont to his *Livre des masques:*

La seule excuse qu'un homme ait d'écrire c'est de s'écrire lui-même, de dévoiler aux autres la sorte de monde qui se mire dans son miroir individuel; sa seule excuse est d'être original; il doit dire des choses non encore dites et les dire en une forme non encore formulée.

21. *Mercure de France,* I (December, 1890), 443.

THE FIRST MONTHS of 1891, a year extremely rich in the annals of symbolism, are largely concerned with the circumstances surrounding the publication of *Le Pèlerin passionné*. Moréas had, it would seem, carefully prepared for much publicity at the appearance of his volume. In late December, 1890, just as the book was coming off Vanier's presses, Anatole France wrote a long article on Moréas for *Le Temps*.[1] Meanwhile Moréas had begun a campaign to celebrate the book and had enlisted the aid of Maurice Barrès and Henri de Régnier in arranging a banquet. In addition, since Deschamps had asked him to edit a special number of *La Plume*, he appears to have retarded his copy until January 1, 1891,[2] the exact moment when the copies of *Le Pèlerin passionné* were put on sale. The issue appeared with the name of Moréas in huge letters on the cover and contained, besides a drawing of Moréas by Gauguin, reprints of articles on *Le Pèlerin passionné*, by France and Barrès [3] and selections from Moréas' published work. An essay by Achille Delaroche, called the "Annales du symbolisme," did contain names of other writers, but again Moréas is mentioned several times.[4]

In the first week of February the banquet, at which Mallarmé presided, was held. The Parnassians had been invited and had sent their regrets; Catulle Mendès arrived at a late hour. Toasts were drunk to Moréas, Mallarmé, Verlaine (who was absent), and to the memories of Laforgue and Baudelaire. Henri de Régnier proposed a toast to Leconte de Lisle and to the fraternity of poets; Bernard Lazare suggested the name of Anatole France and Raoul Gineste that of Félicien Rops. Charles Morice read a sonnet entitled "A Jean Moréas." According to Ernest Raynaud, this event marked the triumph of symbolism rather than of one author, yet many of the two hundred people present could not have failed seeing to what degree Moréas was striving to institute himself as leader of the young poetic generation. His preface to the *Pèlerin passionné* had not been without some pretensions:

Dirai-je, maintenant, de mes innovations rhythmiques, que le los et la complicité des plus affinés jeunes hommes de ce temps les sigillent à la disgrâce de ceux-là

1. On December 24, 1890.
2. During the last months of 1890 *La Plume* apologizes several times for delay of the issue.
3. Barrès' article had appeared in *Le Figaro*, December 25, 1890.
4. A supplement to the issue, "Etrennes symbolistes" by Maurice du Plessys, was also a panegyric of Moréas' work.

qui de prudence s'aggravent! Et n'ai-je, déjà, fait preuve de quelque supériorité en la poétique réglementaire? et qui me saurait tenir en suspicion!

Moréas had loyal friends in Ernest Raynaud of the *Mercure de France* and Léon Deschamps of *La Plume*. Immediate opposition, in February, was expressed in *La Revue indépendante,* where René Ghil with violent scorn and George Bonnamour in a gentler tone of reproof cast doubt on the importance of Moréas and his work.[5] Huret's literary questionnaire later in the year gradually revealed a number of other poets who had little faith in the talents of Moréas, but these judgments were made after schism had split the symbolist ranks with the founding of the "Ecole romane." At the moment of the banquet, although the intention of linking the current period with the Middle Ages and the Renaissance was clearly stated in the preface of *Le Pèlerin passionné,* no one seems to have guessed that Moréas was on the point of forsaking the name he had coined. The title of the issue of *La Plume* was "Le Symbolisme de Jean Moréas," and Gauguin's picture bore the motto "Je suis symboliste."

Although Moréas was succeeding in drawing much homage to himself, the time of his triumph was also that of reverence accorded to those writers whom the symbolists recognized as their spiritual ancestors. The year is the date of Vanier's new edition of *Les Amours jaunes* of Corbière [6] and of Rodolphe Darzens' edition of Rimbaud's work under the title *Le Reliquaire.*[7] The Genonceaux edition of Lautréamont (1890) inspired Remy de Gourmont's article "La Littérature 'Maldoror' " in the *Mercure de France.*[8] Villiers de l'Isle-Adam's name was beginning to be known abroad by such articles as that of Jan Ten Brink in the Dutch magazine *Nederland* and the brief essay by Arthur Symons in the *Illustrated London News* of January 24, 1891. Henry Bordeaux published his essay *Villiers de l'Isle-Adam* at Ghent in November, 1891. The *Entretiens politiques et littéraires,* now in the second year of existence, devoted many pages to unpublished fragments of Laforgue's prose. Al-

5. *La Revue indépendante*, XVIII, 145–152, 160–166.

6. Three of the poems from the volume were printed in *La Plume*, No. 56 (August 15, 1891), pp. 268–269.

7. The *Mercure de France* printed three of Rimbaud's poems from the *Reliquaire* in its issue of November, 1891. A review in the following number of the magazine, by Remy de Gourmont, criticized sharply the preface and indicated little admiration for Rimbaud. The first criticism is amply justified and Gourmont could have spoken of the poor editing of the volume. His article was later revised and became a part of the *Livre des masques.*

Le Reliquaire, in which were certain apocryphal poems, contained a preface signed Rodolphe Darzens. Darzens later protested that he was not the author and asked that the edition be seized as a forgery.

8. The publication of selections from Lautréamont's *Poésies* in the *Mercure de France* (February, 1891), was of some importance, since the famous passage in which the author denied that poetry had made any progress since Racine and in which the poets of the romantic school receive such strange titles was included.

though these fragments had been left by their author in a chaotic state, the critical comments on Baudelaire,[9] Corbière, Rimbaud, Mallarmé, and Bourget are stimulating and suggest astonishing insight and ability.

The prestige of Mallarmé, evident at the banquet for Moréas, continued undiminished. During February and March, in the *Revue indépendante,* was printed the long study by Vittorio Pica.[10] Though some of the critical analyses of the poems were odd, the essay, with its numerous quotations and its enthusiastic admiration, was one of the first attempts to follow Mallarmé's poetic evolution. The publication of *Pages* in Brussels at last brought together some of Mallarmé's prose writings; repercussions of the volume reached the French periodicals. In the *Mercure de France* appeared an essay by Pierre Quillard [11] and in the *Entretiens politiques et littéraires* one by Vielé-Griffin.[12] *La Plume* printed Mallarmé's "La Pipe," and some pages which had appeared fifteen years before in the *République des lettres* were reprinted in the *Mercure de France.*

More equivocal is the situation of Verlaine. With two new volumes of poetry in 1891, and a *Choix de poésies* published by Fasquelle in an edition of fifteen hundred copies, he would seem to be an eminently successful poet. But his new production of verse was remarkably inferior and gave little impression of originality. The poems of *Bonheur* were written in the same mood of penitence as *Amour,* while *Chansons pour elle* seemed only a poor continuation of *Parallèlement.* Critics were aware of this and all that Edouard Dubus could find to say concerning *Chansons pour elle* was the rueful sentence, "Des vers de mirliton par un poète de génie." [13] Only *La Plume,* which had prided itself since the publication of *Dédicaces* on being Verlaine's special protector, used dithyrambic words of praise for Verlaine's new volumes. Thus Léon Deschamps, on receiving a copy of *Bonheur,* wrote his impression:

9. It may seem strange that Baudelaire did not furnish more often the matter for entire critical essays in this period. His name occurs frequently in the periodicals throughout the 1890's and almost always with veneration and respect. But his was a recognized reputation among the symbolists and their principal effort was toward establishing those whose fame was less secure. It is noteworthy how often his poetry seems to have produced, in succeeding young writers, imitations which were almost too close. For example, Camille Mauclair published in 1891 a poem entitled "Spleen" which begins:

> L'amertume et l'horreur des ciels pluvieux
> Que Décembre épandit sur nos fronts effarés
> Evoquent des linceuls moisis et déchirés
> D'où suinterait un sang pâle d'homme très vieux.

La Revue indépendante, March, 1891

10. *La Revue indépendante,* XVIII, 173–215, 315–360.

11. III (July, 1891), 4–8.

12. III (August, 1891), 67–72.

13. Dubus is paraphrasing René Ghil's judgment on Moréas: "Des vers de mirliton écrits par un grammarien."

J'ai pleuré sur ce livre du cher Pauvre qui pardonne à tout et à tous: j'ai frémi de joie céleste en chantant pour moi seul ces divins rythmes d'un poète étrange qui n'est pas le monstre d'orgueil symbolisé par Odilon Redon dans sa puissante *Damnation de l'artiste*.[14]

Verlaine was the object of one of the efforts to relieve the poverty of admired artists, laudable humanitarian efforts which the distress of Laforgue and Villiers de l'Isle-Adam had helped to awaken. Paul Fort's Théâtre d'Art gave a benefit performance on May 21 for Verlaine and the painter Paul Gauguin. The results were negative for the material enrichment of the two. Verlaine's playlet "Les Uns et les autres" was badly presented and Charles Morice's "Chérubin" was a dismal failure; but worst of all the settings for Catulle Mendès' *Soleil de minuit* consumed all the profits. The only happy accomplishment of the venture was the representation of Maeterlinck's "L'Intruse" which was given a cordial reception by the audience. Another charitable effort of the year which also ended in failure was that of attempting to publish the poetry of Germain Nouveau, confined in an insane asylum but for whose recovery some hope was held.

In contrast with this reverence for the past is the emergence of a new generation of poets in 1891. Their arrival is signaled by the foundation of a magazine which proposed to have only twelve issues and to be limited to one hundred copies. Its name was *La Conque* and it has retained some celebrity because of two of its organizers, Pierre Louÿs and Paul Valéry. Their poetry appeared in almost every issue. This periodical of 1891 represents a spirit which is quite different from most of the pretentious and arrogant magazines of 1886 and for good reason, since it did not have the same prejudices to overcome. It was willing to pay homage to talent rather than schools of poetry, and this it effectively demonstrated by initial poems in each issue. These special offerings were signed by Leconte de Lisle, Dierx, Heredia, Mallarmé, Swinburne,[15] Judith Gautier, Maeterlinck, Moréas, Morice, Verlaine, Vielé-Griffin, and Henri de Régnier. While such a list is to some degree the reflection of momentary renown, it is on the whole a very able evaluation of the best writing of the period.

Along with Valéry and Louÿs, frequent contributors to *La Conque* were Léon Blum, soon to become a literary critic of *La Revue blanche,* Eugène Hollande, whose later poetry marked a return to classicism, and Camille Mauclair, one of the devoted admirers, as were in fact most of the contributors of the review, of Stéphane Mallarmé. Mauclair was one of those who in 1891 began

14. *La Plume*, No. 50 (May 15, 1891), p. 169. The work of art by Odilon Redon appeared at the beginning of Iwan Gilkin's *La Damnation de l'artiste.*

15. This is the year when Gabriel Mourey's translation of Swinburne's *Poems and Ballads* appeared in France.

a campaign against Moréas, and Louÿs collected that year his poems into a first volume, *Astarté*. Valéry and Mauclair had both won honorable mention in a sonnet contest conducted by *La Plume* in the last months of 1890,[16] and this was their inconspicuous entry into the world of Parisian letters where they were to become so famous. With them is to be associated their young friend André Gide, who had studied at the Ecole alsacienne with Louÿs and who published the *Cahiers d'André Walter* in 1891. This volume did not bear the name of its author, but it was hailed as the production of a delicate and idealistic spirit and as a point of view opposite from that of naturalism. Critical notes by reviewers as diverse as Paul Redonnel, Camille Mauclair, and Remy de Gourmont were enthusiastic in their praise.[17] Another first volume by an anonymous writer did not awaken the same sort of unified response. This was the play *Tête d'or* which would one day be recognized as an important event in the symbolist theater, but of which the *Revue indépendante* professed not to understand the versification. *La Plume* thought that the unknown author, in order to be different, had caused his book to be printed in an idiotic fashion without margins and page numbers, but admitted that the volume was admired by Stuart Merrill. A paragraph by Pierre Quillard in the *Mercure de France* was one of the rare tributes given to Claudel's first dramatic effort.[18]

Even if Gide and Claudel preferred to remain anonymous in 1891, their books immediately received some comment. Another author, Francis Jammes, began publishing pamphlets of poetry that same year; but printed at Orthez and not placed on sale, these were not known in Paris until several years later. Even in December, 1893, the *Mercure de France* wonders whether the name of Jammes is not a pseudonym. On the contrary, Paul Fort, four years younger than Jammes, and indeed in 1891 only nineteen years old, was creating a great deal of stir with the experiments of his theater. In January his troupe gave Shelley's *The Cenci* in Félix Rabbe's translation, in March a curious program which included the recitation of Mallarmé's "Le Guignon," Rachilde's three-act play *Madame la Mort,* Quillard's *La Fille aux mains coupées,* and a realistic play by Frédéric de Chirac entitled *Prostituée!* The intrusion of this last play in the repertoire of a theater which was combating naturalism and of which poetry and music were important elements may seem strange. The audience hissed the realistic play, and the Théâtre d'Art was accused of having represented the drama to produce just this reaction. The Verlaine-Gauguin benefit performance in May was, as we have seen, not entirely successful except for

16. The winners of that contest were Marcel Noyer, Bénoni Glador, and Jules Laloue. The subscribers to the magazine judged the poems.

17. See *La Plume,* No. 49, p. 154; *Mercure de France,* II, 368; *La Revue indépendante,* XVIII, 405–407.

18. *Mercure de France,* II (April, 1891), 249.

revealing Maeterlinck's dramatic production. If Paul Fort had been able to make a contract with the representative of Villiers de l'Isle-Adam's widow, *Axël* would have been given in July. Toward the end of the year another complex program was presented, with Maeterlinck's *Les Aveugles,* Laforgue's *Le Concile féerique,* Gourmont's *Théodat,* some adaptations of old epic legends by Adolphe Retté, Camille Mauclair, and Stuart Merrill, and of the "Song of Songs" by Paul Roinard. This last number on the program was an attempt to make a synthesis of sensations through musical accompaniment and even diffusion of perfumes from an inadequate atomizer.

A very close bond between literature and art was established during 1891. Even in 1885–86 Téodor de Wyzewa had related the music of Wagner to painting and literature,[19] and during the succeeding years Félix Fénéon had written many art criticisms to show that the independent school of painters was attempting to accomplish in pictorial form the same idealism and suggestion as the symbolist poets. But in 1891 the bonds between symbolism and painting are drawn much tighter and even the titles of articles in *La Plume,* "Théorie du symbolisme des teintes" or "Les Impressionnistes symbolistes à l'Exposition de St. Germain," or an article on Paul Gauguin in the *Mercure de France* which is entitled "Le Symbolisme en peinture," reveal the current of ideas on painting. But the links between painters and poets were on all manner of levels: Eugène Carrière had completed his portrait of Verlaine, Gauguin was completing his etching of Mallarmé in the early months of 1891;[20] there were dinners presided over by Jean Dolent, at which many artists and writers met. At the banquet given in March in honor of Gauguin, who was about to leave for Tahiti, the guests included Mallarmé, Morice, Vallette, Rachilde, Moréas, Dubus, and Retté. The recent deaths of Van Gogh and of Seurat caused much comment in critical columns of periodicals. A special number of *La Plume* was devoted to "Les Peintres novateurs" and contained many short articles on artists, among whom were Seurat, Signac, Luce, Gauguin, Maurice Denis, Cézanne, Pissarro, and Séon.[21] In the *Revue indépendante* Arthur Symons wrote on Odilon Redon and Jules Antoine on Georges Seurat, while in the *Mercure de France* were essays on Gauguin, Dolent, Carrière, Renoir, and Henri de Groux.

Ties were meanwhile strengthened between Belgium and France by such events as Henri de Régnier's becoming an editor of *La Wallonie* and the transfer of *La Revue blanche* to Paris in October, 1891. In his book reviews for the Liége publication Régnier was particularly useful in unifying the Belgian

19. Reprinted in *Nos maîtres* from articles in *La Revue wagnérienne.*

20. See *Mercure de France* II (March, 1891), 189.

21. For details on friendships between painters and writers see Charles Chassé's *Le Mouvement symboliste dans l'art du XIXᵉ siècle.*

and French literary movements. During 1891 he wrote on Quillard's *La Gloire du verbe,* Paul Adam's *En décor,* Vielé-Griffin's *Diptyque,* Mallarmé's *Pages,* and the *Cahiers d'André Walter. La Revue blanche,* in its three issues of the year, not only printed poetry by Merrill, Régnier, Vielé-Griffin, and Kahn, as well as literary notices by Lucien Muhlfeld on new books of poetry, but also an article on "Gentlemen de lettres": Merrill, Régnier, and Vielé-Griffin. The June 15 issue of *La Plume* was entirely devoted to "Les Jeune-Belgique," giving an anthology of poetry and short prose selections with indications of the authors' published work and their collaboration with Belgian periodicals.

Other important components in the literary scene in 1891, perhaps not important for poetry for the year but which furnish the tone or subject matter of some verse, are socialism and occultism. Richepin, Roinard, Camille Soubise, Octave Mirbeau, André Veidaux, and Louise Michel are among the agitators for social reform who knew and associated with many of the symbolist poets. Among the Socialists as among the occultists there were always poetic idealists. Certain forms of humanitarian poetry as well as a kind of false mysticism in the 1890's stem from contacts with the extremists of these groups. A translation of part of the Marx-Engels manifesto was published by the *Entretiens politiques et littéraires* and Henri de Régnier wrote a "Commentaire sur l'argent," in which he contrasted the poverty of the artist of genius with the unworthy holders of wealth. In the same magazine articles by Bernard Lazare pictured the proletariat as the dupe of the rich. The poet of 1891 was usually an idealist and a dreamer; yet few followed Zo d'Axa and Malato to the excesses of anarchism. The same tangent but not all-embracing attitude is visible toward the occultists. Although Péladan, Stanislas de Guaita, and Jules Bois are often mentioned by the symbolist poets, the tone is almost universally one of mockery. The *Revue indépendante* published a long essay extolling the works of Péladan but was careful to head the article as "Tribune libre." [22] The metaphysical poem by Jules Bois, *Il ne faut pas mourir,* published in 1891, excited no comment from other poets; and we have nothing to show that the symbolists flocked to hear Alber Jhouney [23] lecture on "Le Christ esotérique." On the other hand, the selections from Jean-Paul Richter, published in *La Revue indépendante,* [24] and an article by Jean Thorel entitled "Les Romantiques allemands et les symbolistes français," which appeared in the *Entretiens politiques et littéraires,* [25] both are in close relationship with the poetic idealism

22. *La Revue indépendante,* XX (September, 1891), 311–344.

23. Albert Jounet changed his name to this more exotic spelling about 1890. Shortly afterward he, as well as Jules Bois, began giving public lectures. Emile Michelet founded a magazine *Psyché* in November, 1891, and about the same time Péladan announced his "Salon esthétique," of which the program was the rejection of all materialism and the search for the ideal in beauty.

24. *La Revue indépendante,* XXI (October–November, 1891), 70–79, 239–243.

25. *Entretiens politiques et littéraires,* III (September, 1891), 95–109.

and subjectivity of the age. That Tieck and Novalis, Fichte and the great romanticists of Germany had proclaimed the supremacy of poetry and the
revelation of the soul of things had come gradually to the attention of those
who were studying the literary trends in France at the end of the century. In
the efforts of a preceding age and another country the poets of the 1890's were
able to see a movement which paralleled to some degree their own and gave
them added security.

But while this extension in understanding of literature was being attempted,
the adherents of the Ecole romane began to preach a doctrine of two kinds of
literature, that of the North, which was violent and crude, and that of the
South, the only region capable of producing sweet and melodious harmonies,
the only realm of the truly beautiful and mysterious. The French romanticists
had been led astray by allowing themselves to embrace the crudity of the
North; now Moréas proposed to rectify that error. The breviary for the Ecole
romane was written by Charles Maurras and appeared in *La Plume* in an
issue devoted to the Félibrean movement of southern France. It was entitled
"Barbares et romans" and extolled the literary past of Greece and Italy;
Maurras even went so far as to say that Shakespeare was Italian. His remarks
did not go unchallenged; Adolphe Retté published "Le Midi bouge!" [26] written in the caustic tone for which he was later to become known, and Pierre
Quillard with delicate irony asks whether the Middle Ages did not after all
present some trace of the Germanic warrior and should therefore be outlawed
from the doctrine of Moréas.[27]

Maurras thus became the official spokesman for Moréas and the Ecole
romane. He was seconded by Maurice du Plessys with the "Etrennes symbolistes" and the poem "Dédicace à Apollodore," which had been read at the
February banquet, and by Ernest Raynaud, who praised Moréas in an article
in the *Mercure de France*. The opponents to the eulogies given *Le Pèlerin
passionné,* as revealed by the Huret questionnaire, were quite numerous, perhaps sometimes inspired by jealousy but also by the excessive pretentions of a
poet who almost appears a megalomaniac. The expression of discontent with
the art of Moréas, too harshly expressed by Ghil, is best resumed by Camille
Mauclair. In an article [28] he reviews the claims for innovation that have been
made by Moréas and his adulators, shows that others are in truth more original,
and concludes by stating that the author of the *Pèlerin passionné* does not
possess the intellectual depth or the breadth of vision necessary for a great poet.
What Mauclair admires in *Le Pèlerin passionné* is limited to two elements:
the music of certain verses and the settings of some of the poems. He confesses

26. *La Plume*, No. 55 (August, 1891), pp. 251–253.
27. *Entretiens politiques et littéraires*, III (August, 1891), 56–60.
28. *La Revue indépendante*, XX (July, 1891), 29–79.

to have felt that the poetry gave an original effect as he read it, but after reflection he decided that the impression resulted from Moréas' patchwork imitations of a number of different sources. The vocabulary with its obsolete words, according to Mauclair, came from the *fabliaux,* the ingenuous tone of the love songs from Charles d'Orléans; the settings were often suggested by Virgil or Theocritus, the sad or mysterious tone by Baudelaire and Poe. The author's conclusions are that if one must have a poetic leader, it would be better to seek a sincere artist such as Verlaine or Mallarmé, and it would be preferable to admire a poetic work in which there was some thought.

The pompous claims of Moréas, the flattery of his admirers merited much of this adverse criticism. His volume of verse is uneven in quality, but if he had not chosen to make a manifesto and constitute a poetic school it is probable that he would have been recognized as an artist who had recovered some of the charm of sixteenth-century lyrics, who used effects of alliteration and repetition, free verse, and assonance with considerable ability, and who was more interested in the form and sound of his poetry than in expressing an idea. He would have been remembered for his "Etrennes de doulce," for the antique charm of:

> Les fenouils m'ont dit: Il t'aime si
> Follement qu'il est à ta merci;
> Pour son revenir va t'apprêter.
> Les fenouils ne savent que flatter:
> Dieu ait pitié de mon âme.[29]

If *Le Pèlerin passionné* continued to be considered as the volume in which the author had announced that he was not an ignoramus of whom the Muses made fun, the overweening vanity of Moréas is to be blamed. His contemporaries more often remember his expressions of "Ronsard et moi" or "Hugo et moi" than the talent he possessed.

Although Moréas was a successful publicity maker, it is doubtful whether he, any more than René Ghil, did poetry a great service by his histrionics. The writers who spoke with such scorn of *Le Pèlerin passionné* during the Huret inquiry probably felt called upon to reprove conceit. The results of that inquiry inspired George Bonnamour and Gaston Moreilhon to write an article, "Le Fiasco symboliste," [30] which omitted many names but treated scornfully almost all contemporary names except that of René Ghil. They followed this condemnation of symbolism with a long essay [31] on the advocate of scientific and evolutive verse. This article terminated with praise for Ghil in no way less measured than was that of Maurras for the founder of the Ecole romane.

---

29. Jean Moréas, *Poésies 1886–1896,* p. 35.
30. *La Revue indépendante,* XX (July, 1891), 1–29.
31. *Ibid.* (August, 1891), 178–251.

If all the critical literature and all published volumes of poetry had centered about these two strong personalities during 1891, the future of poetry would have appeared black indeed. But about this time it happened that almost all the symbolist group produced new volumes of verse and several interesting newcomers appeared on the poetic horizon. The *Mercure de France* had occasion to speak of some fifty collections of verse during the year; the bibliographical notices were often written by Edouard Dubus, Remy de Gourmont, and Pierre Quillard. With such critics it is not strange that the faults attributed to the Parnassian school are underlined. Thus *Le Poème de la chair* by Abel Pelletier is accused of being too traditional and not musical enough, and *Ce qui renaît toujours* by Jean Carrère of being at times too eloquent and declamatory. *La Joie de Maguelonne* by A.-F. Herold is praised because the author seems no longer under the influence of Leconte de Lisle. A healthy sign in these articles of the *Mercure* is that no volume, if one except Raynaud's essay on *Le Pèlerin passionné,* is given blind, excessive praise or subjected to unjust or biased attack. Remy de Gourmont expresses doubt as to whether the free verse of Dujardin's *La Comédie des amours* reveals much talent, and Pierre Quillard, always very conservative in matters of poetic form, regrets the free meters of Vielé-Griffin's *Diptyque.* Although Ernest Raynaud, in an essay on Dumur's *Lassitudes,* is much too obviously extolling the Ecole romane, it is with some reason that he sees in Dumur a tardy blossoming of the romantic spirit.

The poets born in the 1850's and sixties who are given the greatest praise and in general are accorded most space in the critical articles of the *Mercure de France* are: Moréas, Mikhaël, Raynaud, Quillard, Rodenbach, Tailhade, Vielé-Griffin, Merrill, Herold, Mockel, and Kahn.[32] Henri de Régnier received briefer treatment in 1891 because his publication was a re-edition of *Episodes* and *Sites* with some new sonnets. The qualities which the critics see in these poets are those of personal expression, musical preoccupation in verse, a sense of mystery and suggestion, fluidity and evanescence—in general the qualities which had been associated with symbolist verse.[33] Nor in the reviews of poetry are the ancestors of the movement forgotten; Fernand Clerget's *Les Tourmentes* evokes the memory of Baudelaire for Charles Merki, and Léon Deschamps mentions Verlaine in discussing the same volume.

Recognition of the evolution which had taken place during the years of

32. The volumes by these authors which inspired critical articles in 1891 were: *Le Pèlerin passionné, Œuvres posthumes, Les Cornes du faune, La Gloire du verbe, Le Règne du silence, Au pays du mufle, Diptyque, Les Fastes, La Joie de Maguelonne, Chantefable un peu naïve, Chansons d'amant.*

33. Laurent Tailhade's *Au pays du mufle* is of course an exception, but the reviewers turn from his volume of 1891 to speak of *Au pays du rêve* and ask whether he will not abandon violent satire and return to his earlier poetic manner.

symbolism seems evident from these reviews; yet the great variety in poetic expression, ranging from the simple and direct statement of the emotions to the most ornate and complicated evocations of the mind, kept most critics from trying to formulate definitions. Among those who made such an attempt was Vielé-Griffin in an article entitled "Qu'est-ce que c'est?"[34], which does not find an answer but which suggests the importance of synthesis in sensation and of intuitive qualities in current verse. Vielé-Griffin was inspired to further examining of the question [35] by Brunetière's article of April 1 in the *Revue des deux modes,* and he professes to be in agreement with Brunetière on many points. He admits that the name symbolism is badly chosen and that there is danger of becoming amorphous through using free verse. But one sentence from Brunetière's article shocks him: "Comment serait-on à la fois symboliste et baudelairien?" In reply he quotes part of the sonnet "Correspondances" and then Brunetière's own words which seem to give part of the same message:

L'inconnaissable nous étreint: *in eo vivimus, movemur et sumus;* si nous réussissons, parfois, à en saisir quelque chose, il est également certain que ce n'est pas en observant la nature; mais nous y ajoutons, de notre fond à nous, les principes d'interprétation qu'elle ne contient pas. Et comment le pourrions-nous s'il n'y avait, certainement aussi, quelque convenance, ou quelque correspondance, entre la nature et l'homme, des harmonies cachées, comme on disait jadis, un rapport secret du sensible et de l'intelligible? [36]

It is true that Brunetière, although granting that the symbolists had done good service in suggesting how narrow and superficial was the art of the naturalists, did not intend to become the champion of symbolism. His article is above all a somewhat attenuated denunciation of the innovations in diction and prosody among the symbolist poets. But recognition of certain of their accomplishments, the very appearance in the *Revue des deux mondes* of a serious discussion of symbolism, constituted a triumph. A second recognition of the current trend in poetry came from Anatole France, who in six articles in *Le Temps* [37] discussed "Les Jeunes Poètes." At the outset he announces that since no one knows what symbolism is, he does not intend to find a definition but rather present what the young poets have accomplished. Then, in a series of short essays he takes up forty-two poets and gives examples of their work. Except for three or four names,[38] all those he treats are concerned in the history

34. *Entretiens politiques et littéraires,* II (March, 1891), 65–66.
35. *Ibid.* (May, 1891), 153–158.
36. *Revue des deux mondes,* CIV (April 1, 1891), 684.
37. On September 12, 16, 23; October 6, 7, 8, 1891.
38. France includes Robert de la Villehervé, born in 1849, and more in the tradition of Théodore de Banville than in that of the symbolists, as well as Daniel de Venancourt, born in 1873, whose first volume *Les Adolescents* was published in 1891.

of symbolism. The contributors to the *Mercure de France, La Plume,* and the *Entretiens politiques et littéraires,* several of the Belgian poets such as Giraud, Verhaeren, Mockel, and Maeterlinck, the poets of the Ecole romane, the occultists such as Stanislas de Guaita, Jhouney, and Emile Michelet, and even the old contributors to *Lutèce,* Vignier and Krysinska, are represented. France gives rather more space to Moréas and Maurras than to the others, but his series is a fairly complete picture of current poetry.[39]

But France in his brief notices of separate poets effects no synthesis of currents in lyricism. He does not note for instance a phenomenon which is apparent in the period, a tendency toward a kind of standardized symbolist setting for verse. The poet's dream and a legendary background have become fused by 1891. A contributor to this process was Jean Moréas, who in *Les Syrtes* (1884) and *Les Cantilènes* (1886) had utilized legendary material and had indeed written some poems which resemble the English ballad. Vielé-Griffin with his mythical drama *Ancæus* (1888), Pierre Quillard with his mystery play *La Fille aux mains coupées* (1886, 1891), Morhardt with the dramatic poem *Hénor* (1890), and Henri de Régnier with *Poèmes anciens et romanesques* (1890) also helped to establish a conventional pattern. The problem was to find an appropriate background for highly subjective and personal verse. Gustave Kahn in his *Palais nomades* and Adolphe Retté in *Cloches en la nuit* had attempted to do this through abstruse and unreal settings, but most poets desired a more coherent arrangement than the fugitive symbols of the mind. They did not choose Parnassian plasticity, but as the representation of their dream created a strange realm of forests, lilies, and swans in which roamed princesses and knights. The return to the legendary setting of the Middle Ages might seem a repetition of romanticism, yet in almost all cases the purpose of the poet appears an entirely different one. It is usually not the evocation of the past but an indirect statement of personal mood that was being sought. Idealism at first had found its symbols in religious terms, then had come to the timeless and spaceless setting of a remote era. Only exceptionally was the Hellenic background used, although in the course of the 1890's poets who at first had revolted against the usages of the Parnassians came to recognize the beauty and validity of the antique heritage.

For the moment, however, Greece and Rome remained out of the picture. Merrill, in *Les Fastes,* used Wagnerian and vaguely medieval settings; Kahn those of the remote land of dreams. Vielé-Griffin, in *Diptyque,* created a forest

39. Anatole France, this same year, wrote two articles on Verlaine in *Le Temps.* In the issue of April 19, 1891, he tells the story of "Gestas," thereby giving definite form to the Verlaine legend. In the course of the same article he reviews *Bonheur,* and although he calls Verlaine a true poet and indeed the only Christian poet of the period, he predicts that the new volume will be less well received than *Sagesse.* France's essay of November 15, 1891, is concerned with *Mes hôpitaux* and the curious blend of mysticism and cynicism in Verlaine.

setting which is abstract, and if Ernest Raynaud, in *Les Cornes du faune,* was often inspired by the park of Versailles, his backgrounds remain curiously unreal and only incidental to his theme, the joys and sorrows of amorous possession. Some poets, perhaps unconsciously, perhaps willfully, reacted against the vapory and unsubstantial landscapes of their creation. In a word, and in the most literal sense, they begemmed their poetry. The princesses of Henri de Régnier, Merrill, and Kahn are laden with bracelets and rings; the images in the verse contain the names of precious stones. In this, contemporary art may have had its part; Gustave Moreau was admired by the symbolists and Merrill was well acquainted with the painting of Burne-Jones and the pre-Raphaelites. A paradox in style is created by this poetic manner; the evanescent and ethereal meet the flashing of jewels in the same poem.

The metrical question divides the poetic production of 1891 into two groups. But originality in form, most openly expressed by free verse, is not always accompanied by the most revolutionary expression. This is to be seen in *Diptyque* of Vielé-Griffin, a little pamphlet of two poems printed by the presses of the *Entretiens politiques et littéraires* in 1891. Vielé-Griffin had written more concerning free verse than any poet at this time,[40] for Gustave Kahn, who prided himself on having invented the form and published the first volume illustrating the technique, did not formulate his essay on free verse until the publication of his *Premiers poèmes* in 1897. The execution of Vielé-Griffin's theory is somewhat disappointing. "Le Porcher," the first of the poems of *Diptyque,* is the meditation of a voluntary exile from society, the fugitive memories of his past life, and the statement of the author's belief that in nature is to be found the environment for happiness. The evocations of the swineherd, the wandering themes of his soliloquy bear some relationship with those of Mallarmé's faun, but Vielé-Griffin's shadings are far less subtle and his poetry sometimes becomes didactic. The other poem of *Diptyque* is a dialogue between the poet and the personified form of Art. The theme is again not very original and at times the counsels of Musset's muse seem re-echoed:

> "Te voici, comme au soir de ta première extase,
> Triste du vin de ma beauté;
> Je t'ai donné tout l'or de l'héritage,
> Tout l'or jaloux de la parole,
> Et te voici pleurant vers moi ta pauvreté;"[41]

Even the versification of *Diptyque* is not startling when one considers the great numbers of lines of twelve, ten, and eight syllables. Much more audacious

---

40. The preface to *Joies* and numerous articles in the *Entretiens politiques et littéraires* are his chief contributions. See *Entretiens politiques et littéraires,* I, 3–12, 56–60; II, 155–162, 213–217.

41. F. Vielé-Griffin, *Poèmes et poésies,* p. 220.

is Kahn's second volume of verse, *Chansons d'amant*. As in the *Palais nomades*, the author uses many long lines, identical rhymes, and above all a strange, complicated syntax from which obscurity is not absent. Yet these are love poems, of which the diction does not hide the sensuous note:

> Que tes lèvres demeurent la saveur habituelle
> à mes lèvres sevrées par l'orgueil,
> à mes lèvres scellées par l'oubli,
> et qu'à celui dont les rêves clos ne s'ouvrent plus à la vie habituelle
> il n'est plus qu'un seul fruit,
> le dernier à qui ses enfances encore firent accueil.[42]

Quite often the voluptuous quality of the verse is reinforced by imagery which evokes the Levant. Kahn had, to be sure, spent the years of his military service in northern Africa and the memories of the Arabian civilization he saw there may have left their trace in his poetry. But he was also the poet who had been a student in the Ecole des Langues Orientales, and it would appear that his readings had contributed to lines such as these:

> Les esclaves qui lavent les turbans aux sources inconnues des fleuves
> Les mausolées des ancêtres où stagnèrent les douleurs de veuves
> Mes gazelles et les parures adamantines des ailes
> Qui frôlèrent mes repos près d'elles,
> Au margelles des puits profonds qui s'ignorent en ses yeux inconnus,
> je les oublierai, perdu dans un rêve de bras nus.[43]

By Kahn's preface to his collected poems of 1897 we know that he thought of each poetic line as representing a single impulsion of thought. His long lines gained few adherents among poets, but in 1891 he was recognized as one of the important exponents of free verse. Vielé-Griffin found much to praise in this versification which was so unlike his own, in the unity of the stanzas and in the intuitive and symbolic composition of *Chansons d'amant*.[44] Although Kahn could scarcely have been more conceited than Moréas, he was apparently much more brutal in denouncing the efforts of others and this personal characteristic won him many enemies. Certainly his replies to Huret's questions in 1891 were not models of tact, and the accounts of those who knew him are invariably the portrait of a violent and uncompromising personality.

Much less audacious than Kahn, but still a devotee of free verse, was Albert Mockel of *La Wallonie*. Though his activities were centered about the Belgian literary scene, as the magazine of which he was editor came to have closer and closer contacts with Paris he began to be known in France. Like Edouard

---

42. Gustave Kahn, *Premiers poèmes*, p. 213.
43. *Ibid.*, pp. 177-178.
44. *Entretiens politiques et littéraires*, III (September, 1891), 110-114.

Dujardin, he appears to have come to the conception of free verse through the ideas of synthesis of music and poetry, and his point of departure, like that of Dujardin, was the musical drama of Wagner. Even in 1888 Mockel had begun to preach of "le rythme intérieur" and the restricted use of the alexandrine as a mere stabilizer for multiple eddies of melody.[45] His *Chantefable un peu naïve* of 1891, published anonymously, was his first attempt to place in a book the poetic expression of his ideas. The title "Chantefable" indicates how through prose and poetry he sought to effect a maximum of musical power. The subject matter of his volume is the description of his own emotional life, the joys, affections, and sufferings of a young man, his hesitations and timidities. Among the verses are "symphonic prose poems," the whole work being written with a voluntary artlessness and some archaic constructions. Like Vielé-Griffin and Moréas, he uses traditional refrains from old folk tunes, and he accomplishes musical effects by building poems on only two rhymes: by replacing rhyme with assonance and by alliteration.

With these poets as leading writers of free verse are of course to be counted Henri de Régnier who had published the *Poèmes anciens et romanesques* in 1890, and Edouard Dujardin whose tragedy *Antonia,* written in free meters, was presented in 1891 at the Théâtre d'application. For the moment Moréas appears as a champion of free verse, but already about him is forming the group of Maurras, du Plessys, de la Tailhède, and Raynaud, the school which would attempt to confine poetry in most rigid rules. Other poets in 1891 are only occasionally bold in innovation, but there is a visible effort to vary rhythms and to liberate verse from too narrow rules. Both Stuart Merrill and Ferdinand Herold, in their respective volumes *Les Fastes* and *La Joie de Maguelonne,* use the most exacting of verse forms: the sonnet, the *terza rima,* the *villanelle.* Their quatrains give an appearance of regularity, yet Herold inserted in his volume a few couplets in free verse and used assonance at times instead of rhyme, and Merrill endeavored to give new music to his poetry by mingling at times lines of even and odd syllables:

> Des frôlements de folles étoffes
> Au jeu des bagues d'argent,
> Et l'effroi de somnolentes strophes
> Sur les cordes d'or et d'argent.[46]

The technical matters of versification are treated in almost all critical articles on poetic volumes of 1891, yet one senses that there are more important phenomena which tend to make a fraternity rather than isolated theorists of poets

---

45. See Mockel's article on Fernand Séverin's first volume *Le Lys* (1888). This review appeared in *La Wallonie,* III, 137.

46. Stuart Merrill, *Les Fastes,* p. 59.

in this period. The most important of these is perhaps the alliance of senses, which had been one of Baudelaire's important gifts to later poetry. Even though Ernest Raynaud's *Les Cornes du faune* is entirely in sonnet form, the convergence of sensations of sound and color with visual perception belong to symbolism rather than to the Parnassian school. While the debt to "Correspondances" is not always acknowledged by the poets of the nineties, they are often clearly aware of this synthesis of the senses. Saint-Pol-Roux, writing on Quillard's *La Gloire du verbe* in 1891, expresses this idea in definite terms:

Promptement je répète que les choses doivent être contrôlées et traduites par nos cinq sens. Cette méthode ailleurs étendue, n'est-ce pas la réalisation de la symphonie dans sa plus vaste expansion? Ainsi l'artiste obtient l'œuvre prismatique aux facettes savoureuse-odorante-sonore-visible-tangible; le synthétique bouquet à cinq motifs qu'il parachève et paraphe avec le ruban de son émotion.[47]

Reality transmuted by the emotions is to the poets of the period a necessary part of their artistry. Edouard Dubus finds that although Ajalbert's *Femmes et paysages* is filled with exterior descriptions, at times these become landscapes of the mind for the greater glory of symbolism.[48] The greatest compliment which can be accorded a poet is to call him personal and individualistic. The authors of critical articles in such magazines as *La Plume,* the *Mercure de France, La Revue blanche,* and a little later in *l'Ermitage* were very often poets themselves. This sometimes meant prejudiced judgments but also very keen perception of what was derivative from other writers and what was original. Such a poet as Michel Abadie, whose *Sanglots d'extase* appeared in 1891, was recognized as an able creator of images, but his fellow poets were quick to see how closely he modeled his verse on Raynaud, Merrill, and Verlaine. Raynaud's vocabulary in turn, the mingling of the definite and the indefinite, were noted as in the lineage of Verlaine, and Charles Maurras spoke of Raynaud as the only one who had successfully imitated the author of *Fêtes galantes.* When the impression of debt to one of the recognized ancestors of the symbolists is not too marked, the symbolist critics tend not to be harsh but rather to recognize the validity of such imitative tendency. When it becomes exaggerated, as in the Baudelairian poems of Fernand Clerget's *Les Tourmentés,* the author is usually reminded that he should be original. At times a volume would appear as a kind of parody of another poet, and this was quickly seized upon for caustic comment. Such a volume was Pierre Devoluy's *Flumen,* in which the blind admiration for René Ghil produced lines like the following:

47. *Mercure de France* II (February, 1891), 117–118.
48. *Ibid.* (April, 1891), p. 248.

> Les générations en flottilles compactes
> Voguant vers les Toisons des Futurs fastueux
> Jettent par-dessus bord l'argile des vieux dieux; [49]

Apart from questions of style, the chief complaints of the symbolists against Devoluy and Ghil were concerned with the didactic nature of their verse. For most of the generation of the nineties poetry was an esthetic experience, not a lesson. Very likely the warm reception accorded *Le Pèlerin passionné* at the time of its publication was motivated by the personal note of the volume. But later in the year, with the founding of the Ecole romane and the symptomatic appearance of such poems as Maurice du Plessys' "Dédicace à Apollodore," it became clear that a menace to the intuitive in verse was in progress. Ghil's activity had been isolated, but with the grouping of Raynaud, Raymond de la Tailhède, Maurice du Plessys, and Charles Maurras about Moréas, and the evident intent to make an active campaign that they evinced, a much more powerful poetic force was present.

It is perhaps to be regretted that the Romanist activity began at the very moment when poetry, after excesses, seemed on the point of obtaining some equilibrium in simultaneous portrayal of the external and internal world. Raynaud's articles of 1891 insisted on the necessity of a new school, and Maurice du Plessys announced the advent of Romanism as an inevitable development, but the reasons alleged by them seem inconclusive and specious. Raynaud insists that a pagan incursion was needed since literature was menaced by mysticism.[50] While it is true that poetry among the symbolists had rarely sought its inspiration in mythology, it seemed hardly necessary to make an issue of the myth as opposed to Christian or esoteric backgrounds. Although dramatic poems like Quillard's *La Fille aux mains coupées* and Herold's *La Joie de Maguelonne,* both of which were called "mystères," recall the religious theater of the Middle Ages, a work such as Vielé-Griffin's *Ancæus* found its background in Greece. Raynaud's articles on the new school are not too clear. He speaks of the romantic error, the Parnassian error, and the Symbolist error and says that outside of the Romanists there is no hope for poetry, but one understands with difficulty why he insists that symbolism is gliding into the muddy bogs of Parnassianism. In truth the loyal followers of Moréas seem never to have wished to accept the principles enunciated in the preface

---

49. Concerning Devoluy's admiration for Ghil see *La Revue indépendante,* XXI (October, 1891), 128–133.

50. *Mercure de France,* III, 163–167. Raynaud mentions Barrès, Huysmans, and Bloy as these dangerous forces, and makes no allusion to Jules Bois, V.-E. Michelet, or Péladan. He appears to be thinking of some form of Christian mysticism or, in the case of Huysmans, of satanism rather than the esoteric manifestations of the epoch. Perhaps Paul Adam's pronouncement that the future of literature would be in mysticism served as a point of departure for Raynaud's theories.

of the *Pèlerin passionné* but to legislate and create new refinements of doctrine. This is true with Maurras, who preached against the inspiration of the North and who represented to some readers of 1891 simply a defender of the Félibrean movement of southern France.

A curious year for poetry was 1891. The triumph of symbolism sung at the February banquet and the death knell proclaimed by the Romanists before the passing of many months seem the paradoxical highlights of the period. In truth a new literary chapel had been formed, and while its advent caused much discussion and occasioned useless debate the influence was not by any means decisive. The mysticism so dreaded by Raynaud, the Wagnerianism against which Maurras spoke, continued to be poetic elements, enriched, it is true, by the re-entry of Greek and Roman myth. Nature, as an important part of lyric inspiration, was already heard in the work of Vielé-Griffin, and Henri de Régnier by this time represented a broader appreciation of Parnassian artistry. The importance of 1891 in the history of symbolism is that by that date all its inherent elements had been presented. In form, the double acceptance of free verse and syllabic count was present; rhyme and assonance or even blank verse had all received their consecration in print. The idealism, the suggestion, the synthesis of the senses, the indirect statement of the emotions, the use of symbol to express the emotions had all been amply demonstrated. The efforts to find new musical effects had been multiple and, if not always successful, had indicated most of the possible paths to follow.

HORIZONS, 1892

THE FORMATION of poets into small groups under the leadership of one writer, accomplished in 1891 by the Ecole romane, immediately inspired others to emulation. For a moment Charles Morice considered the formation of an "Ecole française," [1] but quickly found that those whom he had imagined as satellites desired to remain independent. The idea of the literary school was subjected to direct attack by Adolphe Retté in an article entitled "Ecoles"; [2] the author advised both Moréas and Morice to accomplish their work as artists instead of yielding to personal ambition. Alfred Vallette was too canny to make his periodical the organ of the Ecole romane and during 1892 only one article and one poem represent the group. [3] Léon Deschamps and *La Plume* much more openly espoused the cause of the Romanists, not only by critical articles, [4] but by publication of their verse in impressive type on the first page of several issues and by referring to Moréas as the revered leader of the new poetic trend.

The month of January, 1892, saw the founding of a new periodical by a twenty-year-old poet from Aix-en-Provence. Emmanuel Signoret is a curious figure, seen by most of his contemporaries as a kind of megalomaniac, but a talented one. Perhaps today he would be altogether forgotten if André Gide had not written such a laudatory preface for the posthumous volume of his collected verse in 1908. Signoret wished to group the collaborators of his magazine, the *Saint-Graal,* as idealists and dwellers in the world of dream. He tried to bring together those poets who had written religious verse, those who were from his own town (Paul Souchon and Joachim Gasquet), the Romanists, and those lyricists who represented the realm of the unreal (Maeterlinck, Merrill, and Retté). Signoret envisioned a blending of pagan and Christian inspiration in poetry:

> Les antiques héros, par nous ressuscités
> Devant lesquels les champs pleuraient leurs moissons mortes,

1. See *Mercure de France,* V (May, 1892), 6–7.
2. *La Plume,* No. 68 (February 15, 1892), pp. 85–87.
3. The *Mercure* printed W. G. C. Byvanck's interview with Moréas. These pages were a portion of the forthcoming volume, *Un Hollandais à Paris en 1891.* The poem was by Ernest Raynaud, "Consolation à Maurice du Plessys."
4. Moréas wrote an "Eloge de Maurice du Plessys" (No. 70, pp. 129–131). Marcel Coulon's review of *Le Premier Livre pastoral* was dithyrambic (No. 87, pp. 511–512).

Les Nymphes qui portaient en leurs yeux des étés,
Forment au Christ-Jésus de splendides escortes.[5]

While Signoret admired most of the forerunners of symbolism, his especial admiration was for Paul Verlaine. In honor of him he wrote an ode in 1892,[6] and for him he published by subscription the *Liturgies intimes*[7] the same year. Verlaine made seven contributions to the *Saint-Graal*, and Louis le Cardonnel, who was subeditor of the periodical in 1892, published several poems.[8] Charles Morice, one of the companions of Signoret and Le Cardonnel, was also a collaborator. But the *Saint-Graal* never was more than a precarious venture. Signoret, always enthusiastic and in a kind of poetic trance according to those who knew him, was more rich in grandiose ideas than money. Soon he returned to the South and there published from time to time issues of the periodical until his death in 1900.[9]

The staffs of several periodicals in 1892 were filled by a number of critics favorable to the symbolists. Remy de Gourmont wrote a weekly literary column for *La Petite République française*, reviewing in his first article Tailhade's *Vitraux* and Retté's *Thulé des brumes*. Gustave Kahn was entrusted with literary criticism for *La Société nouvelle*.[10] Retté became poetic critic for *L'Ermitage*, which during the year began to assume new importance as an organ for lyric expression, publishing poems by Régnier, le Cardonnel, Merrill, and Retté. Thanks to Albert Saint-Paul, the magazine was able to present some texts and translations from Stefan George's *Pilgerfahrten*, and the readers were informed of the German group which held in such high regard the genius of Baudelaire, Verlaine, and Mallarmé and which was shortly to found the *Blätter für die Kunst*. In Belgium *La Wallonie*, which had announced that it would cease publication at the end of the year, *La Jeune Belgique*, and a newly founded magazine of Liége, *Floréal*, had as more or less regular poetic contributors Vielé-Griffin, Henri de Régnier, Gustave Kahn, and Ferdinand Herold. The *Revue blanche*, in addition to its earlier favorite poets, Romain Coolus and Claude Céhel, gave ample space to the French symbolists, among them Régnier, Mallarmé, Camille Mauclair, Herold, Moréas, and Saint-Pol-Roux. Remy de Gourmont composed an essay,

5. Emmanuel Signoret, *Poésies complètes*, p. 46.

6. First published in *Le Saint-Graal*, March 20, 1892.

7. This first edition of *Liturgies intimes* was a pamphlet of thirty-one pages. The second edition, published by Vanier, was somewhat enlarged.

8. Bibliographical data on Louis le Cardonnel's contributions to *Le Saint-Graal* are to be found in Noël Richard's valuable and complete study of the poet.

9. Eight issues, one a double number, of the *Saint-Graal* appeared during 1892. In later years the issues, intermittently published, often contained only the writings of Signoret.

10. Louis de Saint-Jacques in *Le Passant*, Paul Redonnel in *Chimère*, and Yvanhoé Rambosson in *Revue de la littérature moderne* were also critics favorable to the symbolist school.

"Le Symbolisme," for the magazine and Lucien Muhlfeld reviewed the current volumes of poetry.

Two other types of magazines, not primarily literary, also had a part in the publicity given to poetry in 1892. These were the anarchistic and esoteric periodicals. Their editors felt a kind of communion with the idealists, who suffered from the realities of the world and who were the devotees of the mysterious. These two elements, idealism and mystery, were sufficient to ally the symbolists with Jean Grave of *La Révolte* and Zo d'Axa of *L'En-Dehors* with Papus of *L'Initiation* and Alber Jhouney of *L'Etoile*. A great number of the poets were quite willing to accept as a principle the creed that authority and property had brought out the cruel instincts of mankind; the whole basis of symbolism was in the revelation of the hidden and unfathomable. *La Révolte* had its literary supplement; in the June issue of *Initiation* Tailhade published an essay on Dubus' *Quand les violons sont partis*. *La Plume* devoted an issue to "La Magie" with Papus as guest editor; Paul Fort presented Jules Bois's *Les Noces de Sathan,* which bore the subtitle of "drame esotérique." Some of the collaborators of *La Plume,* the *Mercure de France,* or the *Entretiens politiques et littéraires* wrote articles against governmental control; a few of the poets, among them Edouard Dubus, frequented Stanislas de Guaita.[11]

But the essence of the symbolist doctrine of 1892 is to be found not in the dogma of anarchism, nor in the arcana of the esoteric, but in a broad and generous enunciation of faith in beauty and idealism. The utterance, egotistical however sincere, of René Ghil or of Jean Moréas yields to a more general conception of art. Saint-Pol-Roux in "De l'art magnifique," [12] André Gide in "Le Traité du Narcisse," [13] Stuart Merrill in his "Credo" [14] all seek not aggrandizement of themselves but a deeper understanding of the poetic currents of their epoch. Saint-Pol-Roux, proclaiming the absolute beauty and truth which are the goals of the artist, denies that he wishes to form a poetic school. He makes an indirect attack on Ghil and Moréas by stating that the

11. The alliance of anarchy and the generation of the symbolists was to be much more evident in 1893, although in the *Entretiens politiques et littéraires* of 1892 there are many expressions of sympathy with Grave and Zo d'Axa. In the same magazine Quillard suggested that anarchy could be better accomplished by literary works than by throwing bombs. Kropotkine's *La Conquête du pain* appeared in translation in 1892, which is also the year of several explosions, the execution of Ravachol, and numerous arrests of anarchists. The anarchistic newspaper *L'En-Dehors* counted among its contributors Bernard Lazare, Ferdinand Herold, Emile Verhaeren, and Pierre Quillard, but the examples of humanitarian poetry are not numerous at this time. One can tell from the numerous articles published in the little magazines that the intellectual life of the symbolists extended to consideration of occultism and absence of governmental constraint. Vielé-Griffin described his campaign for free verse as anarchism in literature.

12. *Mercure de France,* IV (February, 1892), 97–104.

13. *Entretiens politiques et littéraires,* IV (January, 1892), 20–28.

14. Quoted in *Les Hommes d'aujourd'hui: Stuart Merrill* (1892). Henri de Régnier wrote this biography of Merrill.

meaning of the poetic epoch in which he is living cannot be derived from the principles of Helmholtz or from Greco-Latin tradition. His message is that in order to make art magnificent, the world of the senses and of the individual must be raised to the realm of the absolute and universal.

Gide, like Roux, is concerned with the change which reality undergoes in becoming poetic. In his article, the poet becomes Narcissus gazing at the reflection of the world and of himself in the waters. The image of realities suggests the dream of paradise; the mirrored face evokes the enigma of human emotions. Each thing contains the symbolic meaning of a higher truth and it is this truth that the poet, or Narcissus, is seeking to comprehend. Much of what Gide says is stated in the brief article of belief in which Merrill asserts his faith in poetry and in the poet's gift of creating perfection from the imperfect phenomena he sees about him. Merrill believes that realism and naturalism are not poetic since they allow the writer to be dominated by the exterior form. The symbolist poet is, on the contrary, able to choose from what he observes only those elements which convey truth and beauty.

At the time when Gide, Roux, and Merrill were announcing their poetic creeds, there appeared in the *National Observer* [15] an important article by Stéphane Mallarmé. Entitled "Vers et musique en France," this essay was soon reprinted in France. [16] Although Mallarmé inserted in it his belief that music and suggestion rather than the vain names of poetic schools are the important elements in current verse, he chiefly examined the transformation in prosody that had taken place after the death of Victor Hugo. Since the article was written for publication in an English periodical, Mallarmé adopted a more simple style than was his wont and documented it with the names of those he considered most important in the evolution of free verse. He suggested the part played by Verlaine, Régnier, Kahn, Moréas, Laforgue, and Vielé-Griffin, and mentioned the names of Morice, Mockel, Verhaeren, Maeterlinck, and Dujardin. Of Rimbaud he said nothing.

In this same essay Mallarmé expressed the opinion that the alexandrine would remain to voice solemn and serious subjects, but he openly approved the liberty which would enable each poet to give individual melody to his thought. An opposite view was expressed by Sully-Prudhomme, at the same time, in a book entitled *Réflexions sur l'art des vers*. Essentially the volume was a long appeal for a return to the traditional laws of French prosody. The author expresses the hope that innovators may be led to see that the formulas given by Théodore de Banville and the liberties taken by Victor Hugo represent the reasonable limits of French versification. Vielé-Griffin, who was the

15. On March 26, 1892.
16. *Entretiens politiques et littéraires*, IV (June, 1892), 237–241.

principal apologist of free verse, wrote an article,[17] deriding the formulas and rules established by Sully-Prudhomme; the *Mercure de France* did not deign to speak of the book.

At this time Léon Deschamps made a successful contribution to friendly relations between the older and younger generations of writers by inaugurating a series of banquets. During 1892 these were presided over by Aurélien Scholl, Zola, Coppée, Claretie, and Auguste Vacquerie. Each of these men of letters made friendly and not overly condescending speeches to a public which had been more hostile than approving during the past decade. The final banquet of the year was to have as chairman Leconte de Lisle, but at the last minute he sent his regrets suggesting Mallarmé to replace him. *La Plume* began in 1892 a campaign to honor the memory of Baudelaire by a monument, named Leconte de Lisle as honorary chairman of the committee (on the recommendation of Mallarmé who had first been approached), and created an executive group which contained the names of those who had been presidents of the banquets and a representative list of the young writers. By the end of the year nearly three thousand francs had been collected, the published lists of contributors revealing a large number of Belgian admirers of the poet. Frequent comment occurred in the little magazines on Brunetière's hostility to Baudelaire's art,[18] the name of Henri Fouquier was still anathema to the symbolists, but a much more amicable spirit is evident toward other older writers.

Echoes of a new literary group in England reached France through the pages of the *Mercure de France* in 1892. They Rhymers' Club, two of whose members were to be influential in revealing French symbolism in England, was described in a short article and examples of poetry by ten of the members given in English text and translation.[19] Meanwhile in the June issue of the *National Review*, Arthur Symons published a sympathetic study of Paul Verlaine. During 1892 the *National Observer* printed not only Mallarmé's "Vers et musique en France" but his "Solennités," "Etalages," "Tennyson vu d'ici," [20] and "Théodore de Banville." These are some of the bonds which helped in establishing the fame of Mallarmé and Verlaine abroad and prepared the way for the lecture tours of both French writers in England.

La Wallonie, with its three editors, Mockel, Olin, and Henri de Régnier, made of its last year of existence a brilliant example of close relations between

---

17. *Ibid.* (May, 1892), pp. 215–220.

18. *Revue des deux mondes*, CXIII (September 1, 1892), 212–224.

19. Signed "The Pilgrim," the translations of these poems are supposed to be the work of Remy de Gourmont. The translation of Ernest Dowson's "Carmelite Nuns of the Perpetual Adoration" is very badly done.

20. Reprinted in *La Revue blanche*, III (December, 1892), 329–333.

French and Belgian poetry. Régnier contributed his dramatic poem "La Gardienne" to the first issue of 1892 and during the course of the year wrote critical reviews of Vielé-Griffin's *Les Cygnes,* Louÿs' *Astarté,* and Gide's *Les Poésies d'André Walter.* The three young men who had been the most active in founding the poetic periodical *La Conque,* Gide, Louÿs, and Valéry, also were contributors to *La Wallonie* during 1892. Verhaeren continued to be the magazine's chief glory; Maeterlinck and André Fontainas each contributed two poems during 1892. Since *La Wallonie* had announced in January that it would cease publication at the end of the year, some of its younger collaborators decided to carry on its tradition with *Floréal.* Paul Gérardy, whose *Chansons naïves* were published in 1892, became one of the editors. Through him relations were established with the group of Stefan George. Translations of Gérardy's poems appeared in the first number of the *Blätter für die Kunst,* and George became a contributor to *Floréal.*[21]

Walt Whitman's death in January, 1892, brought again into the periodicals the name of the poet who had often been called one of the inspirers of the French free-verse movement. Vielé-Griffin published a translation of Whitman's autobiography,[22] while a study by Havelock Ellis of the American poet appeared in the June issue of *L'Ermitage.* In the *Mercure de France* a series of Poe's essays continued the cult begun by Baudelaire and Mallarmé. Among foreign authors, the name of Ibsen was perhaps the most frequent in the little magazines, some of Edouard Tissot's translations appearing in the *Mercure de France* and a complete translation of the *Pillars of Society* in *La Revue indépendante.* Despite many realistic elements in the great Norwegian's dramas, the symbolists claimed him for their own, approving the use of symbolic representation which gives poetry to Ibsen's ideas.

The death of several French writers during 1892 offers curious insight into the favoritism and lack of literary perspective which often accompany judgments in periodicals. When Albert Aurier, one of the founders of the *Mercure de France,* died on October 5, 1892, the magazine announced the event as a great loss to French literature and immediately began plans for publishing the young author's work posthumously. Aurier's death came only a few days after that of Ernest Renan, but to the memory of the latter writer the *Mercure* paid only the dubious homage of reprinting a hostile article by Ernest Hello which had been published in 1863. Léon Bloy had sent this article to Vallette with a letter in which he spoke of Renan as "le Dieu des lâches qu'on vient d'enterrer, avec équité, comme une vieille vache pourrie." [23] The obituary

21. See the issues of September, 1892, and February 15, 1893.

22. In the *Entretiens politiques et littéraires,* IV (April, 1892), 166–169.

23. Bloy's letter is printed as a footnote to Hello's article in the *Mercure de France,* VI (November, 1892), 260.

remark in *La Plume* was somewhat less harsh; Renan was designated as "éminent prosateur mais détestable philosophe." The magazine, however, reserved its tears and admiration for Léon Cladel, to whose memory it devoted an entire issue, even as did the *Mercure de France* to that of Aurier. The *Entretiens politiques et littéraires* continued during 1892 its pious task of publishing the posthumous work of Laforgue: scattered notes, "Pierrot fumiste," and a few poems. Rimbaud's death inspired no critical articles, although Isabelle Rimbaud's protest against Ernest Delahaye's uncomplimentary biographical essays [24] was reprinted by *La Plume* and the *Mercure de France*. Even the Vanier edition of the *Illuminations,* containing both the prose and the poems of 1872, as had the earlier edition of *La Vogue,* elicited little comment. Lucien Muhlfeld, writing in *La Revue blanche,* admits the prestige enjoyed by Rimbaud among current authors, but speaks of "la faiblesse" and "la jeunesse d'exécution" of *Les Illuminations.* Nor was Rimbaud's death, as had been that of Laforgue, followed by the discovery of unpublished works. Only a portion of the poem "Mémoire" was unearthed by *L'Ermitage,*[25] and it was not until the publication of the *Poésies complètes,* in 1895, that further revelation of Rimbaud's writings was accomplished.

Of the volumes of verse published in 1892, three excited most praise and comment in the little magazines. These are Henri de Régnier's *Tel qu'en songe,* Vielé-Griffin's *Les Cygnes,*[26] and *Quand les violons sont partis* by Edouard Dubus. The first two are largely in free verse, but Dubus remained a staunch advocate of traditional metrical form. The sole unifying elements in the three collections are the symbolic expression of the idea, the idealism of the authors, and the dreamlike quality of the poetic settings. Régnier, to celebrate his ideals, his disillusionments, his sorrows, chooses the figure of a proud young knight who is vanquished in a forest, the crumbling stones of a castle, the return of a wearied warrior to his home. Vielé-Griffin, in addition to the two poems of *Diptyque* which are reprinted in the volume, proclaims his search of beauty in a series of songs to the emblematic figure of Helen. Dubus, to describe his love of a beguiling but somewhat cruel woman, creates the image of a Circe-like enchantress.

Most of the critics agreed that Régnier was more successful than Vielé-Griffin in the use of free verse. Many admired the unity of his volume, where three half-legendary, half-dramatic poems are separated by meditations on hopes, despairs, memories, and oblivion. Extremely successful in creating evocative imagery to represent his ideas, Régnier has by 1892 often modified

24. The article signed "M.D." in the December, 1891, issue of the *Entretiens politiques et littéraires.*
25. Published in September, 1892.
26. Not to be confused with Vielé-Griffin's first volume which also bore the same title.

the bejeweled settings of his earlier volumes for a simpler, more direct kind of expression. Thus he describes his palace of memories:

> Dans le silence du vieux et mélancolique logis,
> De salle en salle et d'heure en heure,
> Erre, sourit et pleure
> Le Souvenir avec sa face de jadis
> Et ses sandales
> Muettes auprès de quelqu'un qui dort; [27]

The land to which he invites his soul to come for melancholy contemplation and remorse is in much the same way a blend of the visual and symbolic worlds:

> Je sais de tristes eaux en qui meurent les soirs;
> Des fleurs que nul n'y cueille y tombent une à une,
> Je connais d'antiques miroirs
> Habitués à des faces de taciturne
> Qui viennent s'y songer autres du fond des soirs.[28]

The rhythm, the tone, the imagery of Régnier's free verse bear little resemblance to the poetry of Vielé-Griffin. This was one of the proud contentions of those who preached liberation from syllabic count: that each poet could sing fully the melody of his own mind and that lyric individuality would thus be assured. Régnier's verse gives the impression of careful workmanship, of usage in diction and word order on a purely poetic plane. Vielé-Griffin suggests, on the contrary, the spontaneous utterance of the mind, a lyric form much nearer to the spoken language. He describes his journey in search of beauty in natural, if more superficial, terms:

> Sans doute,
> Le chant des pinsons,
> De bosquet en bosquet, disait la route
> Où nous passions,
> De chansons en chansons,
> Mes rêves et moi, guidés
> Selon l'heure et l'Age
> —Bel attelage!—
> Un double joug enguirlandant leur tête
> Et de pourpre violette bridés,
> Qui traînaient notre char vers des rumeurs de fête! [29]

27. Henri de Régnier, *Poèmes, 1887–1892*, p. 213.
28. *Ibid.*, p. 174.
29. Francis Vielé-Griffin: *Poèmes et poésies*, p. 236.

In contrast with the free rhythms of *Les Cygnes* and *Tel qu'en songe* are the regular lines of *Quand les violons sont partis*. Dubus, who had been one of the principal figures in the poetic quarrels of 1886 and whose verse had so frequently appeared in *Le Scapin* in that year, represents the survival of the poetic forces present at the beginning of the symbolist movement rather than new pathways of lyric expression. That he had a sense of musical effects was undeniable, but his settings recalled rather too imperiously those of the Verlaine of *Fêtes galantes,* and his attitude toward life and the emotions was somewhat too closely modeled on that of Baudelaire. This was to be Dubus' single volume of verse, for, too zealous in search of "paradis artificiels," he was to die from an overdose of a drug in the summer of 1895. Like Aurier, he was considered by his generation to possess considerable talent; like Aurier, the complex tone of irony, bitterness, melancholy, and tenderness that is to be found in the extant work of Dubus gives promise of certain richnesses of poetic expression. The oblivion in which he disappeared is largely occasioned by the constant impression of imitation of Verlaine or of Baudelaire, but the reading of his poetry confirms the impression of beauty, melody, and high idealism which won him passing admiration:

> Tu m'apparus un soir d'hiver mélancolique:
> Envahi par la nuit sinistre, l'occident
> Evoquait ces lointains de vieille basilique
> Où s'érige en splendeur le maître-autel ardent;
> Tu m'apparus un soir d'hiver mélancolique.[30]

The poetry of Dubus recalls by its regular form, its evocations of melancholy, and the dreamy atmosphere which it creates, the verse of Samain. In 1892 Samain, modest and retiring, had not yet published a volume of verse, but thanks to the periodicals which had sprung up, and particularly the *Mercure de France,* he continued publishing from time to time the nostalgic dreams which had first appeared in *Le Scapin* and *Le Chat noir.* Perhaps of all his generation he kept longest that twilight, timeless, and utopian landscape which poets of 1886, in their revolt against exterior descriptive detail, had established:

> Pourquoi nos soirs d'amour n'ont-ils toute douceur
> Que si l'âme trop pleine en lourds sanglots s'y brise?
> La tristesse nous hante avec sa robe grise
> Et vit à nos côtés comme une grande sœur.[31]

Samain's tardy publication of verse in volume form place him, in so far as critical articles on his work are concerned, with a much younger generation

30. Edouard Dubus, *Poésies complètes*, p. 7.
31. *Mercure de France*, IV (January, 1892), 24.

of poets. He was born in 1858, two years before Jules Laforgue, a year before Gustave Kahn. All the generation of the early 1860's—Saint-Pol-Roux, Morice, Dujardin, Ghil, Maeterlinck, Merrill, Retté, Quillard, Raynaud, Henri de Régnier, Dubus, and Vielé-Griffin—were his juniors, but all had been much more active than the timid employee of the city hall of Paris in gaining publicity and in making a career of literature.

The victory of this active group of symbolists was not complete; the conservative and older periodicals still remained closed to them. Yet they had created their own circle and it was a constantly expanding one. They had made a place for the literature which defied reality and declamation. As an example of a work which represents a dubious extreme in symbolist art and yet which excited much favorable comment, one might select Retté's *Thulé des brumes*. This volume of poetic prose was put on sale by the Bibliothèque artistique et littéraire late in December, 1891. In many ways the work represented all that the conservatives called decadent, for it was presented as a series of visions, inspired perhaps by hashish, and its style combined the usual artifices of the prose poem with vocabulary and alliterative effects which properly would seem to belong to the realm of poetry. Later Retté himself was astonished at the extremes to which he had gone,[32] yet the work was treated with interest and respect by many critics during 1892. At least it was not greeted by silence; Maurras in *L'Ermitage*, Lazare in the *Entretiens politiques et littéraires*, Merrill in *La Plume*, Muhlfeld in *La Revue blanche*, Dubus in the *Mercure de France*, all discussed the volume. In Belgium *La Wallonie, L'Art moderne*, and *La Jeune Belgique* included *Thulé des brumes* in their bibliographical notices. In England it obtained attention in the *Saturday Review*. In the provincial periodicals of France the work was likewise given publicity; Louis de Saint-Jacques praised *Thulé des brumes* in *Le Passant* of Marseilles, and Paul Redonnel wrote an enthusiastic article in the *Chimère* of Montpellier. In Paris Remy de Gourmont, Camille Mauclair, and Camille de Sainte-Croix wrote criticisms in which Retté was called a writer of talent. On the other hand, in the *Annales politiques et littéraires* appeared a harsh criticism by Brisson.

When one considers that *Thulé des brumes* was only the second volume of Retté, that the edition did not exceed three hundred twelve copies, and that the subject matter of the work was a series of hallucinatory visions, one can evaluate some of the strength that the intuitive writers had gained. A few years before 1892 it is quite doubtful whether such a work would have met more than disapproving silence or at the most scornful dismissal. It is true that Retté was in 1892 the poetry critic for *L'Ermitage* and had played some part in the foundation of a few ephemeral periodicals, but the attention given him

32. Adolphe Retté, *Le Symbolisme*, pp. 118–119.

stems also from a kind of unity among those of his generation who were preaching a new art form. Through the quarrels and jealousies can be seen another influence, the supremacy of the dream world, which brought together divergent personalities and made for unified action.

It is true that certain poets and indeed certain periodicals represented dominant trends of a more particular nature. The *Entretiens politiques et littéraires* exemplify the preoccupation with free verse and at no time more definitely than in 1892, when the magazine inaugurated a series of "Lectures poétiques." The published poems included "La Mort" by Verhaeren, "La Chevauchée d'Yeldis" by Vielé-Griffin, "Pour l'Ami" by J.-Marius André, and "Proses lyriques" by Claude Debussy, all of which present metrical freedom.[33] On the contrary, in the *Mercure de France* syllabic count and regular stanza form continue to reign supreme. There the free verse of André Fontainas' "Epilogue" and Ferdinand Herold's "La Belle au bois dormant" are exceptions. The preferred poets of the magazine, Aurier, Jean Court, Louis Denise, Ernest Raynaud, Albert Samain, and Saint-Pol-Roux respected syllabic count, not even using the "apocope" which Moréas and Maurice du Plessys were preaching.[34] Though the imagery in most of the poetry is that indeterminate and suggestive vision which sets the symbolists apart, there are evidences of a much more concrete poetic presentation. Four of Heredia's sonnets, inspired by lines from Catullus, and two series of poems by Ferdinand Herold, "Le Livre des Reines" and "Vitrail des Saintes," published during 1892 in the *Mercure de France,* appear to renew the Parnassian tradition of plasticity. Vallette's refusal to enroll his magazine as the official organ of a school of poetry was on the whole more beneficial to lyric art than the obvious preference accorded to Moréas by *La Plume*. Even the *Mercure*'s policy of having only a select group of contributors made for a better magazine; the *Plume* prided itself on the large numbers of unknown poets whose work it printed, but many of these lyrics were of dubious quality, and almost invariably the contributors to the occasional "Supplément poétique" were names which never gained even a small claim to literary fame.

In 1892 the mainstays of poetry in these magazines were principally the group, roughly around thirty years old, who had taken part in the stormy beginnings of the movement, together with the relatively small number of slightly older poets, in their middle or late thirties, who still remained as forces in lyric art. The most productive of this more mature group was perhaps Emile Verhaeren, by 1892 the author of seven volumes of poetry, but whose fame in France was to come only after the *Mercure de France* began republishing

---

33. Even the selection of unpublished poems by Laforgue contains some metrical peculiarities.

34. Raynaud wrote articles in which he defended the suppression of the mute *e*, but his published poetry reveals fidelity to its pronunciation.

his work in 1895. Moréas, who was thirty-six years old in 1892, had succeeded in grouping together some writers ranging in age from twenty-four-year-old Charles Maurras to Ernest Raynaud and Maurice du Plessys, who were twenty-eight. Ghil, thirty years of age, was pursuing his story of the human race and had reached the first volume of *Le Vœu de vivre*, in which he preached the destructive elements in society for the family unit. A new edition of his *Traité du verbe*, under the title of *En méthode à l'œuvre*, continued the promulgation of his theories, admired by only a few obscure authors such as Pierre Devoluy, Mario Varvara, and Jean Philibert.[35] The strength of the symbolists was mainly in those poets not quite thirty years of age and who were publishing actively: Merrill, Retté, Dubus, Régnier, Vielé-Griffin, Herold, and Fontainas.

But there were indications of a younger group of poets among whom were enough vitality and talent to give new orientation to art forms. During 1891 the most interesting manifestation of the newcomers had been Pierre Louÿs' *La Conque*. In it Valéry printed almost the complete production of his verse before the "sincère et durable éloignement" which was to last so many years.[36] But other collaborators of *La Conque* put their poetry into book form during 1892. Louÿs, with his volume *Astarté*, Gide with the *Poésies d'André Walter*, Henry Bérenger with his unsuccessful *L'Ame moderne*, and Eugène Hollande with a volume of poetry called *Beauté*, all of whom had appeared in *La Conque*, received attention from the symbolist critics. Bérenger and Hollande fared badly, the first partly because he sought for inspiration in the material things about him, and the latter because of the didactic and impersonal presentation of his cult for beauty. But the strange and exotic images of Pierre Louÿs and the ironic meditations of Gide were commended.

A periodical of Montpellier called *Chimère*, of which Paul Redonnel was the managing editor, enjoyed some prominence in Paris during the year and a half of its publication, from August, 1891, to January, 1893. Redonnel had been on the staff of *La Plume* before going to the South and had formed many

---

35. Ghil found, for a short time, a champion in Emmanuel Delbousquet, who founded a magazine, *Essais des jeunes*, in Toulouse. Seven issues appeared in 1892. When the magazine was revised in December, 1894, the editors declared that they no longer believed in the "Ecole évolutive."

36. Valéry's publications during the period 1890–92 are often in obscure places. The sonnet "Le Jeune Prêtre," before it was printed in *La Conque*, had been sent to a contest of *La Plume*. "Hélène, la reine triste" appeared in *La Conque* and, with the signature "M. Doris," in *Chimère*. Four of Valéry's poems were printed in *La Syrinx* of Aix-en-Provence during 1892. Some prose fragments, "Purs drames" in the *Entretiens politiques et littéraires* of March, 1892, "Glose sur quelques peintures" in *Chimère* of the same month, and a review of Redonnel's *Liminaires*, in the *Moniteur judiciaire du Midi* in 1891, also belong to this period.

acquaintanceships with the poets of the capital.[37] Thus in the magazine appeared verse by many of the older generation of symbolists: Verlaine, Dubus, Ghil, Merrill, le Cardonnel, as well as by younger writers such as Abadie, Gasquet, Tristan Klingsor, Mauclair, Signoret, André, and Valéry. Another little magazine of the provinces, *La Syrinx,* published at Aix-en-Provence by Joachim Gasquet, contained poetic offerings of considerable interest. Contributors to the publication included Maurras, Valéry, Marius André, Mauclair, Louÿs, Tristan Klingsor, and Souchon, some of whom had represented a temporary group formed around Signoret's *Saint-Graal.* An astonishing number of poets in these regional publications quickly gained a place in the literary life of Paris; Souchon had already published poetry in *La Plume* in 1891 and Tristan Klingsor appeared in the *Mercure de France* in 1892. Mauclair, a Parisian, is on the contrary a contributor to many provincial periodicals. New and important figures appear to be those of Gide and Louÿs, both of whom contributed to the March, 1892, issue of *Floréal.* A whole sequence of admiration and influence is revealed by Valéry's "Narcisse parle," published in the first issue of *La Conque,* Gide's "Traité du Narcisse," in the *Entretiens politiques et littéraires,* and Mauclair's poem "Narcisse," [38] dedicated to Gide.

The Théâtre d'art was not very active during 1892, its chief contribution being the February performance of Van Lerberghe's *Les Flaireurs.* During the summer of 1892 the Théâtre moderne offered the second part of Dujardin's trilogy *Antonia.* Entitled *Le Chevalier du passé,* written in free verse and peopled with abstract personages, this play was considered an example of symbolist drama. It was not a success. The poetry was judged unharmonious, the modern costumes were said to be at variance with the unreal plot, and the action of the play provoked some hilarity in the audience. Dujardin's mistake was in a way comparable to that of Bérenger in *L'Ame moderne.* He attempted to place realistic details on an idealistic plane. His heroine, Antonia, has become a prostitute after the death of her lover; disgusted with her dissolute life, she evokes the dead man's ghost, listens to his counsel, and decides to change her way of life. The great contribution to symbolist drama, though not performed in 1892, was Maeterlinck's *Pelléas et Mélisande,* in which were no clashes of the ideal and real.

Yet it was precisely the alliance of the material and the ideal which Saint-Pol-Roux was preaching at this time and which he thought to discern in the young writers.

37. Redonnel's volume of verse, *Liminaires,* had been published in 1891. Not very original in theme or form, it attracted favorable comment and measured praise in many of the little magazines. Deschamps in *La Plume,* Bonnamour in *La Revue indépendante,* Rambosson in *L'Ermitage,* and Raynaud in the *Mercure de France* were among those who reviewed the book.
38. *La Revue blanche,* III (July, 1892), 43–46.

Prévenus contre l'extrême mystique de l'idéalisme et contre l'extrême athée du réalisme, ces jeunes esprits viennent délibérément à l'Idéoréalisme, présomptif étincelant et salutaire des deux confessions ennemies.[39]

His viewpoint, if not taken too literally, does appear to have some meaning, for among the younger poets was a trend away from the vague and vapory landscape toward greater vitality and concreteness. Gide, with the importance accorded the myth, Louÿs, with his exotic but exact visual effects, the clarity of Signoret, Gasquet, and Souchon indicate a trend toward such an alliance as that foreseen by Roux. Even the young and dreamy Wagnerian who adopted the name of Tristan Klingsor was conscious of an evolutionary aspect in the verse of his contemporaries, observing that the "malaise qui pesait sur l'âme malade des poètes aînés" [40] seemed no longer to have power over the younger writers.

39. *Mercure de France,* V (June, 1892), 156.
40. *Chimère,* No. 13 (August–September, 1892), p. 31.

Chapter XI: CONSOLIDATIONS OF POSITIONS, 1893–94

THE YEARS 1893–94 chiefly present the consummation of several poetic currents which had been in incipient form during 1892. Moréas, wishing to give his *Pèlerin passionné* a unified tone in keeping with his Romanist theories, revised the volume, suppressing the verse which represented his earlier manner and adding several new poems. The excluded items were not disavowed by their author but published separately in a little volume under the title *Autant en emporte le vent.* *La Plume,* through its editor Deschamps, continued to glorify the Ecole romane but did keep among its contributors such a determined enemy of Romanism as was Adolphe Retté [1] and did permit dissenting opinions to be published. Moréas found another ardent champion in Hugues Rebell, whose article on poetry, published in the September, 1893, issue of *L'Ermitage,* was both an attack against symbolism and a eulogy of Romanism.

Rebell's reproaches against symbolist verse are understandable. He is wearied of the eternal, unreal, dream garden which is the setting of so much verse of the period. He is equally satiated with the peacocks, swans, lilies, and floating perfumes, with the princesses and knights errant, with the overadornment of gems and the lushness of vocabulary. It is curious that having seen the dangers of imitation he should counsel following Moréas as a model. Maurice du Plessys, Ernest Raynaud, and Raymond de la Tailhède had already shown that the inspiration of Moréas produced only the most barren of results, poems in which the essential ingredients seemed to be the poet bearing the name of a classical shepherd, the presence of a flute or reed pipe to indicate his art, invocations to Apollo or the Muses, and much mutual bestowing of laurels. Among Moréas' followers, Raynaud perhaps remained the most personal in his themes, but adopting old words and spellings and turns of expression which represent several centuries of French verse, he often succeeded in producing only a kind of anachronistic parody. Such is the case in one of the "Elégies," published during 1893 in the *Mercure de France,* where the poet's description of a disdainful lady presents several of the peculiarities in word order, diction, and rhythm which mark Romanist verse:

1. Retté's article "Le Vers libre," published in July, 1893, in the *Mercure de France* was a summons to each poet to avoid all schools of poetry, all tradition, and endeavor to express only the sincere and individual rhythm of his own mind (*Mercure de France,* VIII, 203–210).

Doulce on la nommerait, n'éstoit qu'aux chalemies
Que j'embouche à son los, elle fait l'endormie,
Et que mes chants n'ont pu, malgré ce que mon cœur
Leur prêtait d'éloquence, entamer sa rigueur.[2]

Of especial interest in this period is the attitude of the young generation
toward the Parnassians and even the romanticists. *La Plume* continued its
literary banquets, with Mallarmé, Verlaine, Francis Magnard, José-Maria de
Heredia, and Rodin presiding during 1893. On June 17 of that same year some
of the young writers organized a dinner to honor the memory of Victor Hugo
and the publication of the last volume of *Toute la lyre.* Although the idea
of the banquet seems to have been inspired partly because Jean Carrère, Stuart
Merrill, Vielé-Griffin, and Pierre Louÿs saw in Hugo the champion of the
oppressed and the apostle of liberty, these same writers expressed in verse the
eulogy of the dead poet's literary genius.

The publication, at long last, of Heredia's *Les Trophées* and the death of
Leconte de Lisle in 1894 brought into publicity the names of two great Parnassians. Save for Coppée and Sully-Prudhomme,[3] none of the major poets
of that school had published very much since the advent of symbolism, and
those two had encountered more hostility than praise among the younger writers. With Heredia the case was quite different; Jean Carrère reviewed *Les
Trophées* for *La Plume,*[4] stating that while he did not approve of the Parnassian school, the sonnets of *Les Trophées* seemed to him far superior to the
work of Heredia's contemporaries; Quillard, in the *Mercure de France,*[5] indicated the reproaches which would probably be addressed to a poet who was
essentially an artisan of visual imagery, but concluded with words of high
praise for this faultless art. The reports of the banquet of *La Plume,* at which
Heredia presided on October 14, 1893, indicate an enthusiastic reception from
the guests. Heredia had expressed during the Huret inquiry of 1891 his regrets
that the young writers had so little respect for their elders; after the banquet
he sent a letter to Léon Deschamps expressing his delight at the polite cordial-
ity with which he had been received.

Although the group of writers associated with *La Plume,* the *Mercure de
France,* the *Revue blanche,* and the *Entretiens politiques et littéraires* appear
to have adopted an attitude of relative mansuetude toward those whose poetic
art was at variance with their own, they continued to consider Parnassianism
as incompatible with true lyric expression. When Leconte de Lisle died, in

2. *Mercure de France,* VII (April, 1893), 366.
3. Coppée was the author of *Contes en vers* (1881 and 1887), *Arrière-saison* (1887), and *Les
Paroles sincères* (1890). Sully-Prudhomme's chief contributions during this period were *Le
Prisme* (1886) and *Le Bonheur* (1888).
4. *La Plume,* No. 94 (March 15, 1893), pp. 119–121.
5. *Mercure de France,* VII (April, 1893), 354–360.

the summer of 1894, articles by Quillard in the *Mercure de France*, Pilon in *La Plume*, and Henri de Régnier in *La Revue blanche* paid tribute to the greatness and nobility of expression of the dead poet but underlined the nullity of his influence on contemporary poetry.[6]

Above all, the poets of 1893 disclaimed the right of Hugo or Leconte de Lisle to be considered as an authority or master to be emulated. This is compatible with the wide opposition toward any form of control which becomes especially marked at this time. *La Plume* manifested this in two special numbers during 1893, the one being a protest against the sentences and fines inflicted on writers and artists for outrage to decency, the other being devoted to defense of the anarchists. The actual effect of subversive political ideas on poetry itself seems negligible, but it is nevertheless true that most of the young writers resented authority and even allied themselves at times with the newspapers which were advocating the overthrow of governmental control. Among these were André Veidaux, Stuart Merrill, Adolphe Retté, Jean Carrère, and Ferdinand Herold. All of them wrote articles which were open attacks against the government, but the *Chevaleries sentimentales* of Herold and *Une Belle Dame passa* of Retté, volumes of poetry published in 1893, could hardly be farther from preoccupation with matters of social and political concern. This is not strange; the one paramount idea of the symbolists seems to have been to avoid the didactic. The whole tenor of their protest against Sully-Prudhomme and René Ghil is predicated on the idea that preaching and lyric expression are mutually exclusive. Even a little later, when humanitarian verse began to be more usual among them, they chose to mask the idea by symbols, Retté choosing the figure of "Le Pauvre" in a forest of enemies [7] and Verhaeren giving to the common occupations of the villager something at once terrible and vast.[8] But meanwhile most of the symbolist poets, in their prose and in their loyalties, were combating the powers which had driven Remy de Gourmont from his librarian's post after the publication of "Le Joujou patriotisme"; the powers which had pronounced verdicts against René Emery of *Fin de siècle*, Jules Roques of the *Courrier français*, and Zo d'Axa, Jean Grave or Jules Méry of the anarchist newspapers; and which thirty-five years earlier had proved harsh toward Baudelaire and Flaubert. In July, 1893, probably through the insistence of Stuart Merrill, *L'Ermitage* carried out a referendum among writers on the question whether a social condition of complete liberty or of control would be most favorable to artists. The answers were largely in favor of freedom from authority, although some, among whom was

6. See *Mercure de France*, XI, 305–310; *La Plume*, No. 127, pp. 308–312; *La Revue blanche*, VII, 97–99.
7. *La Forêt bruissante* (1896).
8. *Les Villages illusoires* (1895).

Merrill himself, admitted that anarchy, good as an absolute ideal, should be tempered in practice by socialism.

This ambiance of subversive doctrine was complemented by the various esoteric groups which were flourishing. The symbolist generation appears to have been keenly alive to the lectures by Jules Bois, the writings of Papus and V.-E. Michelet, the novels and multiple activities of Péladan. A duel between Stanislas de Guaita and Jules Bois, after the former had been accused of the "envoûtement" of a weird ecclesiastic of Lyons, the satirical verse of Tailhade against Péladan, occasioned both jesting and serious comment in symbolist magazines. As in the case of political doctrine, the occult seems to have had little influence on poetry. Edouard Schuré, it is true, abandoned his chief interests, religious philosophy, drama, and Wagner, to publish a volume of verse in 1894. But *La Vie mystique* gained little admiration from poets, who saw as the chief merit of the volume the profound knowledge of mythology and religions which the author of *Les Grands Initiés* had already revealed in 1889.

Leconte de Lisle's death, on the other hand, had literary implications which went much farther than the mere evaluation of his own life and work. One of the immediate issues was the project of selecting a "Prince des poètes" to replace him. While one should not exaggerate the importance of this referendum, which was carried out by *La Plume,* it is still true that through it one hundred eighty-nine writers did express their opinions concerning contemporary poets. Verlaine obtained many more mentions than his competitors, but Heredia was in second place, and Mallarmé in third. It is interesting to note that none of the second generation of symbolists obtained a great number of votes, that Sully-Prudhomme, Coppée, Richepin, Dierx, and Mendès seemed to have greater popularity than Régnier, Samain, or Vielé-Griffin.[9]

The winner of the contest, whom the *Entretiens politiques et littéraires* had unqualifiedly called "notre plus grand poète lyrique" even before Leconte de Lisle's death,[10] was very active at this time. During 1893 Verlaine made lecture tours in Belgium and in England, contributed frequently to magazines, chiefly *La Plume,* and published no less than five volumes of prose and poetry. The next year appeared three other volumes of his verse. None of these works was a masterpiece; two of them were augmented editions of earlier volumes, but with his lyric offerings in such periodicals as *La Revue blanche, La Revue parisienne,* and the *Fin de siècle* they did serve to keep his name in the public eye and to bring in some badly needed money for himself or for his "chères amies" Philomène Boudin and Eugénie Krantz.

Heredia and Mallarmé had also in 1893 been the authors of important

9. See *La Plume,* No. 132 (October 15, 1894), pp. 405–434.
10. *Entretiens politiques et littéraires,* VII (December 10, 1893), 508.

volumes. The perfection of workmanship of *Les Trophées* had received almost general praise, and the publication of Mallarmé's *Vers et prose* had been hailed in the symbolist magazines as the first opportunity for the public to gain a fair idea of the author's original style. But these works had also been the object of some important reservations. Mallarmé's admirers lamented the inadequacy of *Vers et prose* for completely revealing the originality of the author's art; in the eyes of some critics, among them Stuart Merrill, *Les Trophées* represented a more or less sterile triumph of artistry over poetic theme. Of Verlaine much could have been said to his discredit, for his artistic production had not been of very high quality for many years. The silence preserved at the publication of his volumes after 1890 may have been a charitable one; secure in his fame by reason of lovely lyrics which had spanned the years between the *Poèmes saturniens* and *Amour,* established as the poverty-stricken figure who had the flame of genius within him, Verlaine did not have to undergo justified accusations of his failing talent. The epithets showered upon him during the election of the Prince des poètes—terms such as "le grand poète," "le gueux divin," "le sublime mendiant," "ce Pauvre plus riche que nous tous"—showed the kind of admiring pity which endeared him to the younger writers. Some of the newcomers to the world of poetry were unwilling to have him wear the crown alone. Tristan Klingsor and Charles Guérin proposed the joint names of Mallarmé and Verlaine. Other poets who were a little older proposed that he share honors with Sully-Prudhomme, Heredia, or even Mistral, but out of the many conflicting opinions his name emerged triumphant. Immediately after his election, Laurent Tailhade, his old comrade of the days of *Lutèce,* gave a lecture at the "Soirées Procope" [11] and reviewed the story of Verlaine's slow rise to fame.

Meanwhile, in Germany, the fame of the French symbolists was being spread, especially through the able translations of Stefan George in the *Blätter für die Kunst.* The second issue of the magazine, December, 1892, had contained German versions of poems by Mallarmé, Verlaine, Henri de Régnier, and Moréas. In May, 1893, the French authors represented were Albert Saint-Paul, Stuart Merrill, and Vielé-Griffin; in August of the same year Mallarmé was accorded the place of honor, George having translated not only some prose poems but the "Hérodiade" and the "Après-midi d'un faune." [12] Interest in French poetry was far from being restricted to the *Blätter für die Kunst.* In the *Moderner Musen Almanach* for 1893–94 appeared translations from Verlaine by Richard Schaukal and Richard Dehmel and from Baudelaire by Felix

11. On October 25, 1894.
12. The translations from the French in the *Blätter für die Kunst* are fully described in E. L. Duthie's *L'Influence du symbolisme français dans le renouveau poétique de l'Allemagne.*

Dörmann. In the *National Zeitung* Hedwig Lachmann gave a long critical study of Verlaine.[13]

In Belgium, after *La Wallonie* had ceased publication at the beginning of 1893, there was no periodical which well represented the fusion of French and Belgian poetic movements. Paul Gérardy's *Floréal* never attained either the financial security or the importance which Mockel and his associates had succeeded in giving to *La Wallonie*. During 1893, its second and final year of existence, its contributors were chiefly Belgians, although Vielé-Griffin, Henri de Régnier, and Camille Mauclair were represented in its final issues. *La Jeune Belgique,* despite certain admirations among its editors for Baudelaire and Mallarmé, remained quite strongly nationalistic and rather hostile to the younger French generation. True, after Max Waller's death in 1889, it had seemed on the point of becoming more hospitable to French poets, and a few contributions by Henri de Régnier, Vielé-Griffin, Verlaine, and Ferdinand Herold had appeared in its pages. The principal French collaborator in 1891 and 1892 had been Gustave Kahn, but during the following two years the magazine became again almost exclusively Belgian. Valère Gille, Iwan Gilkin, Albert Giraud, and Fernand Séverin were its principal poets and none of these was a wholehearted sympathizer with the generation which had adopted the use of free verse.[14]

Of greater interest in relationships between the poetic movements of the two countries is a little monthly magazine published at Ghent. It had begun to appear in 1891 under the auspices of the "Cercle littéraire français" and it bore the hopeful name of *Le Réveil*. During 1892 Tristan Klingsor, then living at Beauvais, began contributing his eleven-syllable verses to this periodical; and during the following two years *Le Réveil* published poems by Souchon, Henri de Régnier, Ferdinand Herold, Pierre Louÿs, and Vielé-Griffin. Contributors among the Belgian poets included Elskamp, Verhaeren, Gérardy, Mockel, Maeterlinck, and Van Lerberghe. In the grouping of French and Belgian poets *Le Réveil* thus achieved something comparable to that of *La Wallonie.*

The most important new name among the Belgians, in so far as comment in French periodicals was concerned, was that of Max Elskamp. It was not until 1892, when he was thirty years of age, that Elskamp published his first volume, *Dominical*. He was one of those who had helped to found in Antwerp an "Association pour l'art," a group which sought to awake more interest in writing, painting, and music in a city which seemed interested only in industry.

---

13. A portion of this essay was given in French translation by the *Entretiens politiques et littéraires,* VII (December 10, 1893), 508–517.

14. Iwan Gilkin was especially harsh toward free verse, and among its users he singled out one of *La Jeune Belgique's* erstwhile contributors, Vielé-Griffin, for his attacks.

Like many of the other Belgian poets of the period, and especially Rodenbach, Elskamp's poetry evoked the images of melancholy and religious preoccupation in the Belgian towns. Much more daring in securing musical effects than had been Rodenbach, above all much more dependent upon suggestion than upon statement of mood, Elskamp immediately was hailed as an original and promising poet. The year after the publication of *Dominical* there appeared a new volume of verses by Elskamp entitled *Salutations, dont d'angéliques*. This served to give the Belgian poet a definite reputation as a mystical dreamer in the tradition of *Sagesse*. More than one reviewer of his books mentioned the name of Verlaine because of the unpretentious style, the musical utterance, and the candid artlessness of such lines as the following:

> Marie de mes beaux navires,
> Marie étoile de la mer,
> me voici triste et bien amer
> d'avoir si mal tenté vous dire.

In volumes of poetry this was a singularly rich period among the Belgians and although the French periodicals published very little of such productions, they spoke, often with real enthusiasm, of the rebirth in lyricism which had taken place across the border. Even those poets among the Belgians who refused to accept the name and many of the innovations of the French symbolists were not completely antipathetic to the *Mercure de France* or *La Plume*. The atmosphere of terror created in Iwan Gilkin's *Ténèbres* recalled sufficiently the name of Baudelaire; the *Château des merveilles* by Valère Gille held enough of the fanciful not to offend French symbolists by its strict form and somewhat overelegant diction. Rodenbach's *Le Voyage dans les yeux* was both criticized for its Parnassian severity and lauded for its tone of vague melancholy.[15] Such poets received measured approval in France, but real enthusiasm was reserved for those who seemed to the symbolists original and unhampered by tradition—Verhaeren and Maeterlinck.

A thirty-six-year-old French poet, who by reason of his discreet sadness presents many similarities with Rodenbach,[16] offered in 1893 his first volume of verse. Most of the poems had already appeared in periodicals but only when Samain grouped them in *Au jardin de l'Infante* could the reader gain a unified impression of the atmosphere and style of the author. When the *Mercure de France,* of which Samain had been one of the founders, gave a review of the book the critic chosen to speak of Samain was one of the most conservative of

15. See Retté's article in *La Plume*, V, 230, and the review signed "A.S." in the *Mercure de France*, VIII, 185.

16. Guy Michaud, in *Message poétique du symbolisme*, establishes an interesting parallel between Rodenbach and Samain (Michaud entitles the section "Les Poètes du temps perdu," III, 492–501).

its poets, Pierre Quillard. This reviewer, doubtless aware of the reproaches which might be made to Samain for following too closely the romantic and Parnassian traditions, immediately recognized those elements in the volume but insisted on the delicacy and timid aloofness which in themselves created a new and personal charm.[17] Samain's reputation was immediately established by this volume. The poetess Tola Dorian was so impressed by the book that she proposed Samain as Prince des poètes in 1894. Once published, *Au jardin de l'Infante* sold well. A new edition was printed in 1894 and an augmented one in 1897. The almost feminine sensitivity of the verse gained much admiration, especially from women, and Samain's style was not without importance during the last years of the nineteenth century since it presented some affinities with younger poets, among them Charles Guérin and Francis Jammes.

These two poets, Guérin and Jammes, began to gain some slight attention in the symbolist periodicals during 1893 and 1894. Jammes, since 1891, had been publishing the little notebooks of *Vers* at Orthez but had not made any effort to have his poetry put on public sale. The *Mercure de France* really discovered him, first wondering, in 1893, whether the name "Jammes" was a pseudonym, then remarking, in 1894, on the originality of the poet's sincere, profound sympathy with the griefs and joys of his fellow man, and finally, in 1896, publishing a volume of his verse. Guérin, still a schoolboy at Nancy in 1893, arranged for the private printing of his first volume that year. *Fleurs de neige* was signed with the anagram Heirclas Rügen. Quotations at the head of the poems revealed the author's preferences among modern poets: Rodenbach, Verlaine, and Merrill. Imperfections in the volume were quite obvious, yet the bibliographical notices in the magazines indicated a measure of belief in the real poetic gift of the writer. Among these encouraging critics was Stuart Merrill,[18] whose sympathy for Guérin's poems may have been partly occasioned by the excesses in search for musical effect which had been the chief fault of his own *Les Gammes*. Guérin used as his basic form the sonnet but permitted himself assonance instead of rhymes, tried the thirteen-syllable line, and abused the principle of inner rhyme and alliteration. The first stanza of the "Frontispiece" reveals the similarity between his and Merrill's early questing for musical effect:

> Sous les pins fins pleins de plaintes, au sein des landes
> Languissent et sommeillent les filles des neiges.
> Ce sont celles qui souffrent parce qu'elles n'aiment
> Pas. Et leur spleen s'épanouit en larmes blanches.[19]

17. *Mercure de France*, IX (October, 1893), 97–102.
18. In *L'Ermitage*, August, 1893.
19. Charles Guérin, *Premiers et derniers vers*, p. 9.

The twenty-year-old poet had much to discover concerning subtlety in art, but it is to his credit that he learned rapidly and later attempted to buy up all extant copies of the *Fleurs de neige*.[20] His second volume, still signed with the anagram, appeared in 1894. Entitled *Joies grises,* it was a noticeably better production. It was dedicated to Rodenbach, who wrote an encouraging preface for his young admirer. Guérin used in *Joies grises* fixed poetic forms, but with certain liberties and above all with a choice of diction which allied him with the symbolists. That the *Joies grises* contained sonnets, rondels, rondeaux, a sestina, and a villanelle did not seem so important as the engaging melancholy and religious idealism which emanated from the lines.

Both Jammes and Guérin were to have increasing importance during the last years of the century. Their names at this time are quite obscure, but it must be recalled that neither of them sought to migrate to Paris and plunge into the literary groups of the capital. Quite different was the procedure of a poet born only a year before Guérin but who by 1894 was accorded recognition equal to those who were much his senior. This precocious writer was Camille Mauclair, in 1893 the author of a volume of esthetic criticism, *Eleusis,* and in 1894 of the volume of poetry, *Sonatines d'automne.* He was one of the principal contributors to the *Mercure de France* not only of poetry but of artistic and literary criticism. That magazine accorded him a place of honor during 1893 and 1894, his rivals being Samain, Herold, Vielé-Griffin, Fontainas, and Retté.

Among these favorites of the *Mercure de France* Samain stands somewhat apart. His tone of personal confession is far more simple than that of others of his generation, as one is well aware in reading the poetry of his fellow collaborators in the *Mercure de France.* Whatever diversity Retté, Fontainas, Vielé-Griffin, and Herold may present in form and in mood, there is by 1893 striking similarity in their poetic manner. This is all the more strange in that they had seemed a few years earlier entirely divergent. The chaotic, desperate imagery of Retté's *Cloches en la nuit* (1889) had seemed the antithesis of Herold's *Les Pœans et les thrènes* (1890). In the latter work the Hellenic myths and orderly eloquence had appeared the continuation of Parnassianism. Vielé-Griffin's *Joies* (1889), with its spontaneous free verse and images taken from the world of nature, seemingly bore no relationship with the artificiality of Fontainas' *Le Sang des fleurs,* written in sonorous and colorful stanzas. Now, only some five years later, they had arrived at a common ground. The setting of their poetry had become the legendary forest inhabited by more or less unreal figures, a setting out of space and time. The theme had become the author's emotions and ideals, expressed through the medium of the legend.

20. J. B. Hanson, *Le Poète Charles Guérin,* p. 6.

Régnier, Merrill, and Vielé-Griffin had been perhaps the principal forces in establishing this indirect statement of human emotions, and behind them is the influence of the Wagnerian hero, representing both an individual and an idea.

An evolutionary process had occurred in each of these four poets. The greatest change was perhaps in Retté where the clanging bells, stormy waves, evil magicians, and hallucinatory imagery of *Cloches en la nuit* had yielded to the less violent but more poignant emotional story of *Une belle dame passa* (1893). The apparition of the lady, her disappearance, and the emotional effect on the man in whom she has inspired passionate love form the unity and the theme of the volume. But for the statement of this personal adventure a poetic substitution has been made. The lady is a vague kind of princess to whom Retté has given the name of Titania. She, as well as the lover, is the universal as well as the particular figure in this drama of human emotions.

The change in the poetry of Ferdinand Herold is perhaps easier to understand. Myth or legend, the heroes from Greece, Sanskrit literature,[21] the Middle Ages, or the golden legend—all this was the treasure on which he drew for his poetic themes. Certainly his poetry became more warm and more personal after *Les Pœans et les thrènes,* but the sense of his whole work is the adaptation of the myth, the process described in 1892 by Gide in the "Traité du Narcisse." *Chevaleries sentimentales* (1893), with its legendary landscape and its unreal characters, recalled to Quillard [22] the paintings of Puvis de Chavannes, Gustave Moreau, and Burne-Jones, the masters of symbolic representation of figures from legend. Herold's dramatic poem "Floriane et Persigant," first published in Belgium,[23] appeared in pamphlet form from the press of the "Librairie de l'art indépendant" in 1894 and during the same year a revised edition of *La Légende de Sainte Liberata* was published by the *Mercure de France.*

André Fontainas had concentrated most of his poetic activity in his native city of Brussels, but had been one of the noteworthy group from the Lycée Fontanes which comprised Merrill, Ghil, Mikhaël, Darzens, and Quillard. One of the cofounders of *La Basoche* (November, 1884–March, 1886), he had later become one of the contributors to *La Jeune Belgique* and for a short time to *La Wallonie.* With *Les Vergers illusoires* (1892) he had become one of the practicers of free verse, although he never abandoned entirely the alexandrine. In *Nuits d'Epiphanies* of 1894, the Magi become the symbols of a search for the ideal, shadowy figures moving through dark forests and lakes at twilight and expressing anguished realization of transitory human values.

21. Herold published a translation of the *Upanishad* in 1894.
22. *Mercure de France,* VIII (May, 1893), 64.
23. *Le Réveil,* IV (March, 1893), 149–169.

Of these four poets in the group associated with the *Mercure de France,* the change in Vielé-Griffin is perhaps the most slight. The free verse and the type of imagery remain constant after *Joies,* the new elements of *Les Cygnes* (1892), *Swanhilde* (1893), and *La Chevauchée d'Yeldis* (1894) being the inclusion of the narrative element and of personages in his poems. These devices bring them close to allegory. In this respect he had been like Henri de Régnier, whose *Poèmes anciens et romanesques* (1892) contained the dramatic poem "La Gardienne" given by the Théâtre de l'œuvre in 1894. The critics of the *Mercure de France,* in their discussion of poetry of 1893 and 1894, often speak of the unity of the volumes and often this unity is secured simply by the legendary story representing the author's search of an ideal.

During this period of the ascendancy of the dramatic poem, the theater which was called symbolist had undergone some changes. Paul Fort had given up the Théâtre d'art because of financial difficulties and disagreements with the actors of his company. The work he had begun was to be carried on by Lugné Poë, who with Camille Mauclair presented *Pelléas et Mélisande* on May 16, 1893. This performance, given at the Bouffes-Parisiens, inspired much comment, one of the most interesting being the article by Mallarmé in the *National Observer.*[24] In June, 1893, the last play in Edouard Dujardin's trilogy *Antonia* was presented at the Vaudeville, but as in the two preceding years the play was not a success. Alternately accused of childishness and incoherence, Dujardin yet found a defender in Paul Adam, who bitterly criticized the public which had been unable to find inherent qualities of beauty in the play.[25] The theme was in truth idealistic. *La Fin d'Antonia* had as its subject the inability of a soul to find repose in solitude. Dujardin indicated the impediments to an isolation of self by such characters as Hunger, Thirst, Society, and Passion. In using a group of woodcutters to signify the social group and a shepherd to symbolize love, he veiled only slightly the allegorical intent. This at times seems closer to the morality play than to more modern forms of drama. Antonia's recapitulation of the action in the other plays of the trilogy was apparently quite tedious, and the lines appeared to some critics as fragments of sentences held together by rhymes. One may well suspect that limitations in poetic genius, incapable of rising to the heights of great ideas, was the chief fault of the Antonia trilogy. Dujardin, so completely won over to the sonorities and vast horizons of Wagnerianism, appears to have been able to transfer only very incompletely his visions to theatrical presentation.

Of greater moment was the production of *Axël* in March, 1894. The pre-

24. On June 10, 1893. Mallarmé's essay was also printed in the summer (1893) issue of *Le Réveil,* III, 161–164.
25. *Entretiens politiques et littéraires,* VII (July 10, 1893), 42–47.

ceding year, Tola Dorian, who then was associated in Fort's Théâtre d'art, had wished to give the drama but had encountered much opposition from writers who feared that unless a very expensive production was planned justice would not be done to Villiers de l'Isle-Adam. With the aid of Larochelle, who assumed the title role, Mme Tola Dorian carried out her plans and the performance was apparently a reasonable success.[26] The triumph of *Axël*, which had been partly written as early as 1872 and of which the greatness had long been proclaimed by younger writers, including Maeterlinck and Verlaine, seemed to the symbolists the rightful reward of misunderstood genius. Villiers, with Maeterlinck and later Claudel, constituted the rare talents who were able to adapt unreality to the exigencies of the stage.

By the end of 1894 the number of magazines in which the symbolists could express themselves and find a receptive attitude in critical articles was rather reduced. The remaining periodicals, nevertheless, had more vitality and value than the numerous little magazines that had often been hampered by lack of funds and paucity of pages. With the *Mercure de France, La Revue blanche,* and *L'Ermitage* a continued welcome to poetic expression was assured. In Belgium the traditions of *La Wallonie* were perhaps best carried on by *Le Réveil* and *La Société nouvelle*.

Although *La Société nouvelle* had been founded in 1884, its poetic horizon was for a long time limited to Rodenbach and Verhaeren. The magazine commenced to take an active interest in the French literary scene in 1892, the year Gustave Kahn began writing some critical essays for it. That same year Gabriel Randon (Jehan Rictus) sent news of Jules Bois's *Noces de Sathan* from Paris and Vielé-Griffin contributed "Corine de Thèbes," a passage from his forthcoming volume Παλαι. In July, 1892, Kahn established an antagonistic attitude toward naturalism in a review of Zola's *La Débâcle*. In this critical essay he said that one could be the most important naturalist and yet a mediocre writer.

During 1893 and 1894 both French and Belgian poets were given much greater importance by *La Société nouvelle*. Contributions by Henri de Régnier, Vielé-Griffin, André Fontainas, Maeterlinck, Verhaeren, Elskamp, Kahn, Romain Coolus, and Saint-Pol-Roux appeared. An article on Mallarmé by Camille Mauclair, an essay on Villiers de l'Isle-Adam by Kahn, and the text of a public lecture on Mauclair, Gide, and Maeterlinck by Henry Maubel [27] were among the items relating to symbolism. In the critical columns, Kahn discussed novels, political tracts, plays, and poetry under the caption "La Vie mentale," a title he was to retain in later contributions to *La Revue blanche*. In these articles the critic attacked the realistic theater, dismissed Max

26. See *Mercure de France*, X (April, 1894), 358–361 and *La Plume*, VI (April 15, 1894), 153.
27. Maubel gave his lecture at Antwerp on March 16, 1894, and at Brussels three days later.

Nordau's *Décadence* as ridiculous, and carried on his campaign for free verse. After stating that Leconte de Lisle had shown the limits of accomplishment in the use of the alexandrine, Kahn predicts that the twelve-syllable line is on the point of ending its career. In a discussion of Francis Jammes he asserts that the best verse of this poet is in free meters.

The greatest loss to the symbolist poets among the magazines was the *Entretiens politiques et littéraires,* which ceased publication in December, 1893. During its last year of existence, however, it had expanded both in frequency of issue and in the nature of its contents. Published twice a month during 1893, it offered not only the political and literary essays which had been the reason for its founding in 1890 but also fiction and poetry. The critical articles continued to be important, and during 1893 among the most noteworthy might be mentioned four essays on current poetry by Vielé-Griffin, an essay on Baudelaire by Henri de Régnier, and one by Henri Albert on Ibsen. But anarchism, Buddhism, and occultism as well as literary matters were also treated in the magazine, and Paul Adam discussed all kinds of subjects in his "Critique des mœurs." [28] The magazine's poetic contributors included Paul-Marius André, Dauphin Meunier, Emmanuel Signoret, Paul Claudel, Camille Mauclair, and Vielé-Griffin. Saint-Pol-Roux, with installments of his lyric drama *Epilogue des saisons humaines* and selections from *Les Reposoirs de la procession* was a frequent contributor to the *Entretiens* as well as to the *Mercure de France.* Although the outer form of his writing seemed that of prose, by reason of the fact that the content was largely a series of unusual images in which the things of everyday existence were transformed into a poetic idea, he must be primarily considered a poet rather than writer of prose.

When publication of *La Revue indépendante* was suspended in March, 1893, the symbolist press did not express great sorrow. After 1891, when George Bonnamour had begun devoting the magazine to discrediting the accomplishments of symbolism and to championing René Ghil, the magazine had become increasingly hostile to the symbolists. Book reviews of their work were almost always quite harsh. The important part taken by the magazine between 1886 and 1889, with Wyzewa, Kahn, and Fénéon, in the formation of new poetic theory was now forgotten. It had become simply the periodical in which Xavier de Ricard was publishing his memoirs of the Parnassian movement and where the salvation of poetry was predicated on acceptance of the evolutive and instrumental theories of Ghil.

Favorable critics were not lacking for symbolist poetry. In the *Mercure* Remy de Gourmont, Quillard, Herold, and Rambosson, in *La Plume* Adolphe Retté, in *La Revue blanche* Lucien Muhlfeld, in *L'Ermitage* Roland de Marès

28. After the *Entretiens* ceased publication, Adam continued his series in *La Revue blanche.*

and Stuart Merrill formed a resolute body of defenders of liberty in form and of music and suggestion in manner. Vielé-Griffin and Henri de Régnier, soon to take an important part in the *Mercure de France,* distributed articles among both French and Belgian periodicals, and Camille Mauclair's name was often signed to book reviews.

The most curious and most enthusiastic article in defense of poetry at this time came from the pen of Emmanuel Signoret. On July 15, 1894, René Doumic had published an article in the *Revue des deux mondes.* In it he had indicated his opinion that poetry was a dead art. Signoret's answer, printed the following month,[29] was a long list of writers, chiefly poets, with numerous short quotations embracing not only the precursors but the young generation of the symbolists. Among the latter Signoret cites as future leaders Mauclair, Gide, Mécislas Goldberg, Henri Degron, André Ibels, Louÿs, Raymond de la Tailhède, Claudel, Valéry, Souchon, and finally himself. Others whom he admires among the older poets are Merrill, Louis le Cardonnel, Retté, Saint-Pol-Roux, Mallarmé, Tailhade, and Moréas. His "Vers dorés" dedicated to Charles Baudelaire and his "Ode à Paul Verlaine"[30] are other evidences of his enthusiasm. Even if he bestowed his praise rather too generously he succeeded in including almost all the important names in the poetic history of his time. His appreciation of Valéry and Claudel at a moment when both were quite obscure is proof of a splendid intuition of talent. Above all, these lines of admiration for others help mitigate the accusation of megalomania which his prefaces all too clearly suggest. His frequent mention of Dante and Leonardo da Vinci as quasi divinities of the past is proof of a lofty idealism made ridiculous only by the fact that he apparently placed himself on their level. As an expression of suffering of the poet in the century and an awareness of the unconquerable ideal, his message is perhaps no less moving than that of Mallarmé or Baudelaire. His lines appear derivative but not devoid of power:

> Et le monde agonise en un ricanement,
> A nos fronts incompris, il prodigue l'injure,—
> —Le Puits maudit veut rétrécir le firmament,
> Mais l'azur irrité plane et le transfigure.[31]

Overly sensitive, easily offended, Signoret quarreled with almost all those whom he had tried to associate during 1892 in the *Saint-Graal.* Fortunately he found a friend in Léon Deschamps of *La Plume.* In that magazine, during 1893 and 1894, he was one of the most frequent contributors and all of the twelve poems which composed the volume *Daphné* (1894) appear in its

---

29. *La Plume,* VI (August 1, 1894), 305–308.
30. Published by Vanier in 1892.
31. Emmanuel Signoret, *Poésies complètes,* p. 57.

issues.[32] While the place of honor was reserved by the magazine for the poets of L'Ecole romane and the poems of Verlaine were the magazine's chief claim to glory, Signoret was much esteemed. The Bibliothèque artistique et littéraire of *La Plume* published during 1894 Verlaine's *Epigrammes,* Moréas' *Eriphyle,* and Signoret's *Daphné.*

Toward the end of 1894 appeared a book by Vielé-Griffin which resumed many of the current poetic trends. The imagery of nature, the personal meditation of the poet, the use of symbolic figures to convey a dramatic representation of the idea are all present. To some the title Παλαι seemed overly pedantic. It is not inappropriate to the content of the volume, however, since three figures from antiquity, Corine de Tanagra representing experience, Myrtis d'Anthédon representing passion, and a Nestorian man of wisdom called Lassos d'Hermione in turn counsel the poet. Hellenism, much out of favor with the generation which formed the group of the beginnings of symbolism, had never been abandoned by Vielé-Griffin. Without making of it a cult, he had utilized Greek myth as the background of *Ancæus* (1888) and in his later career was to celebrate ancient Greece in a series of volumes. By the time of the publication of Παλαι there were many indications that classic beauty was again assuming an important place in poetry. The inspiration of bucolic poetry was strong among those of the Ecole romane, Quillard and Louÿs were making translations from the Greek, Valéry and Gide had evoked the myth of Narcissus, and Heredia's sonnets had found favor. The unfounded notion that Hellenism implied coldness and plasticity to the exclusion of personal lyricism was past.

Among the ephemeral little magazines which were founded in 1894 there is not much evidence of this return to Hellenism, but there is seemingly a real attempt to admit wider groupings of poets representing great differences in inspiration and form. In the twelve monthly issues of *Album des légendes,* a literary and artistic publication founded by Andhré and Jacques des Gachons, contributions in verse were made by many of the symbolists, Louis le Cardonnel, Merrill, Régnier, and Klingsor but also by Georges Docquois, Marc Legrand, and Gaston Soulier, poets who remained in the Parnassian tradition. In Louis Lormel's *L'Art littéraire,* which at the beginning of 1894 changed from a four-page monthly sheet to a bimonthly magazine of thirty-two pages,[33] selections from René Ghil's work appeared in company with extracts from Saint-Pol-Roux's "Les Reposoirs de la procession," Jarry's "César antéchrist," and lyrics by Kahn, Pilon, Klingsor, and Mockel.

32. Two of the poems also were printed in *L'Ermitage* (June, 1894).

33. *L'Art littéraire* had begun showing interest in poetry as early as July, 1893, when it printed verse by Mauclair and Ghil. During the last half of the year Saint-Pol-Roux, Remy de Gourmont, Léon-Paul Fargue, Alfred Jarry, André Gide, Tristan Klingsor, and Henri de Régnier were contributors.

While *Les Ibis,* founded in 1894 by Henri Degron and Tristan Klingsor, survived for only four issues, it presented a rather impressive list of contributors including Vielé-Griffin, Gasquet, Gérardy, Souchon, Gide, Régnier, Signoret, Dierx, Retté, and Saint-Paul. The magazine also offered translations from the work of Eugenio de Castro and Oliveira-Soarés, two Portuguese poets who were endeavoring to carry the cult of symbolism into their native land. Nicole Chambellan's *L'Idée moderne* is chiefly interesting for several poems by Louis le Cardonnel and an extract from Paul Fort's *Presque les doigts aux clefs.*

Admiration for Saint-Georges de Bouhélier found expression during 1894 in the two issues of a periodical called *Le Rêve et l'idée.* In May, Maurice le Blond announced that the new poetic generation was rejecting the esthetic outlook of both the symbolists and the realists and that Bouhélier would guide the young into new paths of mysticism free of dogma. In October, when the second issue of *Le Rêve et l'idée* appeared, Bouhélier offered a sample of this new mystical outlook in "Pages tragiques." There, in a kind of exalted prose, he proclaimed that divine love had become flesh three times in the heroic figures of Adam, Orpheus, and Jesus. This strange association of names was apparently a demonstration of Maurice le Blond's prediction that Christian dogma was about to be replaced by new ideals of truth and beauty. Although the name of naturism had not been as yet created, Bouhélier's antisymbolist attitude was already launched and was to be much discussed in ensuing years.

Chapter XII: EVOLUTION TOWARD
INTIMATE VERSE, 1895

In 1895, a decade after the first important manifestations of symbolism as a literary movement, a broader view of its accomplishments became possible through the publication of collected editions of some of the important leaders. Under the title *Poèmes 1887–1892*, Henri de Régnier gave a collection of his best verse, the lyrics of *Poèmes anciens et romanesques* and *Tel qu'en songe*. Vielé-Griffin, excluding some of his earliest poems and making rather extensive revisions, was the author of *Poèmes et poésies 1886–1893*. In the reprinting of *Joies*, the second *Cygnes* and the *Chevauchée d'Yeldis*, all of which were included in the volume, a fair representation was offered of his success in the use of free verse and the background of legend. Verhaeren's early work, largely published in Belgium and insufficiently known in France, became available in *Poèmes,* the first of three collections published by the press of the *Mercure de France* between 1895 and 1899. Followed in 1896 and 1897 by *Poésies 1886–1896* of Moréas, *Premiers poèmes* of Gustave Kahn, *Poèmes 1887–1897* of Stuart Merrill, and *Images tendres et merveilleuses* of Ferdinand Herold, these collected editions proved the important accomplishment of the past decade.

Especially noteworthy is the growing importance of Verhaeren in France. His new volumes, *Les Villages illusoires* (1894) and *Les Villes tentaculaires* (1895), gave evidence that the cycle of despair and almost madness, represented by *Les Soirs, Les Débâcles,* and *Les Flambeaux noirs,* was past. The author's art of magnifying the commonplace, the evocation of the fantastic, of the soul of things, had not been lost, but the poet, whether in the presentation of life in the village or of that in the city, was meditating about things beyond the realm of his own personal mood. The evolution in the social structure, the forces which were creating a new era of factories, machines, and trains, the exodus from the farms to the cities appear in the background of his new manner. In thus enlarging the message of his verse, Verhaeren did not become didactic nor did he forget the inner anguish of the individual human soul. His poetry, which had depended for much of its effect on its powerful images, continued to present this same phenomenon; social preoccupation in his verse did not destroy its poetic quality. Already recognized in his own country as its greatest living poet, it was in 1895 that his reputation became firmly established in France. Important in this recognition are the periodical essays which concerned his verse, such as that written by Albert

Mockel for the *Mercure de France*,[1] Henri de Régnier for *La Revue blanche*,[2] and Vielé-Griffin for *La Plume*.[3] The reprinting of the early verse, in which he had expressed the robust vulgarity and mystic faith of the Flemish, at the same time as the publication of his poetry of social change revealed the breadth and capabilities of the poet. This his French admirers were careful to underline.

Both by the extent and quality of their poetic work, as well as by their activity in critical writing, Henri de Régnier and Vielé-Griffin could count as the most important representatives of their poetic generation. When Albert Mockel, examining in *Propos de littérature* (1894) the poetic currents of his time, sought to establish the nature of symbolism he chose as the two noteworthy members of the movement these very poets. Enough contrast was furnished by Régnier's tone of dreamy remembrance and Vielé-Griffin's more vigorous and dramatic statement of idealism to give a demonstration of their individuality, while the parallel use of free verse and the choice of symbols to represent their ideas provided a bond of similarity.

The year 1895 marks a date in the work of Henri de Régnier by the publication of *Aréthuse*. The first and third parts of the volume are dedicated to Heredia and to Mallarmé and are written in alexandrines of polished regularity; the middle portion of the book is a long poem in free verse called "L'Homme et la sirène." Its inscription bears the name of Vielé-Griffin. It cannot be said that Régnier parodied any one of these three poets, but with admirable tact he indicated by small details the admiration he felt for all three. The slight accentuation of mythological detail in the part dedicated to Heredia, the use of dialogue in the poem honoring Vielé-Griffin, the subtle transposition of the visual to the intellectual plane in several poems of the last part of the volume are both clever and beautiful. Nor is there lack of unity in the volume. Régnier includes enough plasticity, enough idealistic suggestion as well as sufficient shading of thought in one and the same poem to satisfy three quite divergent manners. As a simple example one might choose the opening lines of "Métamorphose sentimentale," a poem from the third section of the book:

> Une rose jusqu'à tes lèvres est venue.
> Sois le geste que fut trop longtemps ta statue!
> Les fleurs montent autour du sombre piédestal,
> L'aurore souriante empourpre le métal
> Et le bronze tiédit qui veut être ta chair:
> O toi qui es debout, viens boire au fleuve clair![4]

1. XIV (May, 1895), 190–212.
2. VIII (March, 1895), 213–215.
3. VII (April 1, 1895), 141–142.
4. Henri de Régnier, *Aréthuse*, p. 89.

Commentary on this verse might include the unforseen sequence of the first two lines, with the ellipsis in thought so dear to Mallarmé, the utilization of the Pygmalion theme to suggest the awakening of passion, and the synthesis of ideas of spring and dawn in that of the animated statue. *Aréthuse,* which two years later was to be reprinted as part of the *Jeux rustiques et divins,* marks the abandonment of Régnier's first poetic manner and by comparison with the earlier volumes indicates some of the weaknesses of symbolism in the late 1880's. The new firmness and clarity of Régnier's poetry suggest to what degree it had formerly been vague and difficult for the mind to retain. In attempting to make poetry the province of dream, he, like most of his generation, had left the concrete world too far away. The clouded, melancholy atmosphere of personal mood needed some irradiation of the idea. Régnier captured this in one of his most famous poems written in April, 1895, and published in the *Mercure de France* the next month.[5] "Le Vase," written partly in free meters and partly in alexandrines, is externally the description of a sculptor who is carving a freize on a marble urn. But the poem is applicable to any form of creative effort and its theme embraces the inspiration of the artist, the transfer of his ideas to his work, his enthusiasm during the creation, and his sense of regret at the completion. Régnier did not write an "Art poétique" but he conveyed the ecstasy, the loss of self in search of the beautiful which he felt should animate the artist.

While Henri de Régnier appeared to be turning away from free verse in 1895, other authors remained the firm adherents of the new prosody. Gustave Kahn, who prided himself on having invented free verse and who regarded his discovery as the greatest contribution to the symbolist movement, produced his third and fourth volumes of poetry, *Domaine de fée* and *La Pluie et le beau temps.* For several years he had concentrated his activity in Belgium, sending a poem only occasionally to *La Revue blanche* and giving the greatest part of his poetry and prose to *La Jeune Belgique* or to *La Société nouvelle.*[6] Like *Chansons d'amant* (1891), Kahn's *Domaine de fée* was published in Brussels, but almost all his later volumes were issued from Parisian presses. During the last years of the century he was to become the chief critic of *La Revue blanche.* His verse continued to be more interesting in its form than in its content. In discarding syllabic count and often rhyme, he had retained only the rhythm of the phrase as the basis for poetic music. To define his poetic style is not an easy task, for although he often uses the most sumptuous of imagery and the most unusual diction, he also writes lines of extreme sim-

5. XIV (June, 1895), 266–268.
6. The last of "La Vie mentale," Kahn's regular critical essays for *La Société nouvelle,* appeared in 1895. In them he discussed Léon Dierx, *Gaspard de la nuit* and the prose poem, Régnier, Retté, Elskamp, and Montesquiou.

plicity. This latter trait is particularly visible in *Domaine de fée,* a volume of love songs which terminates with these lines:

> Je t'ai revue et je t'aimais,
> Je t'ai revue, je t'aime encore.[7]

Kahn's poetic work at this time falls into two categories, the emotional statement of his love for his wife Elizabeth and the poetic description of landscapes. In order to give unity to his volumes, he carefully sorted out his love songs for *Domaine de fée* and created a separate volume of the descriptive verse. It is regrettably true that he never composed great poetry, but also true that what he wrote was often a foretoken of the future. His theories of free rhythms were based on the premise that such writing was a spontaneous outpouring of the poetic mind. Had he employed fewer repetitions and somewhat more ellipses in his sequence of ideas, his love poems would present parallels with even such a modern as Eluard. When he did not add the exotic adornments which are so often present in his verse, his lines emerge with a directness which presages modern poetry:

> Je suis celui de ta beauté et rien d'autre,
> le reste des débris du monde n'étant rien
> que nomenclature et que mappemonde,
> je suis celui de ta beauté et rien d'autre.[8]

A volume, also recounting a sentimental adventure, appeared at almost the same time as *Domaine de fée.* It was Stuart Merrill's third volume of verse and was entitled *Les Petits Poèmes d'automne.* Although its prosody depends on strict syllabic count and on rhyme, it offers varieties in rhythm almost as interesting as Kahn's free verse. Apparently wishing to give a vague and uncertain atmosphere to his poems, Merrill used many combinations of odd syllables, completely excluding the alexandrine, favoring especially the enneasyllabic line. Carefully arranged, the volume contained two parts, "Amour d'automne" and "Ame d'automne," separated by a series of little songs.

The general tone of most of the volumes of verse published during 1895 was that of the intimate confession against a rather vague and dreamy background. Merrill's theme was not essentially different from that of several of his juniors who published in that year their first collections of poetry. Two of the newcomers are rather startling since their poetry has been largely forgotten because of their more important works in the realm of drama and fiction. But Henri Barbusse's *Pleureuses* and Henry Bataille's *La Chambre blanche* did not go absolutely unnoticed in the symbolist magazines. Although

---

7. Gustave Kahn, *Premiers poèmes,* p. 335.
8. *Ibid.,* p. 298.

Barbusse was almost immediately identified as a continuator of the Parnassians, after reviews by Chantavoine in the *Journal des débats* and by Catulle Mendès in the *Echo de Paris,* Pierre Quillard underlined the direct and intimate quality of the expression and suggested comparisons with Verlaine.[9] The strict metrical form of the verse may have alienated some of the more ardent innovators, but the vagueness of the background and the equally indecisive note of melancholy would indeed seem to ally Barbusse's volume with the symbolists. Henry Bataille's sensitive and timorous remembrances of his childhood, couched in a direct, almost conversational language, received little attention at the moment of their publication but three years afterward were praised by Remy de Gourmont in his second series of "Masques." [10]

Rather more interesting than the actual poetic production in 1895 was the attitude of the critics toward current poetry. The slight deviation from styles already established, despite lack of unity, produced comments which reveal to what degree the movement seemed to have spent its vital force. Characteristically, it is just at this time that the conservatives began to recognize the activity of the preceding decade. They were not willing to accord wholehearted praise, but René Doumic, in the *Revue des deux mondes,*[11] admitted that the "mouvement de rénovation poétique" was the one interesting literary manifestation which had recently occurred, and Henry Chantavoine, in the *Journal des débats,*[12] accorded a long article to Henri de Régnier and shorter notes to Vielé-Griffin and Charles Guérin. It is true that he reproached the unnamed poets whom he calls "les symbolistes purs" with lack of clarity, and he specifically stated that the real talent of Vielé-Griffin had been vitiated by the currents of symbolism. Even though the fundamental attitude of the press is unchanged, even though the enemies of the new poetry continued to proclaim vagueness as treason to the inherent nature of the French mind, a new tone of respect and willingness to discuss the problem is evident.

Among the poets of the symbolist group Henri de Régnier is the one singled out for most praise. As was evidenced by Doumic's and Chantavoine's articles, together with an essay by J.-H. Rosny in the *Nouvelle revue,* he represented a happy fusion between old and new ideas. Vielé-Griffin, more intransigent and champion of free verse, was not so acceptable. Perhaps as a result of this adverse criticism he continued to take a polemic tone in his critical essays. In "Le Symboliste pur," [13] answering Chantavoine's article, he accused the former enemies of symbolism with lack of sincerity. François Coppée's uncomplimentary remarks about the younger generation of poets, on the occasion

9. *Mercure de France,* XV (August, 1895), 216–219.

10. *Ibid.,* XXV (March, 1898), 694–701.

11. August 15, 1895.

12. April 26 and November 21, 1895 (evening edition).

13. *Revue blanche,* VIII (June, 1895), 490–492.

of Heredia's entrance into the Academy, was further fuel for his wrath. Vielé-Griffin stoutly maintained that the symbolists had not refused respect toward poets of true talent and had been severe only toward those who, like Coppée, did not possess it.

His contention comes at a time when a sudden and unexpected campaign was begun by one writer against, not the Parnassians, but the most venerated of the forerunners of symbolism. Nor was the attacker a Parnassian; he had once been among the most enthusiastic admirers of Mallarmé. On the fifteenth of January, 1895, Adolphe Retté's review of *La Musique et les lettres* was published by *La Plume,* inaugurating a series of hostile articles which were to continue even after Mallarmé's death. Isolated though this manifestation was, it came from a poet who had been the regular poetry critic for *L'Ermitage* in 1892 and who had assumed the following year a comparable position with *La Plume.* Now in 1895 he revealed himself as the enemy of all schools and criticized sharply the Ecole romane. But his condemnation of Mallarmé's style and its influence assumed the proportions of mania; and as his criticism continued, he became a disrupting agent on such symbolist unity as had existed.

Retté's attitude is symptomatic of the times, but less sterile and rather more good-humored criticism was coming from his contemporaries. Lucien Muhlfeld, in *La Revue blanche,* betrayed amused boredom with a certain type of symbolist verse in "Le Petit Symbolard." The poem with the knight and lady in the misty reaches of a dream forest suggests to him a kind of automatic toy in which the movements are all numbered and regulated. Meanwhile Charles Morice was writing against the imitative poetry of the Ecole romane. In *La Plume* a scene from a play, signed "Maurice Mittelinck," parodied the style of *Pelléas et Mélisande.* It is by comparison with such articles that one realizes how much Retté was fighting against windmills of his own imagination. Had he been writing a few years earlier when some of the poems of René Ghil and Camille Mauclair or the prose of André Fontainas were so clearly derivative from those of Mallarmé, he could have gleaned some curious examples of the dangers of imitation. The monotonous repetition of the school of Moréas, the iterations of Maeterlinck, the standardized chivalric settings which had been used by Merrill, Herold, Vielé-Griffin, and Henri de Régnier were far better materials for acid comment than the work of Mallarmé.

Despite opposition from its poetry critic to regimentation by schools, *La Plume* continued to give considerable favorable publicity to the Ecole romane. Léon Deschamps always proclaimed that his periodical would be available for a free expression of ideas, and he seems never to have demanded that Retté speak favorably of the group around Moréas. The presses of *La Plume* had published two books by Ernest Raynaud, *Les Cornes du faune* and *Le Bocage,* as well as Moréas' *Eriphyle* and Raymond de la Tailhède's *De la métamorphose des fontaines,* and it may well be that Deschamps' business instinct was to create discussion around the works of the group. Thus it was that in 1895 both the adverse essays of Retté and a "Défense du système des poètes romans" by Charles Maurras appeared in *La Plume.* The polemics over poetic theory of return to antiquity for inspiration or of reaction against the supposed Germanic influences seem of less moment than the poetic production of the school, for there only could be seen the advantages or dangers of following the dicta of Moréas. Perusal of these works reveals a lack of spontaneity and gives an impression of parody of a bygone age. The Romanists seemed to lack a sense of proportion, as in the following lines addressed by Raymond de la Tailhède to his leader:

> Jean Moréas, par toi le siècle va revivre
> Des victoires, illustre don de Jupiter,
> Et pour hausser ma voix courageuse à te suivre
> Je t'invoque premier devant que de chanter.[14]

The predilection shown by the *Plume* for the Romanists was not shared by the other little magazines. Henri Mazel of *L'Ermitage,* Vallette of the *Mercure de France,* Natanson of *La Revue blanche* followed a policy of eclecticism which represented most of the manifestations of the current poetic movements but did not exhibit the inclination for airing of quarrels which had always been a feature of *La Plume.* True, these magazines sometimes showed a lack of perspective, as was evidenced in 1895 by the *Mercure de France* when one of its founders died. This was Edouard Dubus, the author of *Quand les violons sont partis* (1892). Louis Dumur, in his obituary article,[15] called the volume "une des plus exquises productions de la littérature de ces vingt dernières années." In truth, Dubus' single volume of poetry was quite unequal in quality and perhaps most interesting in derivative manifestations ranging from irony akin to that of Laforgue to muted nostalgia like that of Verlaine's *Fêtes galantes.* At the time of his death, at the age of thirty-one, Dubus was meditating on a volume to be called *Nouveautés prosodiques* which might have proved interesting. He had been one of the few poets of his generation who never deviated from strict syllabic count and his nicety in rhyme had earned him the reproach of being too Parnassian. But he had been one of the leaders in the beginnings of the symbolist movement, a frequent contributor to *Le Chat noir* and later to *Le Scapin.* He was not unadmired by some of the younger poets, among them Tristan Klingsor. Today he is remembered as one of "poètes maudits," for his interest in occultism led him

14. *La Plume,* VII (February 15, 1895), 92.
15. *Mercure de France,* XV (August, 1895), 133–154.

to use drugs and his death was probably from an overdose of morphine. By the death of Albert Aurier in 1892 and Dubus in 1895, the *Mercure* had lost two of its founders. Under the able direction of Vallette, however, it was destined to gain rather than to lose in importance. The end of 1895 marks a change in editorship in another magazine, when Henri Mazel resigned his position to Edouard Ducoté. Mazel's six years of service to *L'Ermitage* had been marked by a gradual affinity with symbolist poetry. Between 1892 and 1896 he had entrusted poetic criticism successively to Adolphe Retté, Louis le Cardonnel, Stuart Merrill, Roland de Marès, and Edmond Pilon, and had printed poetry by Henri de Régnier, Vielé-Griffin, Verhaeren, Kahn, Morice, Mauclair, Charles Guérin, Louÿs, Rambosson, and Signoret. Valéry had been an occasional contributor between 1890 and 1892; Verlaine had contributed poetry for four issues in 1892. Charles Maurras had printed one of his first defenses of the Ecole romane in the magazine, under the title "Le Repentir de Pythéas," [16] but in general a favorable attitude toward the symbolists is present in the bibliographical notices.

L'Ermitage had also shown attentive interest toward the new manifestations in the fine arts, though not to the degree revealed by *La Plume*, which devoted four of its 1895 issues to Puvis de Chavannes, Henri Boutet, modern picture posters, and Andhré des Gachons respectively. Both Mazel and Deschamps envisioned a fraternity of artists and writers and the evening gatherings they arranged were a combination of the two spheres of creative activity. In the *Mercure de France*, with such writers as Camille Mauclair and André Fontainas, and in the *Revue blanche*, with Thadée Natanson, a parallel interest was shown in painting and sculpture which did not represent the academic traditions. The establishment of exact comparisons between literature and the fine arts, except in unusual cases such as that of Félicien Rops, is not an easy task. That artists were attempting rather to convey the atmosphere than a literal transcription of realities and were seeking escape from narrow rules was a sufficient bond between the symbolists and their contemporaries among painters and sculptors.

For a unified impression of the poetic scene in 1895 the twelve monthly articles of Edmond Pilon in *L'Ermitage* are perhaps the most satisfactory. A poet himself, Pilon did not admire all the literary tendencies of his epoch, but he preserved an air of moderation even in his adverse criticism. Although he did not approve of the Ecole romane, he considered Moréas a good poet. He dismissed Raymond de la Tailhède as lacking originality and discovered a vicious Romanist influence in the poetry of Dauphin Meunier. He insisted that the bucolic type of verse, promised by Moréas and his followers, had actually been accomplished by a poet outside their group, Henri Degron. Degron's

16. In the issue of January 1, 1892.

Corbeille ancienne is indeed filled with rural and sylvan landscapes, rapidly traced rather than fully described. In this verse, as in other volumes of the year, Pilon discovers simplicity replacing grandiose evocations. He approves of this, citing as an example Signoret's *Daphné,* which has been freed from the strange mixture of paganism and mysticism in that poet's early work. Pilon's remarks indicate considerable contempt for the followers of Parnassian tradition, for Paul Vérola's *Horizons* and Henri Rouger's *Chants et poèmes.* On the other hand he does not approve of close imitation of the symbolists; he chides Mauclair for having read too well Mallarmé, Laforgue, and Maeterlinck before composing *Sonatines d'automne.* The naturalness and simplicity of *Eveils* by André and Maurice Magre or of *Petits poèmes d'automne* by Stuart Merrill win his admiration.

The summary of Pilon's attitude toward his contemporaries is given in his last article of the year.[17] While he recognizes the accomplishments of the symbolists, he desires to caution them against too much haughty introspection, against overly uniform concentration on suffering and evil. He counsels the poet to go more frankly toward acceptance of nature, a piece of advice not far removed from that repeatedly given by Brunetière. In conclusion, he speaks of two groups, the "bergers candides," represented by Signoret, Gérardy, and Bouhélier, and the "métaphysiciens," led by Gide, Mauclair, and Valéry, who may accomplish this task.

The fortunes of symbolism outside the French frontiers present several interesting aspects during 1895. In Belgium the reactionary attitude of Giraud, Gilkin, and Gille of *La Jeune Belgique* provoked the creation of a new magazine, *Le Coq rouge.* Its program, besides that of attacking *La Jeune Belgique,* was the defense of free verse. The Belgian collaborators of the new publication, Verhaeren, Maeterlinck, Demolder, Eekhoud, and Krains, called upon many of the French poets for contributions. During 1895 Paul Fort, Ferdinand Herold, Gustave Kahn, Camille Mauclair (who sent a series of "Lettres parisiennes"), Régnier, Saint-Pol-Roux, and Vielé-Griffin answered this appeal. Another newcomer among Belgian periodicals, less combative than *Le Coq rouge* but representing the same poetic outlook, contained offerings from five French poets during this year. Its title, *L'Art jeune,* may have been chosen as a kind of rebuke to the conservatism of *La Jeune Belgique.*

The German magazine *Pan,* seeking to effect reciprocal interest in French and German poetic currents, appointed Henri Albert as director of a French supplement to be distributed in Paris. In the four issues which appeared during 1895, Albert made translations of several of Richard Dehmel's poems, but the periodical chiefly printed verse by Belgian and French poets. Verlaine, Maeterlinck, Régnier, Kahn, Hirsch, Roland de Marès, Fort, Vielé-Griffin, Herold,

17. *L'Ermitage,* 1895, II (December, 1895), 289–294.

Elskamp, Klingsor, Louÿs, and Fargue were the principal collaborators, but instead of critical reviews the magazine published representative poems from currently published volumes, thus adding several names to that list. *Pan* set itself no other program than the championship of idealistic poetry in opposition to naturalism. This periodical was merely an attempt to create mutual understanding of poetic currents in two nations.

Enthusiasm for Verlaine and for the symbolists played a part in the founding of a magazine in Coimbra, Portugal, during the last months of 1895. The editors were Eugenio de Castro and Manuel da Silva-Gaio, both destined to have important careers in their nation's intellectual life. Eugenio de Castro had lived in Paris and established many acquaintances among the symbolists. After early poetic volumes, in which the search for rare and musical words was the unusual feature, he had published in 1894 his dramatic poem *Sagramor*. This work received some comment in the little magazines of Paris; it was admired as a message of discouraged idealism, for the hero, Sagramor, vainly seeks from love, wealth, travel, glory, science, faith, and death the key to happiness. Eugenio de Castro consecrated fifty pages of the first issue of *Arte* to the publication of a story by Verlaine, now known as "Conte pédagogique." Friendships which the Portuguese writer had made in Paris account for the rather diversified group of French poets who contributed to the November and December issues.[18] Eugenio de Castro's admirations for French poets were very broad and his own work presents many different points of inspiration in subject and form.

The years 1894 and 1895 mark the beginnings of Valeri Bryusov's endeavors to acquaint Russia with the work of the French. *Romansy kez slov* (1894), a translation of Verlaine's *Romances sans paroles,* was followed by three issues of a poetic miscellany which included imitations and translations of French poets. The pamphlets were entitled *Ruskiye simvolisty* and presage the name given to Bryusov's group a decade later at the founding of *Vesy.*

In the expansion of symbolism outside France, Verlaine's name was more frequently encountered than that of any other French poet. Particularly in 1895 with Eugenio de Castro in Portugal and Bryusov in Russia, the spread of his fame was accelerated. In his own country his situation was somewhat different, for there the writers were not only conscious of the beauty of his past performance but of the mediocrity of his later writing. Verlaine, elected Prince des poètes in October, 1894, was destined to reign only some fifteen months. This period is not marked by any unusual appreciation of his work in the French periodicals. *La Plume* continued to consider itself his special patron and indeed published his *Epigrammes* at the end of 1894. The author

18. Louis-Pilate de Brinn' Gaubast, Remy de Gourmont, Gustave Kahn, Stuart Merrill, Lionel des Rieux, Ernest Raynaud, Saint-Pol-Roux, and Edouard Ducoté.

announced this little volume as a work written by a sick man who needed amusement and as one which was not to be taken too seriously. Of some interest, however, are those poems in which he speaks with patronizing condescension of free verse, the line in which he hints that a line of seventeen syllables may be in reality composed of ten and of seven feet, and the quatrain in which he compares Baudelaire to a discreet Marquis de Sade gifted with the speech of the angels. Many of the autobiographical poems seem negligible except for the unusual combinations of difficult rhymes worthy of Banville.

Immediately before Verlaine's death no long articles on his work appeared. Occasional contributions of his verse were printed in *La Plume,* in Maurice Le Blond's *Le Rêve et l'idée,* and in *La Revue blanche.* Verlaine's series of lectures in England during the winter of 1894, at the invitation of Arthur Symons and other writers, had given him contacts with the *Senate* and the *New Review,* which published several of his poems. Recognition of his worth in his own country is evidenced by the formation of a committee, headed by Maurice Barrès and Robert de Montesquiou, to assure him a modest income. In March, 1895, the Ministry of Public Instruction granted him financial aid. During these last months of his existence, in the *Confessions* published by the *Fin de siècle* press, Verlaine put in print three "Vieilles 'Bonnes Chansons'" which were more frankly sensuous than those of the volume of 1870 but were also evocative of the dim past when he was engaged to Mathilde Mauté. His last days were occupied with the writing of the "Biblio-Sonnets" which he had agreed to compose for Pierre Dauze, a strange occupation for the mind which had so seldom accepted the fetters of restraint.

On January 8, 1896, came the news of Verlaine's death and within a month there began to appear the special issues of magazines and the numerous articles praising the dead poet's work. André Fontainas,[19] Lucien Muhlfeld, Gustave Kahn, Paterne Berrichon,[20] Adolphe Retté,[21] Fernand Gregh,[22] François Paulhan,[23] and Edmond Pilon[24] were the vanguard of Verlainian criticism which found expression not only in France but in England and Germany.

19. *Mercure de France,* XVII (February, 1896), 145–153.
20. Kahn, Muhlfeld, and Berrichon contributed to the February, 1896, issue of the *Revue blanche.*
21. *La Plume,* VIII (February, 1896), 116–118.
22. *Revue de Paris,* III [1] (February, 1896), 658–672.
23. *La Nouvelle Revue,* LXXXXIX (March, 1896), 317–335.
24. *L'Ermitage,* 1896, I (February, 1896), 57–70.

Chapter XIII: SYMBOLISM
UNDER ATTACK, 1896

ESSENTIALLY, from the critical point of view, a year consecrated to the memory of Verlaine, 1896 offers very little in important volumes of poetry save for the second volume of Verhaeren's collected verse. Two series of *Ballades* by Paul Fort elicited many comments on their typographical form and indeed speculation as to whether the works were really poetry or prose. Pierre Louÿs, expressing confidence in Fort's future glory,[1] qualified the new style as "proses libres" while Gustave Kahn preferred the denomination of prose poem, although admitting effects which were closely allied with free verse.[2] Max Elskamp's slender *Six chansons du pauvre homme* continued the style and tone of his earlier poetry; Robert de Montesquiou's *Les Hortensias bleus* was rapidly dismissed as too mannered and Rodenbach's *Les Vies encloses* as overly monotonous. An allegory by Adolphe Retté, written in free verse and entitled *La Forêt bruissante,* suggested to the few who reviewed the book how much the author had lost in poetic beauty by expressing ideas of social reform. In truth it was not until the end of the year, at the appearance of Fernand Gregh's first volume, *La Maison de l'enfance,* that the critics displayed some enthusiasm. Gregh, twenty-three years old, was diversely hailed as a valid descendant of Verlaine, Rodenbach, and Samain and was praised for his intimate, sincere tone and for his nostalgic melancholy.

Emmanuel Signoret, whose *Vers dorés* appeared in 1896, was the recipient of some publicity, but his name was unfortunately associated with an article by André Ibels, published on December 15, 1895,[3] wherein rather damning evidence of plagiarism had been presented against him. That many images in Michel Abadie's *Le Mendieur d'azur* (1888) had been transferred to the pages of *Daphné* was evident, naturally it could not be proved to what extent involuntary memory had been responsible for the borrowings. Jean Dayros, who had read the two volumes at the time of their publication, confessed that he had thought *Daphné* to be an enlarged and emended edition of the *Mendieur d'azur* and had imagined that Signoret and Abadie were one and the same person.[4] Signoret did not make direct refutation of the charges brought against him but, as was his habit, denounced the charges of plagiarism as a

1. *L'Ermitage,* 1896, I (June, 1896), 344.
2. *Revue blanche,* X (February, 1896), 126.
3. In *La Plume.*
4. *L'Ermitage,* 1896, I (March, 1896), 171–172.

wicked plot. His protestations recall those he had made in 1893, when his erstwhile collaborators of the *Saint-Graal* had been offended by an essay in which
Signoret had declared that he esteemed Mallarmé "comme les hautes ruines
et les tombes fleuries." Then, as in 1896, he seemed unable to speak clearly of
the reasons for his unpopularity, and revealed in his open letters merely a
persecution complex and hypersensitiveness which evoke as a parallel the name
of Rousseau. His traits of personality during his lifetime, and even now, obscure the evaluation of his poetic talent, although André Gide, Adolphe Retté,
and J.-M. Bernard [5] have made some effort to judge his work.

In the closing years of the century Signoret's name appeared quite often in
the little magazines. If Paris refused to give him the highest praise, his native
Provence was more kindly. In *Les Mois dorés,* published in Aix-en-Provence
by Joachim Gasquet, he was hailed as a great poet. The first number of the
magazine, that of May, 1896, contained one of Signoret's poems followed by
an article in which Gasquet spoke of the heroic emotion and triumphant
evolution of the spirit discernible in the poet's work. Later in the year, in discussing the *Vers dorés,* Gasquet's praise reached new lyric heights. His expression, "Quelque chose de nouveau s'est intégré au monde: une splendeur
nouvelle s'est manifestée," [6] comes close to Signoret's own estimate of his
genius.

It would be unfair to suggest that a lack of critical equilibrium was confined
to the provincial magazine of Aix. In Paris too one could read some startling
judgments on contemporary poets. In the pages of *L'Ermitage* during 1896
two poets received eulogistic articles. Edmond Pilon wrote on Gustave Kahn,[7]
placing him in the category of the poet as prophet, as the inspired rather than
the meditative lyricist and in the lineage of Tasso, Shakespeare, Petrarch, and
Verlaine. Henri Ghéon, evaluating the work of Vielé-Griffin,[8] called him the
peer of Laforgue, Kahn, and Verhaeren, and not much inferior to Verlaine.
The name of the author of *Sagesse* thus appears unexpectedly and not too
aptly in the course of the year, as though the literary world were unceasingly
conscious of its bereavement.

Meanwhile the shades of other innovators of symbolism were receiving
homage. Camille Mauclair's essay on Jules Laforgue was published in two
installments in the *Mercure de France.* In the same magazine appeared
Maeterlinck's "Introduction à un essai sur Jules Laforgue," and to *La Revue
blanche* Gustave Kahn contributed an essay on Laforgue's work.[9] Paterne

5. See Bernard's *Œuvres II* and Retté's *Le Symbolisme.* Gide's preface to Signoret's collected
poems is perhaps the most interesting testimony of an admirer.
6. *Les Mois dorés,* No. 6 (October, 1896), pp. 161–173.
7. *L'Ermitage,* 1896, I (February, 1896), 72–86.
8. *Ibid.,* 1896, II (September, 1896), 136–145.
9. *La Revue blanche,* X (February, 1896), 122–126.

Berrichon began his fruitless campaign against journalistic articles treating of the personal lives of Verlaine and Rimbaud.[10] In *La Plume* Adolphe Retté published nineteen essays under the general title "Aspects" and devoted many of them to poets and their work. In three of these articles he virulently attacked Mallarmé, and in two others spoke with admiration of Verlaine and Rimbaud. Among the living poets he found kind words for Signoret, Saint-Georges de Bouhélier, and Verhaeren.

Criticism in the little magazines during 1896 was entrusted to a rather small group of writers. Retté's "Aspects," by their number and length, tend to cast other critical articles in *La Plume* into obscurity. In *La Revue blanche* Kahn's series "La Vie mentale" [11] sets the magazine's tone for the year. Even the *Mercure de France* abandoned its custom of entrusting book reviews to many different writers, and from April to December, 1896, Vielé-Griffin composed all the comments on current verse. These three critics were quite friendly toward free verse, but not to the point of condemning regular meters. If they remained cool toward most of the poetry published during 1896 it was not without reason. Volumes by Mathias Morhardt, Edouard Ducoté, Paul Mariéton, and André Lebey, all of which were overly sentimental, offered little in novelty or interest. By comparison Klingsor's *Filles-Fleurs,* with their suggestion of folk poetry and legend, seemed almost sprightly and gay and Signoret's *Vers dorés* splendid and sonorous.

On the other hand, Lionel des Rieux, who wrote the poetry reviews for *L'Ermitage* during the first six months of 1896, consistently condemned liberty in versification. An admirer of the Ecole romane, he blamed his predecessor, Edmond Pilon, for not having appreciated Raymond de la Tailhède's *De la métamorphose des fontaines.* This Des Rieux considered the only beautiful volume of poetry which had appeared during 1895; and since there was little activity among the Romanists during 1896, he devoted his reviews to disparagement of those outside the group. Charles Guérin's *Le Sang des crépuscules* he found obscure and mannered; Edmond Pilon's *Les Poèmes de mes soirs* seemed to him an imitative patchwork of Kahn, Herold, Verhaeren, Merrill, Signoret, and Abadie. For good measure, he asserted that the diction at times suggested Vielé-Griffin. None of the current volumes found grace in these articles by Lionel des Rieux. Klingsor was overly nice and falsely unsophisticated, Ducoté excessively melancholy, and Kahn unpoetic. In his final review he asserted that Edmond Jaloux's *Une ame d'automne* was a continuation of "la poésie détestable" of Verhaeren, Régnier, and Kahn. During the last six months of the year *L'Ermitage* underwent a complete reversal of attitude in

10. *Ibid.,* X (February, 1896), 177–181; XI (August, 1896), 165–173.
11. The same title as that used by Kahn in *La Société nouvelle* during 1894–95.

so far as poetic criticism was concerned. Lionel des Rieux was replaced by Charles Guérin, a poet who, like Pilon, was hostile toward the Romanists. He had accused them of having sent the mystery and soul of poetry into exile and his critical articles were full of praise for the writers against whom des Rieux had been so harsh. Especially did he admire Fernand Gregh's work, for he considered it in the tradition of his favorite poets, Rodenbach, Verlaine, and Samain. But he also praised the simple beauty of Maurice Magre's *Le Retour,* the strength of Verhaeren's poetry, and the independence of spirit he observed in the southern poets, Marc Lafargue and Emmanuel Delbousquet.

Thus the four principal symbolist magazines, entrusting the criticism of verse to five writers during the year, offer a curious spectacle of prejudice. Retté, violently hostile to church and state at this period, was perhaps less interested in poetic problems than in the destruction of authority. His principal contribution in criticism, if it can be called a contribution, was his unjust and ill-mannered attack on Mallarmé. Lionel des Rieux was equally unsatisfactory by reason of his exclusive admiration for the Ecole romane. Guérin's essays were too brief and superficial to be important. Vielé-Griffin and Gustave Kahn, despite their partisan attitude toward free verse, appear the most satisfactory of the five. In his series "La Vie mentale" Kahn is vehement only when he speaks of Robert de Montesquiou's *Les Hortensias bleus,* a volume which in his estimation contains not one good line of verse. He admits laudable poetic qualities in the work of Léon Dierx, a writer whose theories were certainly quite opposed to his own. Vielé-Griffin's comments on twenty-eight volumes of contemporary verse likewise reveal an attempt to be fair and impartial.

Meanwhile in Toulouse a new phase in poetic attitudes was attained by the founding of the monthly magazine *L'Effort.* In the first issue, that of March, 1896, Maurice Magre recalled two earlier attempts of creating a literary periodical in the legendary birthplace of the "jeux floraux." The first had been in 1892, when Emmanuel Delbousquet, Marc Lafargue, Eugène Thébault, and Pierre Dévoluy had published seven issues of the *Essais des jeunes* and had proclaimed solidarity with the Ecole évolutive of René Ghil. A new series of the same magazine had appeared between December, 1894, and August, 1895, when Charles Guérin, Jean Viollis, and Maurice Le Blond became contributors. Repudiating the formulas of Ghil, this new grouping of poets fought chiefly against artificiality in poetry.

Maurice Magre had been a contributor to these earlier magazines, but it was not until 1896 that he pronounced judgment on the symbolists. The preceding poetic generation, he acknowledges, was somewhat constrained by public indifference to the formation of isolated groups and the creation of new magazines. However meritorious such activity may have been it resulted, in Magre's estimation, in hesitations, conflicting currents, pessimism, narcissistic introspection, and finally in a negative attitude toward life. Expressed in the initial issue of *L'Effort,* Magre's opinions are supplemented in the same number by an article signed by Viollis.[12] The accomplishments of the symbolists, as evaluated by Viollis, were the liberation of prosody, the expression of delicate and subtle feeling, and especially the attainment of artistic dignity and independence. Condemning René Ghil as ridiculous and incomprehensible, and blaming the Ecole romane for vitiating such poetic talents as those of Ernest Raynaud and Raymond de la Tailhède, Viollis concludes that the new generation of poets has gained a splendid heritage from symbolism. But poetry, he feels, will be obliged to seek new paths, to react against the currents of pessimism and artificiality which characterized the symbolist period. In December, 1896, Viollis proposed as the best name for this return toward simplicity and love of life the term "Naturisme," [13] thus accepting the word proposed by Bouhélier and Le Blond.

The chief literary criticism of *L'Effort* during 1896 was written by Emmanuel Delbousquet in a series of articles entitled "L'Œuvre et la formule." [14] Successively he examined the work of Heredia, Verlaine, and Mallarmé rather in a spirit of analysis than a tone of controversy. While Delbousquet cannot be said to have shown great originality in his essays, his ideas are sound. He admires the artistry of Heredia, the rhythmic innovations of Verlaine, and Mallarmé's increasing preoccupation with the magic of words. Delbousquet insists chiefly on sincerity in literature, and on this score he is favorably impressed with Le Blond's *Essai sur le naturisme* and is hostile toward the school of Moréas. His views are quite in accord with those of Maurice Magre, who in bibliographical notes commends *La Chambre blanche* of Bataille for its purity and simplicity and Retté's *La Forêt bruissante* for its humanitarian spirit. The group of *L'Effort,* which, besides Maurice Magre, Delbousquet, and Viollis, contained the names of André Magre, Raymond Marival, Henri Mouchart, Marc Lafargue, Jacques Nervat, and Pierre Pouvillon, appeared consistent in its admiration for simplicity and sentiment. Only one member, J.-R. de Brousse, through his imitative poems of antiquity, seemed apart from his fellows and rather close to the spirit of the Ecole romane.

The mild collective protest which was coming from Languedoc was more vehemently expressed in Paris by Saint-Georges de Bouhélier's spokesman, Maurice Le Blond. The latter's *Essai sur le naturisme* was published in 1896

12. *L'Effort,* No. 1, pp. 16–19. The article is entitled "A propos de Paul Verlaine," but wanders far from the immediate subject.

13. *Ibid.,* No. 10, pp. 254–256.

14. *Ibid.,* Nos. 2, 3, 5, 7, and 8.

by the presses of the *Mercure de France*. Accusing the preceding generation of poets of cultivating the unreal, of preferring incoherence to clarity, of frantically searching for the "frisson nouveau," he presages an imminent change toward radiant and gigantic pantheism. As examples of this evolution he cites Gide, Abadie, Fort, and Louÿs, and as guiding spirit he names Bouhélier. Though crediting the symbolists with an attempt to free themselves from the bonds of romanticism, he contends that their lassitude and melancholy is but a continuation of the lyricism which flourished in the first half of the century. The movement of the Ecole romane, the return to antiquity he sees as a new endeavor of liberation but condemns the school as artificial and as contrary to the spirit of literary evolution. Accusing Mallarmé, in his cult of the rare epithet, of creating discord between the poet and nature, blaming Régnier and Moréas for neglecting human emotions, casting disdain on the allegorical aspects of symbolism in general, Le Blond tempers his harshness with some words of praise for certain of his elders: Verhaeren because his poetry gives voice to the soul of a whole race of men; Vielé-Griffin because of his mastery of free verse; Retté because of his independence and humanitarianism; Verlaine because of his rejection of traditional literary conventions —these escape the denunciation which embraces nearly all the poets of the older generation. Le Blond's volume closes with a panegyric of Saint-Georges de Bouhélier, the messiah of a new poetic era.

During January and February, 1896, Le Blond published two numbers of *Le Rêve et l'idée*. In an essay entitled "Epilogue à l'histoire du symbolisme" he rebukes the symbolists for having failed to comprehend that precision is necessary even in the realm of dreams and for not having engendered any new ideas. He indicates Bouhélier as the proper guide to follow and makes the astounding prediction that some of the formulas of that author will be as important in the field of ideas as those of Galileo and Kepler in the physical sciences. These two issues of *Le Rêve et l'idée* also sought to publicize the spread of Bouhélier's ideas in Holland. Translations of some poems by Herman Gorter and a literary essay in Dutch by Joust Verbrughe were printed.

During a few months after the demise of *Le Rêve et l'idée* the naturists found a temporary outlet for their ideas and production in a magazine begun by the artist Maurice Dumont and Paul Fort. The new periodical bore the name of *Le Livre d'art,* a title Fort had used for a similar publication in 1892.[15] In this new series of the magazine, the first, third, and fourth issues contained a section of "Pages naturistes." In them were printed portions of Bouhélier's

15. *Le Livre d'Art,* which had first appeared in May, 1892, had been an outgrowth of the illustrated programs of Fort's theater. While it was chiefly known for illustrations by Emile Bernard, Maurice Denis, Bonnard, Vuillard, and Sérusier, it had printed poems by Roinard, Herold, Gourmont, Saint-Pol-Roux, Morice, Dubus, Aurier, and Quillard.

"L'Hiver en méditation," short extracts from Eugène Montfort's novel *Sylvie,*
and poems by Albert Fleury, Georges Pioch, and Michel Abadie. The naturalists must have received a severe jolt when another of the contributors to the
magazine, Tristan Klingsor, politely intimated that Bouhélier's method of
preaching simplicity was often vainly pompous and complicated and that perhaps everything he was advising had already been accomplished by such a
writer as Vielé-Griffin. Today *Le Livre d'art* of 1896 is chiefly known as the
magazine in which the complete text of Jarry's "Ubu Roi" was first published
and in which poems by Fort, Jammes, Guérin, Klingsor, Pilon, Fargue, and
Ducoté appeared.

The spirit of dissension and irritation which was the poetic atmosphere of
1896 is absent from an ephemeral but interesting quarterly periodical initiated
by Henri Albert in March of that year. Issued in an elegant format, its restricted list of contributors recalls Louÿs' *La Conque* of 1891. The new magazine was named *Le Centaure* and its collaborators included Henri de Régnier,
André Lebey, Jean de Tinan, Ferdinand Herold, André Gide, and Paul
Valéry. Most of the group made contributions both in prose and in verse to
the two issues which appeared. But each number contained over one hundred
twenty-five pages and, aside from this question of volume, the periodical remains noteworthy as that in which Valéry published the poem "Eté," the
sonnet later to be called "Vue," and the prose work "La Soirée avec M. Teste."
In it also appeared Gide's "La Ronde de la grenade," which presaged what
form the lyric utterance of *Les Nourritures terrestres* would take. The magazine's disdain for the literary quarrels of the period was expressed by the
malicious pen of Jean de Tinan. Charles Maurras' harshness toward the work
of Verhaeren, Rodenbach, and Kahn, a letter of protest written by René Ghil
to Robert de Souza, Retté's reply to Vielé-Griffin's unfavorable review of *La
Forêt bruissante,* Viollis' condemnation of the Romanists, and Lionel des
Rieux's championship of the same school are all passed in rapid review under
the heading "Les Poètes." What Jean de Tinan most deplores is the imitative
nature of contemporary poetry, the emulation of Régnier in France and of
Verlaine in England,[16] and what chiefly interests him is the revival of sentiment in poetry, as illustrated by Bataille and Jammes.

This year, so poor in poetic works and so confused in critical appreciations,
witnessed the publication of a series of articles in which was made the first
sustained attempt to delineate the individuality of the writers of the past
decade. They were published not in a symbolist magazine but in *La Revue
des revues.* Their author was Remy de Gourmont. Entitled in the periodical
"Les Nouveaux Venus," [17] these little essays were to furnish more than half

16. *Le Centaure,* II (1896), 124–131.
17. *Revue des revues,* XVI, 124–133, 406–413; XVII, 196–204; XVIII, 493–502 (January–
September, 1896).

the contents of the first *Livre des masques,* published toward the end of 1896. Remy de Gourmont's opening remarks, under the heading "Qu'est-ce que le Symbolisme," were resumed in the broad statement: "En somme, le symbolisme, c'est, même excessive, même impestive, même prétentieuse, l'expression de l'individualisme dans l'art." This viewpoint aids in explaining the author's attitude toward the writers he treats; he wishes to underline their independence of spirit. Verhaeren seems to him the descendant of Victor Hugo and of romanticism, Régnier the lyricist of sumptuous melancholy, Herold the poet of tenderness and gentleness, Vielé-Griffin the expression of joy couched in diction inspired by popular poetry. He praises the synthesis of idea and sentiment in Maeterlinck, he admires the pure sincerity of Samain, he approves the harmony between thought and expression in the work of Quillard. Stuart Merrill, the conflict of a fiery temperament and a gentle heart, and Saint-Pol-Roux, the marvelous inventor of metaphors, warrant, he feels, greater fame than they enjoy. Rather more ironical when he speaks of the claims of the Ecole romane, Gourmont finally accords poetic worth to Moréas. In Gustave Kahn's work he is chiefly attracted by the artistry of the love poems. Retté's untamed spirit and Louis Dumur's obstinate logic claim his attention, while he designates Laurent Tailhade as one of the most authentic glories of current French letters. He does not, following the example of most of the other critics, dismiss Robert de Montesquiou with a few words of scorn. He even defends to a certain degree his preciosity, while deploring the useless adornments which remind him of barbaric tatooing. Not limiting his essays to poets, Gourmont seeks out originality among prose writers. He speaks of the precision and freshness of Jules Renard, the observation and imagination of Paul Adam, the expression of personal wrath, pity, scorn, and love that permeates the work of Georges Eekhoud. In an article outside the series of "Les Nouveaux Venus," he notes the respect accorded to the Goncourts by the symbolist generation.[18] Concurrently with Gourmont's essays, *La Revue des revues* inserted in its issues poetry by Vielé-Griffin, Herold, Régnier, Quillard, Samain, Retté, Montesquiou, and Merrill, giving verse for a short time a place of honor.

The election, early in 1896, of a Prince des poètes to succeed Verlaine provides enlightening commentary on the attitude of writers toward the generation which Remy de Gourmont was discussing. In 1894 the popularity of Verlaine had been unmistakable; now in 1896 it was his memory and not the choice of a successor which was the keynote. In the results of the election, given by *La Plume,*[19] one observes that nearly one hundred writers expressed preference for *Sagesse* in the dead poet's work but that Mallarmé, gaining succession to his title, received only twenty-seven votes. So weakly stated were these

18. *Ibid.,* XVIII (August 1, 1896), 206–211.
19. The issue of February 1, 1896, is entirely devoted to the election.

twenty-seven suffrages that Lionel des Rieux considered only fourteen of them valid and pointed out that fifteen of the nineteen mentions of Moréas were unmistakable nominations for the honor to fall to the leader of the Romanists.[20] The results of the election were all the more curious in that after the names of Mallarmé and Moréas the order of popularity was a combination of Parnassians and symbolists. Sully-Prudhomme, in third place, was followed by Régnier, Dierx, Heredia, and Verhaeren.

Gustave Kahn, who was mentioned by very few of the voters in the election of the Prince des poètes, received a kind of consolatory honor in the form of a banquet, given on February 14, 1896, to commemorate the publication of La Pluie et le beau temps. At this dinner Mallarmé said a few polite words, Pilon made a short discourse in which he linked the names of Verlaine and Laforgue with that of the guest of honor, and Catulle Mendès gave a long and rambling oration in which he explained that although his ideas on poetic form were opposed to those of Kahn, he honored all those who were sincere in their pursuit of literary beauty. At the close of the banquet Kahn proposed a toast to the memory of his friend, Jules Laforgue.[21]

Six days after this banquet Belgian men of letters honored in a similar way the poetry of Verhaeren.[22] Held in Brussels, and primarily a public recognition of the foremost figure in the rebirth of Belgian poetry, the occasion was also recorded in French periodicals. Vielé-Griffin's "Hommage à Verhaeren" was printed in Le Réveil.[23] A less successful dinner was given in Paris on June 15, when Eugenio de Castro happened to visit the capital. His periodical Arte had continued printing contributions by French authors of the symbolist group. In the eight numbers of Arte, between November, 1895, and June, 1896, verse by Gourmont, Kahn, Merrill, Rieux, Raynaud, Louÿs, Vielé-Griffin, Verhaeren, Herold, Pilon, Klingsor, Montesquiou, and Régnier was published. Even Louis-Pilate de Brinn'Gaubast, who had returned to France after several years in the Levant, was represented. The February issue of the magazine was devoted to the memory of Paul Verlaine. But Eugenio de Castro's visit was badly timed, for most of those who contributed to his magazine were not in Paris during the summer and sent cards of regrets. At the banquet, it was Brinn'Gaubast who made the principal speech, calling for French recognition of the author of Horas and Sagramor.

These banquets give somewhat the impression of efforts toward the creation of new altars of devotion after Verlaine's death. As such they were unsuccessful. Indeed, apart from Remy de Gourmont's articles, the year reveals only

20. L'Ermitage, 1896, I (April, 1896), 243–246.
21. La Revue blanche gives in the issue of March, 1896, a complete report of the Kahn banquet.
22. See L'Art moderne, 1896, p. 65.
23. Le Réveil, VI (February, 1896), 87–89.

uncertainty and dissatisfaction with the current state of poetry. At the very end of 1896, after Jarry's *Ubu Roi* was presented on December 10, the term symbolism was brought into the foreground. Among the journalists it was used derisively to convey only the sense of the bizarre and eccentric. The play received its chief support from the group of the *Mercure de France,* but unlike Maeterlinck's theater, Jarry's play seems not to have been accepted as an integral part of symbolist expression.

The year 1896 marks the end of extensive collaboration of French symbolists in Belgian magazines. For a whole decade periodicals in Brussels, Liége, or Ghent had carried on the tradition, begun by *La Basoche* in 1885, of recognizing a parallel literary movement in the two countries. *L'Art moderne,* throughout its long life, gave importance to an international outlook by publishing book reviews, but until 1892 it had been *La Wallonie* with its presentation of poems by French writers which best represented the artistic amity of French and Belgian poets. After *La Wallonie* had disappeared *Floréal,* briefly, and *Le Réveil,* for a longer period, had assumed the task. *La Société nouvelle,* when Gustave Kahn became a regular contributor in 1892, had begun publishing poetry by French authors. Then with the founding of two magazines[24] in Brussels in 1895 an even more extensive field for French poets was created.

Perhaps the hospitality shown by Brussels for Paris during 1896 was in part attributable to French admiration for Verhaeren,[25] but there is much evidence of the Belgians' desire of recognizing the lyric art of their neighbor. Paul Fort was a favored contributor; his "Ballades" appeared in three issues of *Le Réveil,* in two of *L'Art jeune,* and in single numbers of *Le Coq rouge* and *La Société nouvelle.* Contributions by Ferdinand Herold appeared in these four magazines, while Vielé-Griffin's verse was printed in *La Lutte, Le Réveil, L'Art jeune,* and *Le Coq rouge.* Gustave Kahn was a frequent contributor to *La Société nouvelle* although he had ceased being its regular literary critic. Camille Mauclair's poetry was accepted by both *L'Art jeune* and *Le Coq rouge.* Other French writers represented in Belgian periodicals during the year included Ghéon, Ghil, Guérin, Jammes, Klingsor, Merrill, and Régnier.

This abundant collaboration was brought to an end when *Le Réveil,* in its fifth year of existence, suspended activity in December, 1896, and when *L'Art jeune* and *Le Coq rouge,* even by uniting, were able to struggle only until March, 1897. *La Société nouvelle* also ceased to exist in 1897, when one of its founders, Fernand Brouez, became ill. During the last years of the century only a few of Paul Fort's "Ballades" in *Durendal* and several items by Jammes, Vielé-Griffin, and Guérin in *Le Spectateur catholique* remained as vestiges of former international collaboration.

24. *L'Art jeune* and *Le Coq rouge.*
25. Short talks at the Verhaeren banquet, by Vielé-Griffin, Herold and Mauclair, were printed in *L'Art jeune.*

Chapter *XIV:* SYMBOLISM VERSUS NATURISM, 1897

THE VICIOUS ATTACKS on Mallarmé in Retté's "Aspects" of 1896 were destined to have widespread repercussions the following year. Although Retté relinquished his post as critic for *La Plume* in order to contribute to that same magazine his "XIII Idylles diaboliques," his place was taken by a close friend from Marseilles, Louis de Saint-Jacques. The latter, in the first [1] of his twenty literary essays, entitled "Expertises," announced complete solidarity with Retté in respect to Mallarmé. Saint-Jacques, as had Retté, accused Mallarmé of lacking clarity and of deforming the language. At the same time in *La Revue Blanche,* the magazine which had recently published Mallarmé's "Variations sur un sujet," Thadée Natanson was the author of an essay praising the lofty idealism and conception of perfection which were Mallarmé's.[2] Then the *Mercure de France* entered the arena by publishing an open letter from André Gide and subscribed to by Valéry, Schwob, Fort, and Verhaeren. In this letter the signatories condemned the insulting tone of Retté's and Saint-Jacques's articles toward a writer worthy of the highest esteem. Léon Deschamps, the director of *La Plume,* countered with a reply in which he stated that contributors to his magazine were alone responsible for their opinions and that the direction of *La Plume* entertained deep affection toward Mallarmé. Retté also answered Gide's denunciation. His open letter, published in the *Mercure de France* in March, 1897, defended his articles against Mallarmé as the frank expression of a conflicting artistic outlook.

Mallarmé's admirers, meanwhile, had striven to give concrete expression to their loyalty and solidarity, offering the Prince des poètes a banquet on February 2, 1897. Shortly thereafter, twenty-three writers presented Mallarmé with an album of poems and prose passages written in his honor. Among the contributors were Mallarmé's cousins, Paul and Victor Margueritte, and those who had continuously voiced admiration for the poet, Camille Mauclair, André Fontainas, Edouard Dujardin, and Albert Mockel. The Belgians, led by Verhaeren, Maeterlinck, and Van Lerberghe, were also well represented. From the younger group the names of Claudel, who had written an enthusiastic letter to Mallarmé at the time of the publication of "La Musique et les lettres" in 1895, Louÿs, who had composed a sonnet in 1892 honoring Mal-

1. *La Plume,* IX (January, 1897), 20–22.
2. *La Revue blanche,* XII (January, 1897), 79–85.

larmé's fiftieth birthday, and Valéry, one of the assiduous visitors in the Rue de Rome, were conspicuous.

But Retté's erstwhile companions were not absent from this collective homage to Mallarmé. Kahn, Merrill, Régnier, and Vielé-Griffin were also contributors to the album. The diatribes in *La Plume,* however tenacious they were, appear petty and spiteful in comparison with the expression of Mallarmé's admirers, especially when one adds to their number the writers beyond the boundaries of France. During 1896 Mallarmé's essay on Rimbaud had been published in the *Chap Book* of Chicago, while a translation of "Le Phénomène futur" by George Moore and one of the "Hérodiade" by Arthur Symons had appeared in *Le Savoy.*

Saint-Jacques devoted his fifth "Expertise" [3] to "La Protestation mallarmophile de M. Gide et les divagations de M. Mallarmé." In this essay the author poked fun at Mallarmé's long awaited but unpublished masterpieces, recalling that they had been promised by Verlaine in 1884, Wyzewa in 1886, later by Morice, Byvanck, and Mauclair, and even hinted at in Natanson's article three months before. This new tirade reopened the quarrel and Robert de Souza, another of the contributors to the album of homage, became Mallarmé's champion in the pages of the *Mercure de France,* where he was writing the reviews on current periodicals. Accusations and counteraccusations followed. Louis de Saint-Jacques, in his "Expertises," examined the poetry of the year from the viewpoint of reaction against Mallarmé. Nor did Retté remain silent. In the eighth of his "Idylles diaboliques," [4] which might best be described as satirical dialogues, he represented Robert de Souza, under the name of "Norbert de Gloussat," as defending the aridity and vacuous introspection of "Alfane Malbardé."

The ramifications of this somewhat puerile quarrel were numerous and there is evidence of many rifts of friendships because of it. Saint-Jacques, overly zealous in detecting evidence of pernicious Mallarmean influence, stated that Régnier's poetry suggested "Eau froide dans ton cadre gelée." A few months later Régnier, reviewing *Campagne première,* suggested that Retté's return to nature had failed to reveal a personal or interesting note.[5] When Louis de Saint-Jacques insinuated that this hostile tone was the result of his own articles in praise of Retté and that Régnier was attempting to revenge himself by speaking harshly of his friend, a new low in criticism was reached.

Meanwhile, under the direction of Ducoté, the magazine *L'Ermitage* was turning more and more toward interest in the fine arts, to the prejudice of poetry. Offering no opinions on the question of Mallarmé, the periodical

3. In the March 15, 1897, issue of *La Plume.*
4. *La Plume,* IX (August 15, 1897), 537–541.
5. *Mercure de France,* XXIII (August, 1897), 335–336.

limited its critical apparatus to short reviews by Charles Guérin. These expressed admiration for Verhaeren, Régnier, Klingsor, Samain, Vielé-Griffin, and Ghéon, with certain reserves toward free verse and especially toward the eccentricities of Gustave Kahn. Guérin's predilection for tender, personal verse leaves little occasion for a broadly critical outlook. Thus L'Ermitage, through paucity of articles, and La Plume, through the violently prejudiced writings of Retté and Louis de Saint-Jacques, form very unsatisfactory vehicles for presentation of the poetic scene of 1897. But both magazines, by reacting against artificiality and excessive introspection, seemed to be moving in a direction parallel with that of Saint-Georges de Bouhélier and the naturists. It is indeed just at this time of the Mallarmé quarrel and at the moment when Moréas was occupied with the writing of prose that naturism as a movement becomes strong.

Naturism had been making attempts to gain public recognition since 1892, when two very young schoolboys published an ephemeral little magazine called L'Académie française and succeeded in obtaining for the first number a few pages by Camille Mauclair and some sonnets by Edouard Dubus. This issue also contained an article entitled "L'Art se résorbe en Dieu" by Saint-Georges de Bouhélier, one of the magazine's founders. In this grandiloquent and somewhat incoherent essay had been expressed the first conception of naturism, an appeal for a sort of pantheistic mysticism based on comprehension rather than rejection of the external manifestations of nature. The author had at this time one loyal disciple, his friend Maurice Le Blond. The latter was destined to champion the cause of naturism as had Maurras the ideas of the Ecole romane. Between 1892 and 1897 Bouhélier had tried, briefly and unsuccessfully, to ally himself with Signoret's Saint-Graal, had published five numbers of a little magazine called Assomption (1893–94) and four of Le Rêve et l'idée (1894–95). In 1895 Maurice Le Blond had written against artificiality in literature in the Essais des jeunes of Toulouse.[6] In 1896 appeared the same author's Essai sur le naturisme. Gradually the two innovators of the movement had acquired disciples, such as Eugène Montfort and Albert Fleury, or sympathetic adherents, such as Abadie and Gasquet. In December, 1896, Jean Viollis had accepted the name of "naturisme" to describe the trend of the young poetic generation.

The first number of the Revue naturiste appeared in March, 1897, and contained a manifesto by Saint-Georges de Bouhélier, articles by Montfort and Le Blond, and poetry by Abadie. In subsequent issues of the year, Le Blond wrote on the poetry of Michel Abadie while Gasquet offered his "Notes pour servir à l'histoire du naturisme." In poetry supplements Viollis, Fleury, Bouhélier, Maurice Magre, and Edmond Jaloux were prominently featured.

6. Essais des jeunes, No. 4 (March, 1895); No. 8 (July–August, 1895).

The opening articles were generally by Saint-Georges de Bouhélier and took the form of poetic meditations on the glorification of man in nature. If the *Revue naturiste* had been the only outlet for the group's expression, naturism might have remained a closed literary chapel; but Jean Viollis' "Observations sur le naturisme" were printed in the *Mercure de France* [7] and *La Plume* devoted a special number to the movement.[8]

In this issue of *La Plume* Bouhélier discussed "La Révolution comme origine et comme fin du naturisme," Montfort "L'Amour et le naturisme," Fleury "De l'émotion naturiste," while Viollis wrote on the lofty idealistic outlook of Bouhélier. Perhaps the most interesting contribution was Le Blond's "Documents sur la poésie contemporaine," for in it the author depicted the symbolists as having adopted an untenable attitude toward life. His viewpoint was much the same as that expressed the previous year in *L'Effort* and, as then, he cited some exceptions to the currents of pessimistic lassitude, Verhaeren, Vielé-Griffin, and Retté. In the poetic rebirth which he foresees, he names as moving forces Maurice Magre, Fleury, Gasquet, and of course Bouhélier.

The Mallarmé quarrel and the claims of the naturists might seem utterly to have clouded the accomplishments of the symbolists. This is far from true, for 1897 also marks the beginning of close study of the past decade. Among the periodicals it was the *Mercure de France* which best represented the poetic filiations of past and present. The Mallarmé quarrel was wisely relegated to the monthly summaries at the end of the issues and, in addition to the article on naturism by Viollis, the magazine offered many interesting essays on diverse aspects of the literary scene. Vigié-Lecocq's "L'Amour dans la poésie contemporaine" preluded the appearance of a not unimportant volume, wherein was made an attempt to evaluate poetic accomplishments between 1884 and 1896. Remy de Gourmont, continuing the little essays which had been published in the *Revue des revues* during 1896, contributed a series of "Nouveaux masques" to the *Mercure de France*.[9] Among the older writers, Bloy, Fénéon, Rebell, and Dujardin, who had had their moment in the symbolist movement, the author presented younger men of letters such as Jammes, Fort, and Mauclair. In his two volumes of the *Masques,* published in 1896 and 1898, Remy de Gourmont was to collect a portrait gallery which represented fairly completely the innovators, in prose and poetry, of the symbolist period.

The literature on Verlaine persisted during 1897, with articles by Camille Lemonnier [10] and Emile Verhaeren; [11] the enigma of Rimbaud's personality received new documentation, thanks to the affectionate collaboration of Isa-

7. *Mercure de France*, XXI (February, 1897), 304–314.
8. No. 205 (November 1, 1897).
9. In the issues of October and November, 1897.
10. *Mercure de France*, XXII (May, 1897), 299–302.
11. *La Revue blanche*, XII (April, 1897), 409–412.

belle Rimbaud and Paterne Berrichon; [12] the name of Ephraïm Mikhaël, almost forgotten during the years which followed his death in 1890, was accorded commemoration in the February issue of the *Mercure de France* and in the April number of *L'Effort*. Some of those who united in honoring his memory, Delbousquet, Viollis, and Lafargue, were from his native Languedoc; two, Quillard and Fontainas, had been his schoolmates at the Lycée Condorcet; still others were poets who had felt the beauty of the verse by Mikhaël in the *Pléiade* of 1886 or in the posthumous volume of his work published in 1890.

In such studies of the dead poets and in the little essays by Remy de Gourmont, a kind of rebuttal was being made to attacks by the naturists. A more comprehensive answer came in the form of a volume entitled *La Poésie contemporaine* and published in 1897 by the press of the *Mercure de France*. The author, Vigié-Lecocq, in reviewing the past twelve years, based his work on the premise that romanticism, Parnassianism, and symbolism were all parts of a natural poetic evolution and that the differences between the movements were capable of being conciliated. Although he does not attempt to refute the charge, made by Le Blond and his group, that the symbolists catered to small intellectual circles and made little effort toward clarity, Vigié-Lecocq defends symbolist verse as having, by these very faults, avoided mediocrity and overly simplified cheapness. Like Remy de Gourmont, the author of *La Poésie contemporaine* is conscious of the great diversity of temperaments and esthetic outlooks among the poets of the past decade. Qualifying Rodenbach as a melancholy mortal in search of fugitive sensations, le Cardonnel as ascetic and candid, Verhaeren as the multiple expression of power, mysticism, and realism, Vielé-Griffin as the apostle of joyous pantheism and dreamy melancholy, Régnier as the master of sonorities, assonance, antithesis, and imagery, Retté and Maeterlinck as hearts in sympathy with the humble and with human suffering, the author also treats the audacity of Kahn in technical reform, the return to Ronsard among the Romanists, and the elegiac art of Stuart Merrill.

It is to Vigié-Lecocq's honor that, having indicated the divergencies in poetic expression, he attempts to find the directive forces which had produced symbolist verse. In strict opposition to Le Blond and Bouhélier, he adduces them as nature, love, mysticism, and altruism. Then, to explain how these sources of inspiration were utilized by the symbolists, he defines the modern poetic mind in a paragraph which contains comprehension of Baudelaire's role in

---

12. See the *Mercure de France* for October, 1897, and *La Revue blanche* for April, September, and October, 1897. The correspondence between Isabelle Rimbaud and Berrichon (Pierre Dufour), published in the Pléiade edition of Rimbaud, aids in understanding the genesis of these articles.

poetic evolution and suggests some of the contributions made by such great leaders as Verlaine, Mallarmé, and Rimbaud:

La vision du poète s'est amplifiée, ses sens se sont affinés jusqu'à la transposition maladive, son intelligence élargie perçoit l'unité de la vie sous la diversité des formes ondoyantes éparses dans la nature. Il a recréé tout un univers où ne se voient plus seulement des lignes et des couleurs, le jeu des ombres et des lumières à fixer, immuable, sur le canevas poétique, mais où se devinent, dans l'âme secrète des choses, reflétée sur la face mystérieuse de la nature, des idées, des correspondances, des rapports lointains à rendre sensibles par la magie des sons et des mots.[18]

Less successful is Vigié-Lecocq's interpretation of this artistic vision. Reviving the terms which had been bandied about so freely and so often meaninglessly in 1886, he divides poetic artistry into the decadent and the symbolist. The decadent, according to his view, is that which rejects simple feeling and sentiment for the complex, the abnormal, and the rare. This enables the author to group Baudelaire, Rimbaud, Verhaeren, Rodenbach, and Samain in one category. Baudelaire, represented as a divided soul, torn between the mystic and the sensuous; Rimbaud, scornful of what is reverenced by tradition; Verhaeren, whose exceptional imaginative powers approached hallucination; Samain, hypersensitive and excessively delicate; finally Rodenbach, whose melancholy landscapes of the mind contain such refined shadings of feeling— all these seem to Vigié-Lecocq valid examples of decadent art. Far from blaming such poetic expression, the author recognizes that by it is expressed the mysterious, hidden side of human identity, with the tenuous interlocking threads of the past and the present. Since Vigié-Lecocq's discussion comes so close to the problem of the unconscious,[14] it is strange that he does not accord Laforgue a full measure of influence in this lyric manifestation.

Symbolist art is treated in the volume as something more comprehensive than the presentation of exceptional individuality but, like the decadent, opposed to outer reality. By it, according to Vigié-Lecocq, are released the mystical signs of nature. Intuitive and synthetic, it escapes from overly precise detail and from direct confession to create a world of its own, to give new and universal meaning to this created realm, and to reveal hidden relationships between the individual and his universe.

Despite its faults of prolixity, La Poésie contemporaine is an important volume in the history of symbolist criticism. Subsequent essays and studies on poets and poetry of the period appear to stem from Vigié-Lecocq's general premises, the revelation of a peripheral limbo surrounding consciousness and

13. A. Vigié-Lecocq, La Poésie contemporaine, 1884–1896, p. 64.
14. Ibid., pp. 182–183.

the suggestion of unexplained affinities as a result of this new charting of the mind. Somewhat awkward in the labeling of these phenomena, the author at least brought into the foreground the possible relationships among the poetic currents of the century, and by implication gave the lie to those who would see in symbolism only technical reform.

Vigié-Lecocq's volume is, in a sense, a defense of an era which was being currently resumed in collected editions of former isolated volumes. After Henri de Régnier, Verhaeren, and Vielé-Griffin had collected their early verse, came in turn Ferdinand Herold's *Images tendres et merveilleuses,* Paul Fort's *Ballades,* collected in six divisions, André Fontainas' *Crépuscules,* representing his poetic writing between 1892 and 1896, Albert Samain's new edition of *Au jardin de l'Infante,* the first volume of Adolphe Retté's *Œuvres complètes,* Stuart Merrill's *Poèmes, 1887–1897,* Pierre Quillard's *La Lyre héroïque et dolente,* and Moréas' *Premiers Poèmes.* Kahn, simultaneously with the publication of *Le Livre d'images,* released an edition of his early poems. Ernest Raynaud reedited a volume from his pre-Romanist days, *Le Signe.* New publications by other poets of the symbolist era also appeared; Henri de Régnier's *Les Jeux rustiques et divins,* Vielé-Griffin's *La Clarté de vie,* Michel Abadie's *Les Voix de la montagne.* The traditions of the Ecole romane were continued by the *Etudes lyriques* of Maurice du Plessys.

These volumes, coupled with an extensive production by younger poets, tend to make 1897, in contrast with the preceding year, one of the most fecund in the nineteenth century. The most complete picture of the poetic scene is perhaps to be found in the *Mercure de France,* where Henri de Régnier gave reports on some seventy volumes. These are judgments expressed by a poet who had participated in most of the currents of the past decade and whose talent and poetic evolution had finally given him sanctuary in the pages of the *Revue des deux mondes.* Following on the footsteps of Vielé-Griffin as poetic critic of the *Mercure,* he served for only one year, being replaced by Pierre Quillard, who remained in the post well into the twentieth century.

Henri de Régnier, in 1897, is plainly an enemy of poetic schools. When he chances to speak of the naturists, it is with derision; in discussing Fleury's *Sur la route,* he advises that poet to cease believing in the nonsense of Saint-Georges de Bouhélier's group. Equally hostile to the Ecole romane, he laments the influence of Moréas on Maurice du Plessys and on Ernest Raynaud; Lionel des Rieux's *Toison d'or* appears to him not only devoid of talent but a stupid imitation of the Romanists. His words of praise go to verse of flexible, flowing melody, to Herold, to C.-H. Hirsch for his *Yvelaine,* to Vielé-Griffin, and to Samain. He reproves the curious syntax of Kahn, the megalomania of Signoret, the excessive eloquence of Georges Pioch, but is kindly toward the precision and delicacy of Gregh, the gentle simplicity of Viollis, the voluntary awkwardness of Jammes, and the melancholy languor of Charles Guérin.

It is further evident that Régnier's mind is open to diverse types of inspiration and to differing technical manners. He accepts as valid both the *Ame antique* of Marc Legrand, a portion of which consists of translations from the Greek and Latin, and *Les Heures claires* of Verhaeren, which contains poems of personal confession in a gentle tone rarely found in the Belgian poet. Tristan Klingsor's dexterous handling of free verse and Paul Fort's mingling of poetic and prose techniques in the *Ballades* appear to interest him as much as traditional forms. The question of influences of the immediate past is constantly present in Régnier's mind. He speaks of the inspiration of Baudelaire and Verlaine in Fernand Gregh's work, of the Verlainian quality of Léopold Dauphin's *Raisins bleus et gris,* and of the intellectual and verbal interplay, stemming from Mallarmé, in the poetry of Fontainas. He does not always approve of this ascendancy of older on younger poets; Marcel Réja's violent imagery in *La Vie héroïque* provokes his comment that the poet has read too much Verhaeren, and of course any imitation of Moréas is frowned upon by Régnier as a fundamental error. It is to Régnier's credit that he observes relationships with the more remote past among his contemporaries; Signoret's verse seems to him sometimes allied with that of Lamartine's *Harmonies,* and another side of the great romanticist's art is recalled to him by Saisset's *Au fil du rêve.*

The protest against schools of poetry was not confined to Paris. In Le Havre, Yves Berthou founded in January, 1897, a monthly magazine whose very title, *La Trêve-Dieu,* was a summons to cease poetic quarrels. Like most of the regional magazines, this little periodical during its year of existence tended to lack of perspective by championing local writers. But while the poems of Camille Maryx were overly emphasized, the magazine did offer verse by poets as diversified as Rodenbach, Réja, Vielé-Griffin, Raymond Bouyer, Jammes, Fort, Raynaud, Guérin, Pilon, Remy de Gourmont, Stuart Merrill, Charles Vellay, and Edouard Ducoté. Paterne Berrichon, carrying none too successfully into poetry his cult of his dead brother-in-law, contributed "En la gloire d'un poète maudit"; Robert de la Villehervé appeared in three numbers of the little periodical.

Although the question of poetic technique is treated almost everywhere, by 1897, as a matter of secondary importance, Gustave Kahn in his articles in *La Revue blanche* remained the firm partisan of free verse. It is true that, after discussing the alexandrines in C.-H. Hirsch's *Yvelaine,* he stated that the two manners, free verse and regular syllabic count, had won their places in French literature and that therefore discussion was no longer necessary.[15] But he prefaced the edition of his *Premiers poèmes* with a long essay on free

15. *La Revue blanche,* XII (March, 1897), 402.

verse,[16] and in his critical articles revealed a decided bias in favor of complete liberty in prosody. He found the rhythms of Merrill's *Petits poèmes d'automne* too mathematically precise and praised the free meters of Pilon's *La Maison d'exil*. When he discussed the Academy's reserves in honoring Gregh's *La Maison d'enfance,* he again announced himself as the discoverer of free verse.

The position of Mallarmé during his second year as Prince des poètes is a curious one. He had not at any time deigned to answer Retté's and Louis de Saint-Jacques's attacks in *La Plume*. His poetic production of 1897 is limited to the "Tombeau" in honor of Paul Verlaine and the revolutionary "Un Coup de dés jamais n'abolira le hasard." The latter poem appeared in the May issue of *Cosmopolis*. A short preface to Léopold Dauphin's *Raisins bleus et gris,* and the volume of *Divagations,* so harshly criticized by Louis de Saint-Jacques, complete his publications for the year. His prestige is witnessed by few articles. Alfred Athys, writing on the development of the prose poem, credited him with genuine contribution to that form and praised his experiments in distilling the essence of meaning from the crude matter of words.[17] Eight of Mallarmé's poems and prose poems were the inspiration of *Images d'après Mallarmé,* a collection of etchings by R. P. Rivière and J. F. Schnert. The lone essay by Thadée Natanson, already referred to, is the most important essay of the year in his honor. Perhaps the greatest compliment paid to his art occurred in Joachim Gasquet's "Notes pour servir à l'histoire du naturisme." There Mallarmé's poems are called the purest monument which the French language possesses, and Gasquet adds that only certain verses of Ronsard, Racine, or Signoret may be compared to them.[18]

16. Kahn's preface was subjected to criticism in the October, 1897, issue of *La Revue blanche*. Remy de Gourmont, the author of the essay, pointed out that alexandrines, when recited, have different lengths, by reason of mute *e*'s and lengthened syllables. Gourmont appeared unconvinced that free verse was the best manner of poetic reform.

17. *La Revue blanche,* XII (May, 1897), 587–592.

18. Gasquet's essay was first published in January, 1897, in *Les Mois dorés,* the magazine he was editing in Aix-en-Provence. In the ten numbers which appeared during 1896–97, the naturists, Signoret, and Mistral are given high praise. Gasquet accuses the symbolists of having lacked will power, but isolates from them his hero, Stéphane Mallarmé.

Chapter XV: THE DEFEAT OF NATURISM, 1898

IN THE ANNALS of poetic history, 1898 is remembered as marking Mallarmé's death. This is justifiable, for, as in the case of Verlaine, the circumstance released a quantity of critical judgments on the value and meaning of the dead poet's work. But Mallarmé's death did not occur until September 9, and during three-quarters of the year, not he, but symbolism and naturism were the subjects of poetic controversy.

During 1897 the naturists had been fully as violent against symbolists as the latter had at one time shown themselves against Parnassianism. Probably the vehemence of Maurice Le Blond had played its part in Henri de Régnier's attitude toward the naturists and had led him, in his final chronicle in the *Mercure de France,* to defend the poetic attainments of his generation. When Camille Mauclair, in an essay entitled "Réflexions sur les directions contemporaines," [1] expressed the opinion that the symbolist group had completed its contribution to literature, the naturists seized on this avowal to strengthen their position. Then, just as 1897 was drawing to its close, appeared *Eglé ou les concerts champêtres.* Here at last was a volume of poetry by the leader of the naturists, by the writer who had proclaimed himself and had been denominated by Le Blond as the messiah of a new age in poetic expression.

In January, 1898, Saint-Georges de Bouhélier's volume was reviewed in the *Mercure de France* by Pierre Quillard and in *La Plume* by Louis de Saint-Jacques. Quillard called the book incoherent and monotonous, while the critic of *La Plume* insisted rather on the all too evident imitations of other poets, the errors in syntax, and the poverty of vocabulary. In March, H.-D. Davray reviewed the book in *L'Ermitage* and found that Bouhélier had contributed nothing new either in substance or in form. Kahn had already, in December, 1897, spoken briefly of the volume in *La Revue blanche* and his report was as discouraging as those of the other critics. This universal condemnation of *Eglé* established the tone for many of the critical articles of the year and its repercussions involved not only naturism but romanticism, symbolism, and in particular the worth of Francis Jammes's poetry.

In speaking adversely of Saint-Georges de Bouhélier's volume, Louis de Saint-Jacques did not take up the defense of symbolism. In truth, using

1. *Mercure de France,* XXIV (November, 1897), 379–390.

Stuart Merrill's collected verse as a contrasting problem, he pictured Bouhélier as arriving on the poetic scene at a propitious moment and Merrill as having been the victim of deplorable influences during the symbolist era. Saint-Jacques defines the symbolist movement as a reaction against the literature of observation, represented in prose by Zola and in poetry by Coppée. This definition was complemented the next month by Maurice Le Blond, who stated that the only reason for existence that could be offered for symbolism was that of opposing the esthetic outlook of the "Rougon-Macquart" series.

This remark by Le Blond occurred in a series of articles in *La Plume* entitled "Emile Zola devant les jeunes." In them the author made the claim that the younger writers were at last recognizing the great worth of the naturalist novelist. It is quite true that in the little magazines the name of Zola was being treated with new respect, but the reasons seem hardly literary. Zola's stand in defense of Dreyfus, the pamphlet *J'accuse,* the ensuing prosecution and condemnation of the author on February 23, 1898, provoked widespread expressions of sympathy. The little magazines were largely liberal in political thought, antimilitary, and certainly in favor of freedom of expression. The result was that the writer, whose work they had so often condemned, emerged in 1898 as a hero.

After his defense of Zola, Le Blond assumed the post of chief literary critic of *La Plume,* entitling his essays "La Parade littéraire." Louis de Saint-Jacques had written the last of his "Expertises" for the April 15 issue, expressing contentment at leaving his post and saying a definite good-by to literature. Retté, although contributing a series of "Arabesques" to the magazine, was devoting more of his attention to praise of rural life and to social problems than to literature. This left the field free for the champion of naturism, just after the devastating criticism leveled at Bouhélier's *Eglé.*

The first essay of "La Parade littéraire" [2] might lead the reader to think that Le Blond intended to present an eclectic and unbiased viewpoint, for the author gives as his aims the reconciliation of traditional and revolutionary currents, the consideration of social as well as esthetic problems in literature. But in his second article, which appeared on June 15, such illusions were shattered by his accusations that the symbolists, unable to find sufficient talent in their own ranks, had annexed Francis Jammes. Le Blond contended that the praise accorded Jammes during recent months (he was probably thinking especially of Henri de Régnier's articles in the *Mercure de France* during 1897) had been activated by the sole desire of injuring young poets of real talent. Although he was careful not to bring into the foreground the name of Saint-Georges de Bouhélier, Le Blond reserved his words of praise for those who had, at least in part, accepted the theories of naturism; Lafargue, Viollis,

2. *La Plume,* X (May 15, 1898), 300–302.

Souchon, and Nervat. In part this was an act of gratitude since the group from Languedoc had been hospitable to Le Blond by publishing his two essays on "La Littérature artificielle" in the *Essais des jeunes* during 1895. Later in *L'Effort,* in the first issue of 1897, Delbousquet had spoken favorably of the *Essai sur le naturisme.* Still the point of view of "La Parade littéraire," which attacked Jammes with such ferocity and which preferred the poetry of Jacques Nervat and Henry Cabrens to that of Henri Ghéon, was extremely biased. It was only when Le Blond spoke of the poetry of Robert de Souza as detestable or when he indicated the close imitation of Verlaine in Fleury's *Impressions grises* that he aligned himself with the critical opinions of his contemporaries.

Le Blond's contention of a wicked plot against the naturists stimulated some reproving letters in the "Tribune libre" of the *Mercure de France* and a mocking retort by Ghéon entitled "Le Naturisme en danger ou comment les symbolistes inventèrent Francis Jammes." [3] Gide's third "Lettre à Angèle" [4] was also very likely inspired by Le Blond's articles. The leader of the naturists, Saint-Georges de Bouhélier, did not contribute very much to the quarrel until November, when his article "Inutilité de la calomnie" attempted to explain why he was hostile toward both Retté and Gide. His account would lead the reader to believe that perusal of the "XIII Idylles diaboliques" had alienated him from Retté and that the lack of religious faith in Gide's work made him unacceptable to the naturists. His remarks are conditioned by a previous accusation, made by Stuart Merrill, that Bouhélier's change of attitude toward Retté was to be attributed to piqued vanity. In reply to this charge Bouhélier offered another example to substantiate his fairness of attitude. Although Emmanuel Signoret had spoken badly of him, Bouhélier stated that he still considered him a good poet.

These are some of the aspects in the childish and useless backbiting which filled so many pages of the poetry magazines of 1898. In place of constructive criticism an atmosphere of pettiness, wounded feelings, and thwarted ambitions seemed to reign. Again, as during the preceding year, exception must be made for the *Mercure de France,* where Pierre Quillard had replaced Henri de Régnier as poetry critic. Never a partisan of free verse but sensitive to innovations in melody, Quillard began his long term of service to the *Mercure* by recalling the poets of his generation: the dead, Mikhaël, Dubus, and Aurier; the living, Merrill, Mockel, Van Lerberghe, Vielé-Griffin, Régnier, Saint-Pol-Roux, Verhaeren, Kahn, Maeterlinck, Retté, Samain, Collière, Ghil, Dumur, Gourmont, Fontainas, Herold, Albert Saint-Paul, and le Roy; and finally those who had quickly passed into other fields of literary activity, Ajalbert,

3. *L'Ermitage,* 1898, II (August, 1898), 123–129.
4. *Ibid.* (September, 1898), pp. 210–214.

Darzens, and Lazare. Evidently Quillard's list contains several names which had small importance in the poetic field, but naturally those with whom he had been associated in *La Pléiade* and later in the *Mercure de France* presented themselves first to his mind.

With Quillard came a larger sense of reconciliation between the traditions of symbolism and Parnassianism. Although opposing verse of too didactic a tone, Quillard accepted as valid the inspiration of antiquity and found generous praise for *Le Bouclier d'Arès* of Sébastien-Charles Leconte and for *Le Bois sacré* of the Vicomte de Guerne. On the other hand, he calls the *Entrevisions* of Van Lerberghe exquisite, admires the contemplative aspect of Charles Guérin's *Le Cœur solitaire,* and comments on the charming facility and abundance in rhythms in the poetry of Francis Jammes. The inspiration of older writers does not, in his eyes, constitute a fault, unless, as in the case of Fleury, it is carried to the point of imitation.[5] From the poetic utterance of the immediate past, Quillard kept the taste for suggestion rather than the complete statement of the theme. Discussing the verse of Yvanhoé Rambosson, he reproves the overly visible allegory; in the work of Ghéon he finds as a virtue the absence of much description. Neither a partisan nor an enemy of free verse, his personal taste prefers syllabic count. He asks why Paul Fort should choose to hide perfectly good alexandrines in the outer form of the prose poem.

In view of the large number of poets who had accepted as equally useful the free and regular meters, it is somewhat strange that the question should occupy the critics in 1898. Two events, however, served to orient discussion into this domain: Le Blond's statement that free verse was not acceptable to the young generation [6] and the reservations made by the Academy in giving an award to Fernand Gregh's *La Maison d'enfance.* Le Blond's appellation of free verse as a "genre bâtard" brought rebuttal from Marc Lafargue in Toulouse.[7] In Paris Vielé-Griffin, nettled because the Academy took the view that Gregh was to be honored in spite of his use of free verse, countered with an article entitled "Le Mouvement poétique." [8] In this essay the poet who had fought so ardently for liberation from syllabic count in the pages of the *Entretiens politiques et littéraires* (1890–93) took the stand that free verse was

5. Fleury's *Impressions grises* do at times give almost an impression of a parody of Verlaine. For example:

> Ciel gris et morne,
> Comme on s'ennuie!
> Dans l'air atone
> Filtre une pluie.

6. *La Revue naturiste,* No. 11 (January, 1898). The essay is entitled "Sur la rime."
7. *L'Effort,* No. 25 (March, 1898), pp. 88–94.
8. *Mercure de France,* XXVI (April, 1898), 5–10.

but the evolution foreseen in the "vers brisés" of Victor Hugo and that the Academy's conservatism was indefensible.

Symbolism, in its larger aspects, found no such ardent defender. With Le Blond attacking in the name of the naturists, already weakened by Retté's and Saint-Jacques's campaign against obscurity as epitomized by Mallarmé, under fire in such articles as Marcel Proust's "Contre l'obscurité" of 1896, and Mauclair's "Reflexions sur les directions contemporaines" of 1897, the movement in 1898 was definitely on the defensive. The *Revue blanche*, although appending a note denying solidarity with the opinions expressed, printed a French translation of the tenth chapter of Tolstoy's *What Is Art?* [9] In it the Russian author attacked the very fountainheads of the symbolist movement, stating that not one of Baudelaire's poems could be understood without effort and that the results of that effort were scarcely ever rewarding, that Verlaine was affected and obscure, and that Mallarmé and Maeterlinck had raised lack of clarity to the position of dogma. According to Tolstoy, this perversion of the artist's purpose had penetrated the realm of the fine arts; he cited notes from his daughter's diary of a visit to the symbolist, impressionist, and postimpressionist painting exhibitions of 1894 to substantiate his contentions.

Meanwhile, in *La Plume*, in those of the "Arabesques" which were devoted to literature,[10] Retté voiced the opinion that symbolism had finished its course. Although crediting the movement with having released lyric expression from the gelid objectivity of the Parnassians, his attitude is one of defeat. He blames the symbolists for having isolated themselves from the world in which they lived, for never having formulated a doctrine which could obtain adherents from the new generation, and for having been hypnotized by Mallarmé. At the beginning of the year he voiced some hope for the future of poetry in the tenets of naturism, but his quarrel with the leader of that group soon nullified such championship. Retté's attitude is to some degree echoed by writers in *L'Ermitage*. There, H.-D. Davray, although hostile to the naturists, finds that poets of 1898 have awakened to love of life after a period of weariness and discouragement. It is Vielé-Griffin whom Davray indicates as having first sounded this note of hope in the symbolist era. Gide, in the same magazine, praises the verse of Signoret for its enthusiasm, that of Jammes for its moving simplicity, and that of Ghéon for its sincerity. Gide's fourth letter to Angèle, which speaks of these three writers, gives the impression that the *Vers dorés, De l'Angélus de l'aube à l'Angélus du soir*, and *La Solitude de l'été* offer real elements of change in poetry.

In this period of confusion and bickering, when the poetic world seemed in the difficult position of denying the past and yet finding no common ground

---

9. *La Revue blanche*, XV (February, 1898), 251–268. The extract is entitled "Les Décadents."
10. See "Arabesques," I, II, IV, XI, *La Plume*, for 1898, pp. 5–10, 33–37, 129–133, 468–473.

for action in the future and when the only solution appeared to be the broad eclecticism implied in Quillard's critical judgments, came the death of Mallarmé on September 9, 1898. The remainder of the year is more or less, in so far as poetry is concerned, consecrated to his memory. To the *Mercure de France* Henri de Régnier contributed a short but appreciative essay.[11] In the same magazine Albert Mockel's long study, "Un Héros (Stéphane Mallarmé),"[12] voiced not only profound veneration but consciousness of the perfectionism which was both the glory and the defeat of the dead writer. Pierre Louÿs published a sonnet to the memory of the poet who had honored Poe and Verlaine in that form. In the *Revue blanche,* where a few months before Mallarmé's "A la nue désolante tu" had been held up to derision in Tolstoy's essay, Thadée Natanson exalted the lofty artistic idealism of Mallarmé, and Remy de Gourmont, writing a kind of rebuttal to Tolstoy's assertions, entitled his study "Stéphane Mallarmé et l'idée de décadance."[13] According to Gourmont's point of view, decadent poets are those who compose imitative verse and the term is most inapt for a writer of such eminent originality as that of Mallarmé. Simultaneously with Gourmont's essay appeared in *L'Ermitage* a study [14] by André Gide which pictured Mallarmé as an inspirational force, while in Belgium Edmond Picard published an essay [15] giving a bibliography of articles on Mallarmé which had appeared in *L'Art moderne.* Among the Parisian newspapers *Le Gaulois* was noteworthy in that it reprinted two of Mallarmé's poems in its literary supplement of September 17 and published a little essay by Mme Catulle Mendès extolling the charming character of the dead writer.

In contrast with the tone of veneration and praise for the late poet, *La Plume* printed the sixth of Le Blond's "Parades littéraires" in which the champion of naturism stressed the lack of affinity between the young French poets and Mallarmé, making the prophecy that complete oblivion would soon engulf the name of the late Prince des poètes.[16] Moréas, who was contributing to the magazine a series entitled "De Fil en aiguille" and which generally took the form of aphorisms, devoted a few pages to his personal contacts with Mallarmé but offered no critical judgments. Nor did Léon Deschamps' magazine take the initiative, as it had done in 1894 and 1896, for the election of a new Prince des poètes. It was instead a journalist, Raoul Aubrey, who assumed charge. He sent out sixty letters, principally to those who had voted in the elections of 1894 or 1896, but only forty-one answers contained possible names of candi-

11. *Mercure de France,* XXVIII (October, 1898), 5–9.
12. *Ibid.* (November, 1898), pp. 362–391.
13. *La Revue blanche,* XVII (November, 1898), 428–436.
14. *L'Ermitage,* 1898, II (November, 1898), 225–230.
15. *L'Art moderne,* September 18, 1898, pp. 299–301.
16. *La Plume,* X (October 1, 1898), 597–598.

dates.[17] Léon Dierx was accorded fifteen votes and given the title; Heredia, in second place, received seven. Régnier was third with six ballots, Moréas received four votes, and Sully-Prudhomme two. This meager showing is in striking contrast with the election, held only four years before, when Verlaine had received more than twice the number of votes of the total for these five leading candidates. The names of the poets who suggested Dierx provide some interest, for the list contains several of the symbolists: Saint-Pol-Roux, Vielé-Griffin, Stuart Merrill, Pierre Quillard, and Emile Verhaeren. Among the Parnassians who favored Dierx were Catulle Mendès, Armand Silvestre, and José-Maria de Heredia. Two naturists, Saint-Georges de Bouhélier and Maurice Le Blond, also suggested his name. René Ghil divided his poetic affections between Dierx and Strada. Among those who abstained from voting were Régnier, Retté, Tailhade, Kahn, and Georges Vanor.

That the election was inconclusive, that it was carried out in great haste, that it did not even approach a great number of young poets, and that it was engineered by a journalist who probably was regarded as a potential enemy by several of the prospective voters does not hide the fact that past enthusiasm had become a kind of torpor. The *Mercure de France,* the *Revue blanche,* and *L'Ermitage* made little comment on the new "Prince," and it was only Maurice Le Blond, in *La Plume,* who gave Dierx the honor of an essay, calling him the most naturist of the Parnassians.[18] Yet there were hidden admirations for Dierx. Francis Jammes, in a letter to Samain in 1897,[19] had named Dierx and the author of *Au jardin de l'Infante* as the two living examples of the great classical tradition; at the time of publication of Dierx's *Œuvres complètes* in 1896, bibliographical notices by such poets as Kahn and Vielé-Griffin were filled with respectful admiration; in the election which gave the title of Prince des poètes to Mallarmé, Dierx had been mentioned enough times to warrant him fifth place.

The publication of poetry in the magazines outside the realm of the little reviews reveals to what degree the symbolist generation, despite its courage and enthusiasm, had had to remain a somewhat isolated group. The *Revue des deux mondes* had finally accepted two offerings by Henri de Régnier in 1896 and published some of his poetry during the following three years. Samain was the other symbolist poet who penetrated that holy of holies twice during 1897 and once in 1898. The *Revue de Paris* offered poems by Fernand Gregh in six of its issues between 1894 and 1899. In the same magazine during this period verse by Ferdinand Herold appeared once and poems by Rodenbach

17. Reports of the election and texts of the letters received are to be found in *Le Temps* for October 11, 12, 13, and 21, 1898.
18. *La Plume,* X (November 15, 1898), 644–645.
19. Jules Mouquet, *Albert Samain et Francis Jammes: correspondance inédite,* p. 96.

three times. Rigorously opposed to free verse, the conservative reviews preserved silence on such writers as Verhaeren, Kahn, and Vielé-Griffin.

This hostility toward freedom in versification is more or less shared by the newspapers. Journalists occasionally spoke of current poetry but they almost altogether ignored the symbolists. In an article entitled "Critique littéraire" [20] in *Le Journal*, Armand Silvestre chanced to speak of the Vicomte de Guerne, Vielé-Griffin, and Jehan Rictus' *Soliloques du pauvre* in the same column. Praising the nobility and sincerity of *Les Siècles morts* and confessing that he was profoundly moved by Rictus, whom he places in the tradition of Villon, Silvestre states that he is embarrassed in speaking of Vielé-Griffin's poetry. At most he accords him a sincere feeling for nature; yet he cannot find any music in his lines. He says in conclusion that in his opinion a foreigner is incapable of writing good French verse. Shortly afterward [21] Silvestre spoke of Henri Rouger's *Poèmes fabuleux* and praised the excellent craftsmanship of that conventional poet. François Coppée, also in *Le Journal*,[22] took up the question of free verse in discussing Paul Fort and Francis Jammes. He professes admiration for their talent but voices the opinion that the innovators will finally come to the writing of lyric prose. In support of his statement he refers to the typographical form of Fort's *Ballades*. Still a third writer in *Le Journal*, this time André Theuriet, largely devoted his criticism to the craftsmanship of verse. Citing Henri de Régnier as an example of gradual acceptance of traditional meters, he laments the fact that Ghéon's lines are not true verses and finds the versification of Guérin's *Le Cœur solitaire* much more competent.[23]

The resistance toward liberty in prosody is well illustrated by the words of Gaston Boissier, the secretary of the Academy, in awarding the Archon-Despérouses poetry prize to Albert Samain in November, 1898.[24] After complimenting Samain on having a place of honor among the young poets, Boissier observed that like many of his contemporaries Samain sometimes took liberties with traditional French versification. These liberties the orator found quite unnecessary, since in his opinion the poems of impeccable form in *Au jardin de l'Infante* are the best. When one considers that Samain's most venturous innovations are in sequences in rhymes or in extensions of the sonnet form, Boissier's reproofs seem harsh and unnecessary.

But the prestige enjoyed by Samain, his acceptance by Coppée and Heredia, his verse in the *Revue des deux mondes*, the prize accorded his volume of poetry, all present an interesting commentary on current attitudes toward sym-

20. August 30, 1897.
21. October 4, 1897.
22. October 7, 1897.
23. July 15, 1898.
24. Boissier's speech is printed in *Le Temps*, supplement for November 18, 1898.

bolism. On the one hand, by his adherence to the alexandrine and his some-what conservative form of lyric expression, he was considered a derivative of the Parnassian school. Yet on the contrary, in seeking the fine shadings of feeling, in his extraction of the quintessence of emotion, he seemed to belong to another school, one which had as its ancestors Baudelaire and Verlaine and which had been baptized as decadent. Despite several cruel judgments on his art in our century (one thinks of Paul Morand's "Lamartine pour impériales d'omnibus" or Derennes' "Samain est le dernier des derniers, parce qu'il a mis le symbolisme à la portée des sous-préfètes . . ."), most of the critics in 1898 and in later years have seen in his work a fortunate blending of diverse currents, new and traditional. Alone in 1898 Charles Maurras, whose championship of the Ecole romane made most of his articles extremely biased, wrote [25] that Samain's poetry was an unendurable blend of empty pose and imitation.

Among the little magazines the places of honor accorded Samain, Gregh, Ghéon, and even Charles Guérin at the end of the nineteenth century show the hiatus left by the deaths of Verlaine and Mallarmé. In general, in these periodicals it was not the long-debated question of free verse but rather the setting and the presentation of the poetic idea which were the basis of current admirations. Vielé-Griffin's legendary landscapes were not so acceptable as the background of Orthez. If the landscape of the mind were to be left indeterminate, it should at least be so charged with personal emotion that its message was definite. The question of clarity, which had been the principal objection offered the symbolists by the conservative press—the very one on the basis of which Tolstoy had attacked the innovators in French poetry—is still vitally important in 1898. The excesses of symbolism, its search for strange words, its use of unusual syntax, and its too radical departures from reality all had ceased to have defenders.

On the other hand, even in admitting the elements which had acted to the discredit of the movement, critics such as Quillard and Gourmont realized the important principles, not only for poetic form but for its expression, that had been contributed. The presentation of feeling, not through descriptive elaboration, but through suggestive power of words, their music and their arrangement, was still recognized as the most valid and durable of symbolism's lessons.

25. In the *Revue encyclopédique,* January 22, 1898.

Chapter XVI: THE END OF AN ERA

THE SYMPTOMS of decline in the estate of poetry, visible since 1896, continue until the end of the century. The Dreyfus case, with its resultant breaks of friendships, the death of several important writers, the increased space given in the periodicals to social and political problems or to foreign literatures, all tend to make the change appear more striking. The reasons for the lethargy lie deeper however. Symbolism seemed to have built its altars for a few poets of genius who belonged to an older generation. The younger votive priests, several of whom had aspired to become the new objects of veneration, had proved more or less unequal to the honor. Be it said to their credit, they had not been slavish imitators and, in their search for originality, had indicated new paths of expression. Among them were many good poets but none who was transcendent.

The year following Mallarmé's death shows little interest in poetry. Rodenbach's death elicited a few articles in which respect but not enthusiasm was voiced. In the *Mercure de France,* except for two articles by Adolphe Retté entitled "Sur le rythme des vers" and one by Vielé-Griffin, "La Désespérance du 'Parnasse,'" no very interesting essays appeared. In the *Revue blanche,* except for the bibliographical notices of Gustave Kahn, complete silence was preserved on problems of poetry. In *La Plume* the last two of Le Blond's "Parades littéraires" were followed by Henri Degron's "Paysageries littéraires." In his closing articles Le Blond did not speak directly of poetry, although in praising Montfort's *Essai sur l'amour* he introduced another panegyric of Bouhélier and naturism. Degron's criticism of poetry embraced little beyond the favorites of *La Plume*: Verlaine, Retté, and Signoret.

On December 28, 1899, *La Plume* lost its founder and director by the death of Léon Deschamps. An epoch was closed in the life of a magazine which had been at the same time too partisan and too eclectic, which had often erred against good taste, but which had published in its Bibliothèque artistique et littéraire volumes by Verlaine, Moréas, Retté, Raynaud, and Signoret, which had honored the memory of a great precursor in *Le Tombeau de Baudelaire,* and which, for better or for worse, had fostered the Romanists. The attack against Mallarmé was, in a sense, continued by the periodical until the time of the founder's death, for Retté was contributing a novel, in serial form, called *La Seule Nuit* and which contained a thinly disguised portrait of his pet hate under the name of "Abscons Lunaire."

In the little magazines the space devoted to poetry was rather more limited than in previous years. There had always been a tendency to give prominence to favorite poets of the separate periodicals, but by 1899 the phenomenon is accentuated, *La Plume* seeming to have little to offer beyond extracts from volumes published by its own presses: from Signoret, Raynaud, and Maurice Magre; and *La Revue blanche* finding room for only seven poets: Kahn, Romain Coolus, Fleury, Retté, Robert Scheffer, Tristan Klingsor, and Francis Jammes. In the *Mercure de France* the situation appears to be parallel, as is evidenced by a letter sent to Samain by Vallette on February 8, 1900. Having obtained the insertion of some poems by Albert Fleury in the *Mercure,* Samain made a second effort on behalf of the young poet but Vallette refused, saying that the complicated and difficult question of insertion of verse in the magazine was already between fourteen and sixteen months behind schedule.[1]

One of the Paris magazines, *L'Ermitage,* published a considerable quantity of verse during 1899. The periodical was placed that year in the hands of twelve writers. Ducoté remained as managing editor and all contributions, save for two poetic supplements, were made by himself and the eleven others. At that time nine of the group were primarily interested in verse; thus it happened that extensive selections of poetry by Fort, Ghéon, Guérin, Jammes, Merrill, Verhaeren, Vielé-Griffin, Signoret, and Ducoté were interspersed among prose offerings by the same writers. In the supplements hospitality was offered to poets outside the closed group of the twelve. These guests included many of the young poets of the provinces (Berthou, Delbousquet, Fleury, Gasquet, Lafargue, and Viollis), as well as some of the older generation of Paris (Dujardin, Fontainas, Herold, Régnier, Saint-Pol-Roux, and Robert de Souza). Such a representation gave a fairly comprehensive picture of poetry at the end of the century, both as to form and content. Vielé-Griffin's "La Partenza" and "Wieland le forgeron," Signoret's "Tombeau dressé à Stéphane Mallarmé," Verhaeren's "Sur les côtes de la Flandre," Jammes's dramatic poem "La Jeune Fille nue," and eight short poems by Charles Guérin range from the eloquent to the elegiac, from the abstract to the concrete, and from free to the most regular of meters. That four of *L'Ermitage*'s editors were also contemporary contributors to the *Mercure de France,*[2] that one was a protégé of *La Plume,*[3] and that Jammes and Vielé-Griffin had been many times represented in the pages of *La Revue blanche* enhanced the prestige of the group.

Although *L'Ermitage* stands alone in 1899 as the Parisian magazine which printed a considerable quantity of verse, it, like its sister periodicals, did not

1. Jules Mouquet, *Albert Samain et Francis Jammes; correspondance inédite,* p. 140.
2. Guérin, Jammes, Merrill, and Verhaeren.
3. Signoret.

offer much discussion of poetry. In it, strictly speaking, there was but one critical essay, "Le Vers libre et la tradition" by Vielé-Griffin.[4] This article is written in an aggressive tone, for the principal defender of free verse was somewhat nettled by the lack of enthusiasm shown toward that medium by Remy de Gourmont and Gide, and the more open hostility displayed by Gasquet in *Le Pays de France* [5] and by André Beaunier in *La Revue bleue*.[6] Remarks on current literature in the magazine, generally limited to a few sentences, were couched in the informal "Lettres à Angèle" of André Gide and the "Lettres d'Angèle" of Henri Ghéon.

There is at this time in *L'Ermitage* no discussion of symbolism, naturism, or Romanism. To find a positive attitude toward poetic doctrine one is obliged to leave Paris and turn toward Aix, the capital of Provence. There, under the leadership of Joachim Gasquet, was published a magazine during 1899 which was an organ of decentralization, a mouthpiece for the *félibrige,* and at the same time a refusal of symbolism and a qualified acceptance of naturism. To Gasquet the poetry of the immediate past represented a kind of postromantic age, in which the pessimism of Schopenhauer had been superimposed on the "mal du siècle" and in which Lamartinian union of the soul with God had been rarefied into vague Plotinian ecstasy.[7] From his immediate predecessors Gasquet isolates two poets for special commendation. One seems an entirely natural choice, the enthusiastic southerner, Emmanuel Signoret. The other, Vielé-Griffin, in view of Gasquet's attitude toward free verse, is more surprising. Gasquet vindicates his choice, however, by stating that the two poets had both brought into poetry the beauty of song.

The principal ideas of *Le Pays de France,* Gasquet's monthly magazine, concern respect for old traditions, the belief that cosmopolitan Paris is a destructive agent, and an appeal for enthusiasm and cult of beauty rather than pessimism. Even if Gasquet disapproves the invitation to disorder in Bouhélier's *Eléments d'une renaissance française* [8] and is somewhat skeptical of Montfort's *Essai sur l'amour* because of its impractical idealism, these are the voices he respects. In Souchon's *Elévations poétiques* and Maurice Magre's *Chansons des hommes* he finds the most important collections of 1898. A curious article by M. Demolins in *Le Pays de France* [9] supports Gasquet's attack against pessimism, for in that essay the author takes Villiers de l'Isle-Adam to task for the rejection of life which terminates *Axël.*

These voices from the extreme South made little impression on Paris, save

4. *L'Ermitage,* 1899, II (August, 1899), 81–94.

5. No. 6 (June, 1899), pp. 382–388.

6. In the issue of March 4, 1899.

7. Gasquet's ideas are chiefly expressed in his monthly essays, "Les Idées et les faits," in *Le Pays de France.*

8. Published in *L'Evénement* during 1897 and collected in book form the following year.

9. No. 11 (November, 1899), pp. 645–662.

in the one poetic supplement of *L'Ermitage* which included the names of Gasquet, Delbousquet, Nadi, Vellay, and Viollis, all contributors to the *Pays de France*. The latter magazine is noteworthy, not for the influence it exercised, but because in this group of young writers is the only evidence of enthusiasm and of faith in a poetic renaissance. That they were repudiating the art of their predecessors in favor of more natural expression, more optimistic acceptance of life, presents analogies not only with the viewpoint of young poets in Paris but also with the evolution of some of the older writers, Merrill, Retté, Kahn, and Henri de Régnier—in fact the very ones against whose past performance the southerners were reacting.

The end of the century witnessed publication of a few volumes of poetry by some of these more mature writers. Two, Verhaeren and Samain, were over forty years old, and six, Saint-Pol-Roux, Régnier, Vielé-Griffin, Jammes, Merrill, and Herold, had passed their thirtieth year. Signoret, Fagus, Fort, and Gregh were still in their late twenties. In the older men is especially to be seen the change in outlook, the more calm setting, the identification of the poet with his surroundings, and a greater acceptance of life. In Verhaeren's *Les Visages de la vie* much of the violence and hallucination which had given the atmosphere to *Les Flambeaux* and *Les Soirs* has disappeared. Samain's *Aux flancs du vase,* many poems of which had been published in the *Mercure de France* and the *Revue des deux mondes* during 1897 and 1898, offers a setting of antiquity quite remote from the personal melancholy and despair of many of his earlier poems. It is true that his verse retains a note of personal confession; Samain designated the poems of his new volume as little pictures of daily life and explained the classical atmosphere as a means of removing overly patent reality.

Régnier, slightly younger than these two poets but whose first volume of verse had been published as early as 1885, offers a similar example of evolution. A collection of his *Premiers poèmes* (1899), appearing a few months before a new volume, *Les Médailles d'argile* (1900), accentuates the impression of transition from dreamy unreality to a more plastic and concrete form of expression. Stuart Merrill also, in his *Les Quatre Saisons* (1900), demonstrates a change from the artificial and bejeweled artistry of his early volumes to direct transcription of emotion in the presence of nature. Still interested in rhythmic innovations, Merrill attempted in this volume a system based upon the number of sonorous syllables in the line. His final poem showed the social preoccupation that was later to become dominant in his work. Ferdinand Herold's *Au hasard des chemins* (1900) begins with a poem on the childhood of Odysseus and ends with one on the modern city, with a series of "chansons" separating the two. Few traces remain of the atmosphere of the Middle Ages, formerly dear to the author of *Images tendres et merveilleuses*.

On the other hand, Vielé-Griffin's *Wieland le forgeron* and Saint-Pol-Roux's

La Dame à la faulx continue, in form and in content, the kind of dramatic legend which had long been in favor. The latter volume, a drama in the tradition of Maeterlinck and Van Lerberghe, was given greater praise than any volume of lyrics published during 1899 or 1900.[10]

Two poets who seemed on the point of gaining a considerable amount of renown died in 1900. They were Emmanuel Signoret, one of the favored poets of *La Plume,* and Albert Samain, whose verse had appeared every year in the *Mercure de France* since its founding in 1890. Samain's volume of poems *Le Chariot d'or* and his lyric drama *Polyphème,* which was to be set to music by Jean Cras in 1921, were published posthumously in 1901. Signoret's swan song took the form of the *Tombeau dressé à Stéphane Mallarmé,* a poem regarded by André Gide as one of the most beautiful in the French language, and *Le Premier Livre des élégies,* another example of Signoret's talent for transforming the commonplace into radiant imagery. Other voices which had played their part in the poetry of the immediate past were stilled for other reasons. Adolphe Retté's last volume of poetry, *Lumières tranquilles,* appeared in 1901. The last twenty-five years of his life were to be consecrated to the composition of prose volumes on religious subjects. Louis le Cardonnel, whose poetry had not yet been collected in volume form, had disappeared from the Parisian scene and had become a priest. His name was but rarely mentioned in the periodicals, although Paul Souchon devoted a laudatory article to his verse in *La Plume* of 1900.

That there was a sense of a closing epoch in poetic history is demonstrated in many ways during the last years of the nineteenth century. After Remy de Gourmont's two volumes of the *Livre des masques* came the publication in England of Arthur Symons' the *Symbolist Movement in Literature* and in France the initial volume, destined to triple in size during the first third of the twentieth century, of Van Bever's and Léautaud's *Poètes d'aujourd'hui.* A little after the turn of the century Gustave Kahn's *Symbolistes et décadents* and Retté's *Le Symbolisme* began the vogue of retrospective volumes which have created a vast literature on the subject.

Symons, the poet who had visited France when the symbolist movement had been at its height and whose own manner of writing had been influenced by admiration for Verlaine, was conscious that Paris had contributed much to the poetry of his own country and that such a movement as Yeats's Irish renaissance owed much to the French. The *Symbolist Movement in Literature* is devoted to essays on eight of the writers who had given impetus to the new poetic manner: Gérard de Nerval, Villiers de l'Isle-Adam, Rimbaud, Verlaine, La-

---

10. See Degron's "Paysagerie littéraire VII," in *La Plume* for March 15, 1900, Edmond Pilon's "Bibliographie," in *La Vogue* for January 15, 1900, and Kahn's comments in *La Revue blanche* for November, 1899.

forgue, Mallarmé, Huysmans, and Maeterlinck. His inclusion of Nerval may
have been occasioned by the appearance, two years earlier, of the *Poésies de
Gérard de Nerval*, edited by Remy de Gourmont, but it is indeed strange that
Baudelaire did not furnish him a chapter. Symons attempts little in the way
of synthesis except for a few pages of introduction which condense his general
ideas on the importance of music and suggestion in the authors he is about
to study:

All the art of Verlaine is in bringing verse to a bird's cry, the art of Mallarmé in
bringing verse to the song of an orchestra. In Villiers de l'Isle-Adam drama becomes the embodiment of spiritual forces, in Maeterlinck not even their embodiment, but the remote sound of their voices. It is all an attempt to spiritualize literature, to evade the old bondage of rhetoric, the old bondage of exteriority. Description is banished that beautiful things may be evoked, magically; the regular
beat of verse is broken in order that words may fly, upon subtler wings.[11]

Written in English and published in London, this volume can have had
only a very limited public in France. A few months later, however, Henri
de Régnier gave in Paris a lecture in which he attempted to explain and
evaluate symbolism.[12] After having credited the Parnassians with having
brought order into poetry and having blamed them for wishing to impose
their art for eternity, the lecturer emphasized the fetish of observation which
had become a form of slavery among the naturalists. In excuse of the excesses
of symbolism's early years, he demonstrated the general lack of interest in
poetic expression and the low estate into which poetry had fallen during the
decade preceding 1885. After an epoch in which Silvestre kept repeating "la
même chanson sonore et vide," in which Coppée made lyric expression overly
vulgar, while Leconte de Lisle remained silent, according to Régnier any
liberty to awaken interest seemed valid.

In symbolism itself Régnier finds individuality and idealism as dominant
factors. In the tone of verse, the change from the authoritative to the suggestive
appears to him most important. Myth and legend, instead of being narrated
and described, have been utilized for their eternal meanings. The poetic line
has become more vague, uncertain, fluid, and delicately shaded in expression
of mood. From Verlaine poetry had learned a new musical art and from Mallarmé mysterious possibilities of verbal utterance. But the lecturer was conscious that by 1900 poetry was undergoing a change. Writers such as Gregh,
Jammes, and Guérin had begun to sing of mankind through his thought, his
emotions, and his senses rather than in terms of symbols. Wisely, Régnier did

11. Arthur Symons, *The Symbolist Movement in Literature*, p. 9.
12. The lecture was delivered on February 6, 1900, for the "Société des Conférences" and was
published in the *Mercure de France*, XXXV (August, 1900), 321–350.

not attempt to make any forecast of future trends; he merely indicated the phenomena of change.

The greater part of Régnier's lecture is a recapitulation of the past and his tone is somewhat one of apology for a poetic movement which had ceased to dominate the scene. The month before Régnier delivered his address, Henri Degron had published in *La Plume* one of his "Paysageries littéraires," which strove, through accumulation of names, to glorify the poetic age of the past fifteen years. By including the esoteric poets, such as Jules Bois and Emile Michelet, and those whose work had not yet been collected in a volume, particularly Paul Roinard and Louis le Cardonnel, he made up a very impressive catalogue of names. In contrast, when he arrived at the younger generation, he seemed able to summon forth only the naturists and the group from Provence which was publishing *Le Pays de France*. In later essays of his series, which continued until July, 1900, Degron examined current poetic production but showed little enthusiasm except for Saint-Pol-Roux's *La Dame à la faulx* and Fleury's *Confidences*.

La Plume, after the death of Léon Deschamps, ceased to have the particular character which the preferences and antipathies of its founder had impressed upon it. The change was toward greater eclecticism, for the new director, Karl Boès, made Paul Fort his managing editor and enlisted Kahn, of *La Revue blanche,* for a series of art criticisms. Retté, Moréas, Merrill, and Signoret, the habitual poets of the magazine, were supplemented by many others, including Verhaeren, Fontainas, Quillard, Maurice Magre, Jammes, Vielé-Griffin, Herold, Guérin, Gourmont, Lorrain, Fargue, Morice, Fleury, Mauclair, Montesquiou, and Klingsor. Long selections from the "Ballades" of Paul Fort, a fragment from René Ghil's second volume of *Le Dire du mieux,* and a poem by Valéry dated 1893 were also published by the magazine in 1900. Together with such a wide selection of poetic tone and manner came the cessation of the aggressive critical articles, which, though often futile, had enlivened the magazine's pages. The new director, intent on giving a broad and dignified tone to the periodical, yet preserved some of the traditional features, such as that of the special issues. But even these, devoted in 1900 to Grasset, Rodin, and Sarah Bernhardt, present a serious and calm tone unlike that of Deschamps' regime.

In Boès' abandonment of poetic criticism, though not in the increased publication of verse, is evidenced another aspect of the times. The *Mercure de France, L'Ermitage,* and even *La Revue blanche* were also reflecting a state of equilibrium, in regard to verse and versification, to the exclusion of the polemic spirit. Poetry in free verse and in alexandrines, verse symbolizing ideas or expressing personal emotions were considered equally valid. The spirit of combat was gone.

The founding, in Paris and in 1899, of a new periodical in which poetry was given a place of prominence does little to alter the general picture. The newcomer bore the name of *La Vogue*, a title which had been used by Kahn's and d'Orfer's important magazine of 1886 and Kahn's and Retté's ephemeral periodical of 1889. This third *Vogue* was largely edited by a poet, Tristan Klingsor. During the first of its two years of existence, the twelve monthly issues offered verse by Merrill, Fleury, Albert Saint-Paul, Jacques Lamer, Léopold Dauphin, Moréas, Jammes, Kahn, Charles Vellay, Robert de Montesquiou, Alfred Mortier, Retté, Verhaeren, Mockel, Louÿs, Boès, Gregh, and Gabriel de Lautrec. The curious aspect of this verse, coming from writers of such varied ages and of whom many had been revealed as such strong individualists in their early writing, is the general levelness of tone. Largely poetry of intimacy and confession, the background of nature enjoys an importance it had been formerly denied. The collaborators, despite innovations in form, seem closer to the romantic age than to symbolism. During its second year *La Vogue* absorbed the *Anthologie-Revue* [13] of F. T. Marinetti and Edouard Sansot-Orland, thus adding new contributors but printing little that was strikingly original.

The general atmosphere—that of rejection of poetic ideas which had once been so enthusiastically proclaimed and of the twilight of a literary movement which had probably spent itself all the more quickly in its feverish search for novelty—is not without a defeatist aspect. But in considering the excesses, the errors if one will, of the symbolist period, it would be utterly false to neglect the positive contribution it had made. Poetry between 1885 and 1898 had undergone an experience from which it was to emerge conscious of new possibilities and powers. Through prose poems, free verse, and even prose rich in metaphors the poetic idea had been revealed as capable of multiple forms of expression over and above the count of syllables. This expansion, not only visible in the huge production of free verse in our century but also in the cadenced prose of such writers as Péguy or Claudel, is the most evident phenomenon which emerged from the symbolist period. The question of exterior form, however vital a contribution it may have been, requires less comment than the more intimate problems of poetic thought and its expression. Here perhaps symbolism made its worst mistakes through excess, but gave the lyric tonality which lasted beyond its own era.

Poetry on the eve of the twentieth century, despite the strong trends toward intimate utterance and the background of visible nature, did not return to the tone of romanticism. Even if the symbolists had gone too far afield in their

---

13. This periodical, published in Milan and Paris, was an unsuccessful attempt to give the reading public samples of current French and Italian literature. It had no literary allegiances and sometimes merely reprinted French poems which were well known in France.

rejection of reality, they had shown the validity of the veil interposed between the visual world and the reader. When one compares the importance given to description by the followers of the romantic school and the minor Parnassians with the evocative details in the nature poems at the end of the century, he cannot fail to seize the diversity of treatment. Although certain lines of Albert Samain suggest the romantic era, the dominant impression is that of the poet who loves "l'indécision des formes grêles." Even in the case of a poet in whose work plasticity played a great part, the *Astarté* of Pierre Louÿs for example, the message of suggestion, the supremacy of the idea evoked over the detail of description is ever present. Henri de Régnier or Ernest Raynaud, choosing the definite background of Versailles for many of their poems, never let description dominate emotion and atmosphere. The more typical setting for poetry during the period, most apparent in Merrill, Herold, in the early work of Régnier and Vielé-Griffin, and in the songs of Klingsor—that of the dim reaches of the medieval—had lent its passing note of the unreal. By the end of the century the fashion had somewhat changed but the dream of a world apart from actuality was not lost. As for that poetic realm, out of time and space, suggested in the *Palais nomades* of Kahn or *Cloches en la nuit* of Retté, brought on the stage by Maeterlinck and Van Lerberghe and unsuccessfully attempted by Dujardin, it has marked subsequent French poetry even to our day.

The symbolist age had reacted sharply against two preceding currents, the didacticism of Sully-Prudhomme and the banality of Coppée. That strange outgrowth of the period, the instrumentalist and evolutionary poetry of René Ghil, remained as an isolated phenomenon, gaining few expressions of admiration except in regard to the sincerity and perseverance of the author of the "Œuvre-une." Apart from the strange syntax and interminable sentences of Ghil's lines, the principal complaint made against his poetry was that it was expository. Even when poets such as Stuart Merrill began to include in their verse matters of social concern, they avoided the preaching tone as antipathetic to the spirit of poetry; sometimes, as did Retté in *La Forêt bruissante,* they cloaked their message under the symbol of the knight errant, or else, as had Verhaeren, enveloped the idea in magnificent and strange imagery.

The definite aversion toward the triviality and sentimentality of Coppée had sometimes led poetry too far in unusual and even fantastic realms, but had avoided the pitfall of triteness into which verse seemed to be falling in the 1870's. Justly the symbolists might be accused, in their avoidance of reality, of having rejected the challenge of a poetic problem. Only a few writers (Saint-Pol-Roux, metamorphosing the commonplace by lyric metaphor, and Verhaeren, casting a hallucinatory aura over the visual world) refused evasion. It was finally Francis Jammes, the voice from distant Orthez, who revealed to Paris what could be done in poetry with the detail of everyday occurrences. It seems fair to think that the success of *De l'Angélus de l'aube à l'Angélus du soir* was predicated in part on the book's appearance at a moment when the poetic setting had become to a degree stereotyped in the misty reaches of Thule. But the admiration accorded Jammes, whose subject matter is often as commonplace as that of Coppée, also comes from the recognition of an art which, through avoidance of narrative and descriptive elaboration, seeks rather to evoke a deeper and more personal significance.

In their reaction against Parnassianism the symbolists often rejected a source of eternal beauty, the Greek and Roman heritage. Their desire to create new poetic expression, their will to escape traditions and transgress rules, perhaps played their part in this refusal, for the symmetry and order of classicism were not sympathetic to the spirit of untrammeled liberation. But this exclusion was neither long in duration nor by any means complete. Vielé-Griffin composed *Ancæus,* Régnier gradually gave his verse more and more the flavor of antiquity, Moréas and the Romanists quickly reacted, Gide offered the myth of Narcissus as an example of the poetic spirit, Valéry and Louÿs, arriving on the poetic scene, gave the lie to those who made synonyms of impassivity and classical myth, and Heredia silenced objections by the very art of his expression.

Each restriction by the symbolists seems to contain its part of error but each innovation gives its measure of truth. The reentry of poetic sources such as the folk song, the verse of the troubadours, and the balladry of Heine penetrated literature in many and diverse ways. Laforgue, Vielé-Griffin, Klingsor, and Gérardy, though unequal in talent, offered examples of this enrichment of expression. Wagnerism, not valid in itself to become a poetic cult, at least gave poetry a whole new grouping of myths and imagery.

Almost all the poetry of the symbolists is idealistic and, quite naturally, sometimes religious in tone. The admiration expressed by so many of the poets for Baudelaire and especially for Verlaine's *Sagesse* would seem to have its part in this form of expression. Rimbaud's religious impact on Claudel looms as an isolated case. The religious currents, strong in Max Elskamp in Belgium and in Louis le Cardonnel in France, found their way into the imagery of many poets, among them Retté and Tailhade. Prevalent as such images are, they seldom represent deep sincerity or true mysticism. Often simply a question of ornament, perhaps in the final analysis merely the replacement of temporarily discredited Hellenism by the symbols of Christianity, these outward signs assume only superficial importance. The symbolists appeared more interested in Huysmans' *A rebours* than in *La Cathédrale.* In most cases the question of religious faith is coupled with some form of weakness, which leaves the question as equivocal as that of Verlaine. Satanism, dipsomania, and sensuality were the customary stations to the altar, and the poetic utterance was reminiscent of these paths.

In a less specific sense, as an outlook on life rather than a religious orientation, the symbolist period merits the denomination so often bestowed upon it of mystical. From the first to the last the negation of visible and outward form, the search for an understanding of existence through intuition, the abstention from the rational and the dogmatic gave their imprint to poetic writing. The sources in the world of philosophy are not always easily discernible, although Hartmann in the case of Laforgue and Schopenhauer in the early work of Moréas are evident. Of all the poets of the period it is perhaps Maeterlinck who has left, in *Le Trésor des humbles* (1898), the clearest picture of the themes and authors who conditioned his writing. The revelations of silence, the unexplored realm of the soul, the tragic aspects of everyday existence, the search for beauty are subjects in which his knowledge of Plotinus, Carlyle, Novalis, Emerson, and Ruysbroeck is constantly evident. Many other poets of the symbolist era, who have not left so tangible a record of their literary preferences, offer so many points of contact with the essays of *Le Trésor des humbles* that the volume is a sort of symbolist breviary. Like Maeterlinck, the poets appear as explorers in realms beyond mere sensation and reason. His chapter headings, such as "La Bonté invisible," "La Vie profonde," or "La Beauté intérieure," suggest with their qualifying adjectives the areas of interest in the poetry of his contemporaries. Such realms aid in explaining the vagueness which has been regarded as symbolism's greatest charm or its worst fault.

Idealism, revolt against realism, eager search for new forms of poetic expression, suggestion as opposed to direct statement, exploration of fine shadings of sentiment—these are the patent elements in the poetic rebirth which had taken place. Yet symbolism remains today, as in 1886 and 1896, a word of difficult definition, for individuality and the resolve not to allow admiration to become imposition of leadership were the keynotes of the age. André Fontainas, writing in 1928 his memories of symbolism, explains the term as the rallying cry of a generation enthusiastic in its devotion to art. Remy de Gourmont, in the preface to the *Livre des masques*, had made symbolism a synonym of originality. Other writers who have left their reminiscences of the period, Raynaud, Kahn, and Retté, are no more successful in defining the movement in which they had played a part. Varying importance accorded free verse, the exploration of musical effects, evocation or suggestion as opposed to declaration, the banishing of the banal—all give facets of truth but no satisfactory explanation of the term.

The difficulty of definition is the logical consequence of the strong individualistic note of the period. Efforts of ambitious figures, presaged by the curious attempt of Anatole Baju, to regiment poets met with constant failure. Ghil's instrumentalist theories, after some brief adherents, remained without disciples; Signoret's attempt to obtain united expression rapidly terminated in his solitary editorship of the *Saint-Graal;* Saint-Georges de Bouhélier's doctrine of naturism, despite Le Blond's ardent championship, completely collapsed. The loyalty of the little group around Moréas, abetted by the critical articles of Maurras and the support of Léon Deschamps, gave an impression of firmness and cohesion but was universally deplored by those outside the small circle. As for those poets of greater stature, whose influence dominated the whole period, it is evident that admiration did not usually mean slavish imitation. Isolated cases did occur: the early sonnets of Ghil and Mauclair which were closely modeled on Mallarmé's verse, passages by Fontainas which almost parodied the prose style of the same writer, close reminiscence of Rimbaud's prose poems in the earliest work of Paul Fort, and Fleury's Verlainian verse. In a more general way, the influence of Baudelaire, Verlaine, Mallarmé, and Rimbaud is constantly present. The shadings in meaning, the elements of fluidity and suggestion, and the search for new verbal effects all show the powerful directive forces which created symbolist verse.

The period was very rich in poetic tonalities. Merrill's early poems of ornamentation and sumptuous imagery, Klingsor's return to the candid expression of the troubadours, Vielé-Griffin's utilization of dramatic dialogue, Verhaeren's metamorphozed visual world, Roux's brilliant succession of shining images, Régnier's more sober adventure in the realm of dream and meditation, Maeterlinck's exploration of a fantastic realm of fable, and Kahn's renewal of the love song offer examples of lyric individuality which have rarely been equaled in literature. Despite the petty quarreling, the multitude of antagonistic literary circles, and the seemingly aimless search for theory, the symbolist poets had accomplished an important literary step. The resolve not to accept a pattern was stronger than the desire to create a formula. Remy de Gourmont, in calling individuality the significant aspect of the period, had spoken wisely and indeed had understood what was to be perhaps symbolism's greatest contribution to the twentieth century. The outstanding French writers of verse after the symbolist period would continue to reject the idea of regimentation. Each in his own way, Apollinaire, Claudel, and Valéry demonstrated their faith in the magic power of the word freed from traditional associations. The liberation of poetry from overapparent sentimentality, pomposity, and preaching had been a positive contribution from their immediate predecessors, valid for them as for Yeats or Eliot.

In our realization of such symbolist errors as artificiality, excess in ornamentation, dubious vagueness, it would be unwise for us to dismiss their effort too hastily. Not only for France, but for England and America, symbolism has been of prime poetic importance. The impact of Verhaeren on F. S. Flint, of Remy de Gourmont on Aldington, of Tailhade and Corbière on Ezra Pound, of Henri de Régnier on "H. D.," of Laforgue on T. S. Eliot, as well as Amy Lowell's *Six French Poets* and John Gould Fletcher's *La Poésie d'André Fontainas* indicate sufficiently the persistent radiation of a group which had deep faith in poetry and equally profound belief in new possibilities for its expression.

APPENDIX

*A Chronological List of the Most Important Periodicals
in the Symbolist Movement, 1881–99*

1. *L'Art moderne, 1881–1914*
Picard's Belgian magazine. It did not publish poetry but was rich in critical commentary on the French poetic movement. The articles are usually unsigned. Some of the most important essays are by Emile Verhaeren.

2. *Le Chat noir, 1882–95*
The weekly literary sheet published by Rodolphe Salis' café. Between 1882 and 1886 contributors included Rollinat, Moréas, Morice, Krysinska, L. le Cardonnel, Verlaine, Samain, Denise, Ajalbert, Tailhade, and Dubus. After 1886, more serious periodicals having been founded, *Le Chat noir* offered mostly light verse and was important only for items by Verlaine.

3. *La Nouvelle Rive gauche,* November 9, 1882—March 30, 1883
   Lutèce, March 30, 1883—October 3, 1886
Under these two titles appeared the weekly periodical of Rall and Trézenik. Moréas, Morice, and Verlaine during 1883, supplemented by Vignier and Tailhade during 1884, and by Laforgue, Vielé-Griffin, Raynaud, and Régnier in 1885, are the important contributors of poetry. The magazine is famous for having first printed Verlaine's essays on Corbière, Rimbaud, and Mallarmé under the title "Les Poètes maudits." Brief revivals of the magazine in 1886 and 1897 are unimportant for symbolist poetry.

4. *La Revue indépendante* (first series), May, 1884—April, 1885
Poems by Verlaine, Moréas, Morice, and Tailhade. Mallarmé's "Prose pour des Esseintes." Essay on Verlaine by Louis Desprez.

5. *Les Taches d'encre,* November, 1884—February, 1885
Four issues composed solely by Maurice Barrès. Important for the long essay on Baudelaire, in which current "decadent" poetry was discussed.

6. *La Basoche, 1884–86*
The first Belgian periodical establishing definite bonds with the French poetic movement. Poetry by Fontainas, Merrill, Mikhaël, and Quillard. Ghil's first manifesto, entitled "Sous Mon Cachet."

7. *La Revue wagnérienne, 1885–88*
Dujardin's magazine, famous for its suggestive criticism on the bonds between music and poetry. Mallarmé's "Richard Wagner, rêverie d'un poète français." Eight famous sonnets of homage to Wagner by Mallarmé, Verlaine, etc.

8. *Le Scapin, 1885–86*
Poetry by Dubus, L. le Cardonnel, Ghil, and Verlaine. Vallette's essay on symbolism.

9. *La Pléiade,* 1886
Mikhaël, Darzens, Quillard, Roux, Ghil, Maeterlinck, and Van Lerberghe. Ghil's *Traité du verbe.*

10. *Le Décadent* (first series), 1886
Founded by Anatole Baju. His critical articles are ridiculous, but contributors to the thirty-five issues include du Plessys, Aurier, Verlaine, Brinn'Gaubast, Ghil, Mallarmé, Dubus, Laforgue, Vignier, Merrill, and Raynaud.

11. *La Vogue,* 1886
Directed by Léo d'Orfer and Gustave Kahn. Important for publication of Verlaine, Rimbaud, Laforgue, Mallarmé, Kahn, Moréas, Dujardin, Morice, Vignier, and Ghil. "Les Illuminations," published for the first time, and the reprinting of the very rare *Une Saison en enfer* made Rimbaud's work available. Wyzewa's "Notes sur Mallarmé."

12. *La Décadence artistique et littéraire,* 1886
Interesting as the organ in which Ghil contested Moréas' claims to leadership of the new poetic school.

13. *Le Symboliste,* 1886
Moréas and Adam oppose Ghil.

14. *La Wallonie,* 1886–92
Mockel's important Belgian periodical. Mockel cemented relations between poets of his country and the French symbolists by publishing and discussing their works.

15. *La Revue indépendante* (new series), 1886–93
Between 1886 and 1889 the editors of the magazine were Dujardin, Wyzewa, Kahn, and Fénéon. Publication of Laforgue's posthumous work. Mallarmé's essays on the theater as well as some of his most important later poems. After 1889 change of ownership and reversal of literary attitudes. Bonnamour's championship of Ghil. During this last period in the magazine's existence occurred, however, the publication of Vittorio Pica's essay on Mallarmé.

16. *Les Ecrits pour l'art,* 1887–92
Ghil's magazine, published at irregular intervals. The six issues of 1887 are of general interest, since they contain Mallarmé's preface for the *Traité du verbe,* as well as contributions by Régnier, Vielé-Griffin, Verhaeren, and Merrill. Subsequent issues are concerned with Ghil's unsuccessful attempts to constitute a school of poetry.

17. *Le Décadent* (new series), December, 1887—March, 1889
Baju's first series of this magazine had been a four-page weekly issue. This new series was published bimonthly in smaller format but with more pages. Many contributions by Verlaine, Raynaud, and Tailhade. The Rimbaud sonnet hoax was perpetrated in the periodical.

18. *La Cravache,* 1888
An ephemeral little periodical, created by Lecomte and Retté, for publication of symbolist poetry and criticism.

19. *La Jeune Belgique,* 1881–97
Founded by Max Waller, the magazine underwent several changes in editorial policy after his death in 1889. While Verhaeren was a contributor to *La Jeune Belgique,* between

1890 and 1894, the French symbolists were welcome collaborators. Between 1894 and 1897 Gilkin, Gille, and Giraud carried on an energetic campaign against free verse and excluded the French poets.

20. *Art et critique*, 1889–92
Jean Jullien's periodical, more concerned with the theater than with poetry, contains criticism favorable toward Verlaine, Mallarmé, V. de l'Isle-Adam, and Maeterlinck.

21. *La Vogue*, 1889
Founded by Kahn and Retté, the magazine had only three issues. Vielé-Griffin, Régnier, Vanor, Saint-Paul, and Delaroche were contributors.

22. *La Pléiade*, 1889
A collective enterprise of Brinn'Gaubast, Aurier, Dubus, Dumur, and Leclercq, who were also the chief contributors. Five issues were published. Some of the group set about securing the services of Vallette for a new periodical. The result of their efforts was the *Mercure de France*.

23. *La Plume*, 1889–1905
Founded by Léon Deschamps, this magazine became one of the four important magazines of the symbolist movement during the eighteen-nineties. The others were the *Mercure de France, La Revue blanche,* and *L'Ermitage.*

24. *Mercure de France,* 1890–
Vallette's magazine, much more mature and broader in scope than any other in this list, is the richest source of published poetry and critical comment on verse during this period.

25. *L'Ermitage,* 1890–1906
Founded by Mazel. Directed after 1896 by Ducoté. Like *La Plume,* this periodical was important in revealing both literary and artistic currents.

26. *Les Entretiens politiques et littéraires,* 1890–93
Founded by Régnier and Vielé-Griffin. The periodical contains many essays on poetry and particularly on free verse by the codirectors as well as political and literary studies by Bernard Lazare and Pierre Quillard. Among interesting items in the magazine are Gide's "Traité du Narcisse," Mallarmé's "Vers et musique en France," Saint-Pol-Roux's "Epilogues des saisons humaines," and much of Laforgue's hitherto unpublished work.

27. *La Revue blanche,* 1891–1903
While the poems, essays, and book reviews by Gustave Kahn constitute the most extensive contribution by a single author to *La Revue blanche,* almost every symbolist poet or critic is represented in the magazine.

28. *La Conque,* 1891–92
Famous for the early poems of Valéry, Louÿs, and Gide. Mauclair and Quillot were also frequent contributors. Limited to one hundred copies and with a restricted list of collaborators.

29. *Le Réveil,* 1891–96
A literary magazine published at Ghent. Important for the French movement between 1892 and 1896, when Régnier, Vielé-Griffin, Klingsor, Souchon, Herold, and Louÿs were among its contributors.

30. *Chimère,* 1891–93
Founded by Paul Redonnel at Montpellier. Many contributions from Parisian poets as well as from southern French writers.

31. *Die Blätter für die Kunst,* 1892–1919
George's German magazine was published at irregular intervals over a period of years. For French verse, the years 1892–93 are the most important.

32. *Le Saint-Graal,* 1892–99
Founded by Emmanuel Signoret. The eight numbers of the magazine published during 1892 are of general interest since contributors include Verlaine, Morice, L. le Cardonnel, Gasquet, Souchon, Retté, Maurras, Moréas, Vicaire, and Degron. The twelve issues published between January, 1893, and March, 1899, were composed by Signoret alone.

33. *Floréal,* 1892–93
Founded by Gérardy in Liége. *Floréal* attempted to continue the friendly bonds between French and Belgian poets established by *La Wallonie.*

34. *La Syrinx,* 1892
Founded by Gasquet in Aix-en-Provence. Contributors included Maurras, Valéry, Louÿs, Klingsor, Souchon, and Mauclair.

35. *Les Essais des jeunes,* 1892
Founded in Toulouse by Delbousquet. The seven issues proclaim solidarity with René Ghil's theories. Maurice Magre was one of the contributors.

36. *L'Art littéraire,* 1892–94
Founded by Louis Lormel in October, 1892. Contributors include Ghil, Mauclair, Saint-Pol-Roux, Régnier, Gourmont, Fontainas, Gide, Fargue, Jarry, Mockel, Pilon, Kahn, and Klingsor.

37. *La Société nouvelle*
A Brussels periodical, founded in 1884, but important for French symbolism only between 1892 and 1895. Gustave Kahn's critical essays and contributions by Régnier, Vielé-Griffin, and Saint-Pol-Roux occurred during these four years.

38. *Les Ibis,* 1894
Founded by Degron and Klingsor. Poetry by Vielé-Griffin, Gasquet, Retté, Gérardy, Souchon, Régnier, Dierx, Signoret, and Saint-Paul.

39. *Le Rêve et l'idée,* 1894–95
Maurice Le Blond's attacks on symbolism and his championship of Saint-Georges de Bouhélier are the most important features of the four issues of the magazine.

40. *L'Idée moderne,* 1894
Founded by Nicole Chambellan. Chiefly important for contributions by L. le Cardonnel.

41. *Essais des jeunes* (second series), 1894–95
This revival of the Toulouse magazine, showing sympathy with the naturists, repudiated its earlier championship of Ghil. Contributors include Guérin, Viollis, Delbousquet, Magre, Lafargue, Le Blond, and Régnier.

42. *Album des légendes,* 1894
   Le Livre des légendes, 1895

Successive titles of an artistic and literary periodical founded by Andhré and Jacques des Gachons. Among the symbolists who appeared in its pages were L. le Cardonnel, Merrill, Régnier, Klingsor, Degron, and Vielé-Griffin.

43. *Le Coq rouge,* 1895–97

Founded in Brussels as a protest against the reactionary attitude of *La Jeune Belgique.* Friendly toward French contributors, among whom were Régnier, Vielé-Griffin, Gourmont, Souza, Fort, Gide, Herold, Kahn, Ghéon, Jammes, and Mauclair.

44. *L'Art jeune,* 1895–97

Another little magazine published in Brussels and similar in aims to *Le Coq rouge.* Among its French contributors were Fort, Ghéon, Gide, Mauclair, Régnier, and Vielé-Griffin.

45. *La Coupe,* 1895–98

Founded at Montpellier by Joseph Loubet. Local poets were often contributors, but Vielé-Griffin, Gide, Klingsor, Verhaeren, Valéry, Régnier, Kahn, Degron, Guérin, Retté, Jammes, Souchon, Signoret, Ducoté, and Jaloux are each represented.

46. *La Lutte,* 1895–97

Founded in Brussels by Georges Ramaekers. Chiefly Belgian contributors, among whom were Verhaeren and Elskamp. Vielé-Griffin, Régnier, and Ghéon were the principal collaborators from France.

47. *Arte,* 1895–96

Founded in Coimbra, Portugal, by E. de Castro and M. da Silva-Gaio. Verlaine, Gourmont, Kahn, Merrill, Raynaud, Saint-Pol-Roux, and Ducoté were among the French contributors.

48. *L'Effort,* 1896–98

Founded at Toulouse by Delbousquet and others. Continued the formulas established by the second series of the *Essais des jeunes.* Magre, Viollis, Delbousquet, and Lafargue are the principal poets and critics of the magazine.

49. *Les Mois dorés,* 1896–98

Founded at Aix-en-Provence by Gasquet and d'Arbaud. Eleven issues were published. Signoret, Mistral, and the naturists are the recipients of praise in the magazine.

50. *Le Livre d'art,* 1896

An earlier series bearing the same title had been issued by Paul Fort in 1892, but its interest was rather artistic than literary. In the series of 1896 there is a section called "Pages naturistes," as well as poetry by Jammes, Fort, Klingsor, Guérin, Fargue, and Ducoté. Jarry's "Ubu Roi" was published in the magazine.

51. *Le Centaure,* 1896

Founded by Henri Albert. The list of contributors was quite restricted, and included Régnier, Valéry, Herold, and Gide.

52. *La Revue naturiste,* 1897–98

Chief contributors were Bouhélier, Montfort, Le Blond, Viollis, and Fleury. The periodical contained a poetic supplement of naturist poetry.

53. *La Trêve-Dieu,* 1897

Founded at Le Havre by Yves Berthou. Much mediocre poetry but some noteworthy items by Vielé-Griffin, Jammes, Fort, Raynaud, Guérin, Pilon, Gourmont, Merrill, and Ducoté.

54. *Le Pays de France,* 1899–1901

Founded by Gasquet at Aix-en-Provence. Gasquet's critical articles attack the symbolists for their pessimism. His admiration goes to Souchon, Magre, Vielé-Griffin, and Signoret.

55. *La Vogue,* 1899–1900

Klingsor, Merrill, Pilon, Fleury, Moréas, Kahn, Verhaeren, Mockel, Louÿs, Jammes, Gregh, and Gasquet were all contributors to this third *Vogue.*

A SELECTIVE BIBLIOGRAPHY of Books
concerning the History of the Symbolist Movement

NOTE: *Place of publication is Paris unless otherwise indicated.*

Part I: GENERAL REFERENCE

Aeschimann, Paul. *Vingt-cinq ans de littérature française* (article "La Poésie"). Librairie de France, 1926.

Barre, André. *Le Symbolisme.* Jouve, 1912.

Beaujon, Georges. *L'Ecole symboliste.* Bâle, 1900.

Beaunier, André. *La Poésie nouvelle.* Mercure de France, 1902.

Braunschvig, Marcel. *La Littérature française contemporaine.* A. Colin, 1929.

Casella, Georges et Gaubert, Ernest. *La Nouvelle Littérature, 1895–1905.* Sansot, 1906.

Charpentier, John. *Le Symbolisme.* Les Arts et le Livre, 1927.

Clouard, Henri. *La Poésie française moderne, des romantiques à nos jours.* Gauthier-Villars, 1924.

Dérieux, Henry. *La Poésie française contemporaine, 1885–1935.* Mercure de France, 1935.

Fontainas, André. *Dans la lignée de Baudelaire.* Nouvelle Revue Critique, 1930.

Fort, Paul et Mandin, Louis. *Histoire de la poésie française depuis 1850.* Flammarion, 1926.

Le Cardonnel, Louis et Vellay, Charles. *La Littérature contemporaine.* Mercure de France, 1905.

Marie, Aristide. *La Forêt symboliste, esprits et visages.* Didot, 1936.

Martino, Pierre. *Parnasse et symbolisme, 1850–1900.* A. Colin, 1925.

Michaud, Guy. *Message poétique du symbolisme.* 3 vols., Nizet, 1947.

——— *La Doctrine symboliste.* Nizet, 1947.

Mornet, Daniel. *Histoire de la littérature et de la pensée française contemporaines.* Larousse, 1935.

Osmont, Anne. *Le Mouvement symboliste.* La Maison du Livre, 1917.

Poizat, Alfred. *Le Symbolisme.* Renaissance du Livre, 1919.

Raymond, Marcel. *De Baudelaire au surréalisme.* Corréa, 1933.

Schmidt, A. M. *La Littérature symboliste.* Presses Universitaires, 1942.

Séché, Alphonse. *Les Caractères de la poésie contemporaine.* Sansot, 1913.

Sénéchal, Christian. *Les Grands Courants de la littérature française contemporaine.* Malfère, 1941.

Thompson, Vance. *French Portraits.* Boston, Richard G. Badger & Co., 1900.

Van Bever, Adolphe et Léautaud, Paul. *Poètes d'aujourd'hui.* 3 vols., Mercure de France, 1945.

Vigié-Lecocq, E. *La Poésie contemporaine, 1884–1896.* Mercure de France, 1897.

Visan, Tancrède de. *L'Attitude du lyrisme contemporain.* Mercure de France, 1911.

Walch, G. *Anthologie des poètes français contemporains.* 3 vols., Delagrave, 1906.

Part II: REPORTS FROM PARTICIPANTS IN
THE MOVEMENT

Ajalbert, Jean. *Mémoires en vrac: au temps de symbolisme, 1880–90.* Albin Michel, 1938.

Bouhélier, Saint-Georges de. *Le Printemps d'une génération.* Editions Nagel, 1946.

Dujardin, Edouard. *Mallarmé par un des siens.* Messein, 1936.

Fontainas, André. *Mes Souvenirs du symbolisme.* Nouvelle Revue Critique, 1928.

Fort, Paul. *Mes Mémoires.* Flammarion, 1944.

Ghil, René. *Les Dates et les œuvres.* C. Crès et Cie, 1923.

Gourmont, Remy de. *Le Livre des masques.* Mercure de France, 1896.

—— *Le IIᵐᵉ Livre des masques.* Mercure de France, 1898.

—— *Promenades littéraires.* 4ᵉ série, Mercure de France. 1912.

Huret, Jules. *Enquête sur l'évolution littéraire.* Charpentier, 1891.

Kahn, Gustave. *Symbolistes et décadents.* Vanier, 1902.

Laforgue, Jules. *Lettres à un ami, 1880–1886.* Mercure de France, 1941.

Larguier, Leo. *Avant le déluge.* Grasset, 1928.

Lévy, Jules. *Les Hydropathes.* Delpeuch, 1928.

Mallarmé, Stephane. *Œuvres complètes.* Editions de la Pléiade, 1945.

Mazel, Henri. *Au beau temps du symbolisme.* Mercure de France, 1943.

Merrill, Stuart. *Prose et vers. Œuvres posthumes.* Messein, 1925.

Moréas, Jean. *Les Premières Armes du symbolisme.* Vanier, 1889.

Morice, Charles. *La Littérature de tout à l'heure.* Perrin et Cie, 1889.

Mouquet, Jules, ed. *Albert Samain et Francis Jammes, correspondance inédite.* Emile-Paul
  Frères, 1946.

Raynaud, Ernest. *La Mêlée symboliste.* 3 vols., Renaissance du Livre, 1920.

—— *En marge de la mêlée symboliste.* Mercure de France, 1936.

Régnier, Henri de. *Nos rencontres.* Mercure de France, 1931.

Retté, Adolphe. *Le Symbolisme, anecdotes et souvenirs.* Messein, 1913.

Tailhade, Laurent. *Quelques fantômes de jadis,* L'Edition Française Illustrée, 1920.

Tellier, Jules. *Nos poètes.* Dupret, 1888.

Vanor, Georges. *L'Art symboliste.* Vanier, 1889.

Verlaine, Paul (Adolphe Van Bever, éd.). *Correspondance.* 3 vols., Messein.

—— *Œuvres complètes.* Messein, 1911.

—— *Œuvres posthumes.* 3 vols., Messein, 1923.

Wyzewa, Téodor d' *Nos maîtres.* Perrin, 1895.

Part III: MONOGRAPHS

Bocquet, Léon. *Albert Samain.* Mercure de France, 1921.

Bonneau, Georges. *Albert Samain.* Mercure de France, 1925.

Cours, Jean de. *Francis Vielé-Griffin.* Champion, 1930.

Cornell, Kenneth. *Adolphe Retté.* New Haven, Yale University Press, 1942.

Estève, Edmond. *Un grand poète de la vie moderne: Emile Verhaeren.* Boivin, 1928.

Etiemble, Paul et Gauclère, Yasu. *Rimbaud.* Gallimard, 1936.

Fontaine, André. *Verhaeren et son œuvre.* Mercure de France, 1929.

Georgin, René. *Jean Moréas.* Nouvelle Revue Critique, 1929.

Henry, M. L. *Stuart Merrill.* Champion, 1927.

Lepelletier, Edmond. *Paul Verlaine et son œuvre*. Mercure de France, 1907.
Martino, Pierre. *Verlaine*. Boivin, 1924.
Mondor, Henri. *Vie de Mallarmé*. Gallimard, 1941.
Richard, Noel. *Louis le Cardonnel*. Didier-Prévot, 1946.
Starkie, Enid. *Arthur Rimbaud*. New York, W. W. Norton & Co., 1947.
Zweig, Stefan. *Emile Verhaeren*. Mercure de France, 1910.

INDEX OF NAMES